FRENCH LITERATURE

AND ITS

BACKGROUND

EDITED BY

JOHN CRUICKSHANK

〰〰〰

. 2

The Seventeenth Century

OXFORD UNIVERSITY PRESS

LONDON OXFORD NEW YORK

1969

Oxford University Press

LONDON OXFORD NEW YORK
GLASGOW TORONTO MELBOURNE WELLINGTON
CAPE TOWN SALISBURY IBADAN NAIROBI LUSAKA ADDIS ABABA
BOMBAY CALCUTTA MADRAS KARACHI LAHORE DACCA
KUALA LUMPUR HONG KONG TOKYO

First published by Oxford University Press, London,
as an Oxford University Press paperback, 1969

PRINTED IN GREAT BRITAIN

Contents

Introduction

THIS is the second of six volumes bearing the collective title *French Literature and its Background*. It deals with various literary, intellectual, and social aspects of the seventeenth century in France, and it does so in a way that aims less at full coverage than at raising a variety of questions; it seeks to challenge as well as to inform. Inevitably, since a detailed literary history of the seventeenth century was not the main purpose, some of the chapter-headings may suggest a rather arbitrary picture. In fact, with the exception of one chapter, this volume was written by a group of scholars working in the University of Sussex, and they were left free to write in the way they chose on aspects of seventeenth-century France which they found particularly interesting. At the same time, individual contributors consulted one another a good deal, and I hope that the picture which emerges is reasonably coherent, though it is necessarily incomplete.

Given certain limitations of space, we decided in the course of several discussions that complete chapters could be devoted only to Corneille, Racine, Molière, La Fontaine, and Pascal. It is clear that a strong case could be made for similar treatment of Descartes, for instance—possibly even at the expense of La Fontaine—but we finally kept to our assessment of La Fontaine as a major poet and agreed that the significance of Descartes's ideas would emerge most clearly in a chapter ('Towards the Enlightenment') dealing with the growth of critical and sceptical thought. Other topics which seemed to merit detailed discussion were the acute consciousness of language during the period and its rhetorical use for a number of different purposes, the domination of literature and the arts by the existence of a court society, the growth and nature of the aphorism, and the development of prose fiction.

Since so much writing in the seventeenth century is either theological in character or refers to the nature and status of the Church and of religious ideas, a chapter on 'Religion and Society' appeared to be an essential part of the background material. Similarly, we thought it necessary to give some account of the social and economic 'infrastructure' of the *grand siècle*, which has too often been presented in terms of unquestioned social stability and aristocratic exclusiveness. Hence the chapter on 'Social Structure and Social Change', which makes a number of important points about the wider social spectrum while also indicating the general direction taken by some of the most lively and original French scholarship in this area in recent years.

As with the other volumes in this series, various chapters are complementary to one another, so that a single author or theme will be seen from more than one angle in more than one chapter. For example, there are comments on Corneille, Molière, and Racine in the chapter entitled 'Louis XIV and the Arts' as well as in the separate chapters devoted to them. Similarly the Jesuit/Jansenist conflict is discussed both in 'Religion and Society' and in 'Pascal'. This means, of course, that the Index to the volume should be frequently consulted.

Finally, attention should be drawn to the 'Chronology', which is designed to serve various purposes. It enables the reader to relate seventeenth-century French literature to historical events (mainly French), to English literature of the period, to the main contemporary painters and composers, and to major works of ideas which influenced European intellectual life in the seventeenth century.

JOHN CRUICKSHANK

University of Sussex
March 1968

1. The Language of Literature

QUOI qu'il en soit, si la langue française n'est pas encore la langue de tous les peuples du monde, il me semble qu'elle mérite de l'être. Car à la bien considérer dans la perfection où elle est depuis plusieurs années, ne faut-il pas avouer qu'elle a quelque chose de noble et d'auguste, qui l'égale presque à la langue latine, et la relève infiniment au-dessus de l'italienne et de l'espagnole, les seules langues vivantes qui peuvent raisonnablement entrer en concurrence avec elle?

(Bouhours, *Entretiens d'Ariste et d'Eugène*, 1671)

These are familiar notes. Over the years the world has become accustomed to hearing the French praise their language—and many who are not French have taken up the refrain. From Rivarol (1753–1801), confidently affirming the universality of the French tongue, to General de Gaulle, insisting that French scientists at international conferences should use their own language, so remarkably well-suited by virtue of its clarity and precision for the expression of scientific thought, the position has remained substantially the same. Today the confidence is dwindling.

It was in the seventeenth century that these claims were first made on behalf of French. When Du Bellay and the Pléiade defended their native language in 1550 and attacked the entrenched superiority of Latin and Greek, they were gambling on what French might become. By the time of Bouhours the potential had been realized; in the view of Ariste and Eugène, French had in fact, as well as in promise, become an instrument equal to the ancient languages and superior to the modern. Under the Sun-King it had reached a state of near-perfection: 'Si la langue française est sous son règne ce qu'était la langue latine sous celui d'Auguste, il est lui-même dans son siècle ce qu'Auguste était dans le sien.'

Bouhours probably spoke for most cultivated French speakers of the seventeenth century in his eulogy of his language; he certainly reflected their interests in devoting a large part of his *Entretiens*, which are presented as the seaside talks of two men of the world, to questions of grammar and eloquence. These were indeed among the main subjects of conversation in polite society. Even today the educated French appear to show more interest than many of their neighbours in questions of language, and daily newspapers carry regular features devoted to good French. In the seventeenth century this interest went much further.

To start with, most children's education was dominated by grammar and by rhetoric, the art of prose eloquence. Whether the emphasis was on Latin, as in the Jesuit colleges, or on French, as at Port-Royal, the training given was essentially linguistic. The boy read with a view to learning a standard of correctness and he culled from his textbooks turns of phrase, devices of eloquence, or historical examples which he might use when he came to practise the art of the word—as he did at school by inventing suitable speeches for imaginary occasions. In particular, rhetoric taught the art of amplification—how to expand a theme or make something of nothing. To this end the orator might use (among other devices) comparisons, rhetorical commonplaces, historical precedents, or enumeration of the different aspects of his subject. The art of amplification was central to the literature of the period.

All this had its effect in training people to be highly conscious of language and its proper use, but it was pedantic stuff. Far more elegant discussions of language went on in books for the general educated public (books like Bouhours's *Entretiens*) and in the salons and other places where society met. Indeed it was in the salons that much of the grammarians' work was done. In spite of the emphasis which we naturally give to poets and those who signed works which codified *le bon usage*, the real authority for linguistic matters was vested in polite society. Vaugelas (1585-1650), the most important grammarian of the century, presents himself—perhaps with excessive modesty—as no more than an assiduous observer of the language of 'la plus saine partie de la Cour', which for him included 'les femmes comme les hommes, et plusieurs personnes de la ville où le Prince réside, qui par la communication qu'elles ont avec les gens de la Cour participent à sa politesse'. The Académie Française was in its early days a sort of extension of the salons, a specialized high-level language salon which would take over linguistic points that had been discussed at the Hôtel de Rambouillet and in its turn provide subjects for discussion there.

This state of affairs had important implications for literature. In the mid-sixteenth century the ideal literary language was widely held to be a learned, esoteric creation which was clearly set apart from the usage of the Court, where poets had until then acted the part of entertainers. But the public resisted and it was not long before these high ambitions were reluctantly abandoned by many poets. In 1565 Ronsard wrote in his *Abrégé de l'art poétique*: 'Mais aujourd'hui, pource que notre France n'obéit qu'à un seul roi, sommes contraints, si nous voulons parvenir à quelque honneur, parler son langage courtisan', even if this means that 'il faut bien souvent ployer sous le jugement d'une demoiselle ou d'un jeune courtisan'. The tide was running strongly in this direction well before Malherbe (1555–1628) set himself up as legislator, but Malherbe was an important figure in the movement. Nor should we be misled by his often-quoted remark that his linguistic arbiters were the market porters. All that this signified was a minimum standard of intelligibility; essentially his efforts were directed towards elaborating a poetic language which would satisfy those who were not poets but men and women of the world.

And for all the fierce protests of Montaigne's adoptive daughter, Mademoiselle de Gournay (1566–1645), who accused Malherbe and his camp of beggaring the French language, it was Malherbe's line which prevailed. The language of seventeenth-century French literature was dictated by the usage of a relatively small section of Parisian society, the group defined above by Vaugelas, the *honnêtes gens*. At one time literature and learning had been despised by such people, but increasingly during this century it was considered necessary for them to be capable of appreciating contemporary literature and speaking French correctly and elegantly. And with this greater cultural awareness came the power to impose their standards of speech on literature.

Nor were those works, such as burlesque poems, 'realistic' novels, or satires, which used the language of inferior beings, in any way a revolt against what might seem to us now the tyranny of polite usage. They were rather conscious deviations from a norm, deviations which gained their effectiveness from the existence of the norm. Reading them, the well-bred audience enjoyed being able to step outside the pale of *le bon usage*, just as the highly civilized *habitués* of the Hôtel de Rambouillet indulged in the crudest practical jokes.

In general, then, seventeenth-century French literature presents the modern reader with a strange spectacle, one which may perhaps arouse in him scorn, perhaps envy—that of a series of great writers using a language which had been worked out for them by their audience. Of course, they helped to form or to consecrate usage and increasingly towards the end of the century they provided models, but essentially they were writing to please or persuade a small known group and felt obliged to use the language of that group. Hence the language of their books is in many ways like the language of polite conversation, which is governed by a commonly accepted rhetoric. All the great writers of the classical period showed themselves aware of the paramount importance of pleasing—and although pleasing did not necessarily involve obeying the rules of Aristotle, it did call for a high degree of linguistic conformity. Writers felt themselves vulnerable to the needling grammatical criticism which was the dominant mode of literary analysis—the best-known case is probably that of Racine sending one of his plays to Bouhours with a modest request:

Je vous envoie les quatre premiers actes de ma tragédie, et je vous envoierai le cinquième, dès que je l'aurai transcrit. Je vous supplie, mon Révérend Père, de prendre la peine de les lire, et de marquer les fautes que je puis avoir faites contre la langue, dont vous êtes un de nos plus excellents maîtres.

So there were severe limits on the individuality of an author's use of words. The word could not be dwelt on, an object of delectation in its own right; it was above all a rhetorical instrument, and this instrument had to be used in the accepted manner—with the variations appropriate to the author's skill and his field of discourse. In return he had many compensations. He was sure of his audience as his audience was sure of him; he knew for whom he was writing and knew that he could expect a full response to the formal qualities of his writing from an audience trained to notice words and enjoy their manipulation.

How, then, did the language of this polite society develop and take shape? The mid-sixteenth century had seen a powerful movement, led by poets and scholars, to enrich the vocabulary of French. Ronsard once said: 'Plus nous aurons de mots en notre langue, plus elle sera parfaite', and in his *Abrégé de l'art poétique* he advocates borrowing from 'les artisans de tous métiers', from the 'dialectes de notre France', and from 'nos vieux romans'. Where the poet cannot borrow, he can invent, either in imitation of Greek and Latin or by formation from existing words—thus 'sur les vocables reçus en usage, comme *pays*, *eau*, *feu*, tu feras *païser*, *eaüer*, *foüer*, et mille autres tels vocables qui ne voient encore la lumière faute d'un hardy et bienheureux entrepreneur'. It had been an age of linguistic individualism, exemplified in the rich, original, and sometimes grotesque vocabulary of the poet Du Bartas (1544–90), who wrote, for instance:

> Cette antipéristase (il n'y a point danger
> De naturaliser quelque mot étranger,
> Et même en ces discours, où la gauloise phrase
> N'en a point de son cru qui soient de telle emphase). . . .
> (*La Première Semaine: Second Jour*)

But by the time that this was written the movement of enrichment had slowed down, and the following century was to see a widespread and prolonged effort to consolidate and to impose a uniform standard.

This effort applied in the first place to vocabulary. Here the aim was partly to clarify the meaning of words, distinguishing for instance between *jardin* and *jardinage*, *plainte* and *complainte*, *chaire* and *chaise*, *consommer* and *consumer*. But more important was the deliberate rejection of many words from the vocabulary of polite or literary language, words which had been quite at home, for instance, in the essays of Montaigne. The principle of exclusion did much to mark off *le bon usage* from ordinary speech. The voluntary impoverishment of literary French went to extraordinary lengths.

A vast number of words were thus categorized as 'sales', 'mal-honnêtes', or simply 'bas', which might mean that they held disagreeable associations (*poitrine* was taboo because it made Malherbe think of *poitrine de veau*) or that they were words used only by the bourgeois or the common people—only in comedy could a writer use *m'amie*. Technical terms were undignified; in particular the language of the law was considered pedantic or grotesque and unsuitable for polite conversation, even though many of those who helped to form polite usage were themselves lawyers. The cultural domination of Paris was emphasized by the exclusion of all forms of dialect, notably the Gasconisms which had come to Paris with Henri IV. Nor, in spite of the regrets of Vaugelas and others, was any mercy shown to expressions which had for some reason come to seem old-fashioned, however useful they might have been.

Not that newly invented words fared much better. The learned neologisms of the Pléiade were scorned, and throughout the seventeenth century it was extremely difficult to introduce new words into French. At most one might combine words in a new way, coining ingenious periphrases to replace single words—but even this freedom was severely limited. Thus the group known as the *précieux* (or *précieuses*), who were prominent in the hunting down of low words, displayed a certain amount of skill in the attempt to enrich the language with new, usually metaphorical, turns of phrase (for example *travestir sa pensée*). But it was not far from this to more doubtful creations such as *les portes de l'entendement* (ears), and from these to the parodies of Cyrano de Bergerac and Molière.

It is in the lexical field that the restricting and standardizing tendencies of the seventeenth century can be best seen, but the same process was at work on every element of the French language. The *Remarques sur la langue française* of Vaugelas (for this was a century of remarks, comments, and queries rather than of formal grammars) deals with all sorts of questions; alongside the sifting of vocabulary we see the gradual fixing of a standard of correctness in grammar and syntax. To take a few examples among many, Vaugelas condemns the contracted futures of *donner*, *je donray* and *je dorray*; he declares that *l'ébène* is feminine, even though the ebony-workers use both genders; he attempts to sort out *d'où* and *dont*, and he rules that one should not say 'les plus grands capitaines de l'antiquité, ce fut Alexandre, César, Hannibal', but 'ce furent'. Behind some of this legislation lay certain vague notions of logic, but far more important for Vaugelas and for almost all the grammarians of his time (with the Port-Royalists providing a partial exception) was the desire to reach an agreement on forms which would be acceptable to, and thence binding on, all educated users of language.

Correctness, then, was the first requirement. In elaborating *le bon usage*, grammarians were concerned not so much with the language of literature as with the French of polite conversation and letter-writing. As we have seen, however, their pronouncements could, with certain modifications, be applied to the language of the pulpit, the law-courts, the madrigal, the theatre, or the epic poem. Rhetoric and poetics were not always clearly differentiated in the seventeenth century, and for some theorists the language of poetry should be virtually identical with that of prose—thus Bouhours: 'Nous avons fort peu de mots poétiques; et le langage des poètes français n'est pas comme celui des autres poètes fort différent du commun langage' (*Entretiens d'Ariste et d'Eugène*).

Nevertheless, certain important distinctions were made in the field of literary language. It was not simply a question of sorting out acceptable and unacceptable words and expressions; the acceptable ones in their turn were arranged in classes. As Hugo wrote in his picturesque *Réponse à un acte d'accusation*: 'Les mots, bien ou mal nés, vivaient parqués en castes.' The normal classification took account of three styles—the elevated, the mediocre, and the humble (not counting the incorrect style of burlesque and satire). The three correct styles had been depicted schematically in the Middle Ages on 'Virgil's wheel', on which they were represented respectively by the *Aeneid*, the *Georgics*, and the *Eclogues*. Different words are allotted to the different segments of the wheel according to their degree of elevation: *equus* is elevated, *bos* is mediocre, and *ovis* is humble.

Such a categorization was noted in French dictionaries of the seventeenth century and universally accepted by writers of the time. It went with a clear view of the distinction of the genres and the suitability of certain forms of treatment for certain subjects. Such clear distinctions made it possible for burlesque and mock-heroic writers to win easy laughs from incongruity of style and subject-matter or deliberate juggling with different styles. More subtly, Racine for instance was able in his tragedies to obtain powerful effects from shifts of stylistic level, such as the descent to a style which is nearer to the humble than to the elevated:

> Avec quelle rigueur, Destin, tu me poursuis!
> Je ne sais où je vais, je ne sais où je suis.
>
> (*Phèdre*, IV. i)

A clearly defined linguistic system, while it may limit a writer by making it impossible for him to use serious language about certain subjects (for example the love-affairs of lawyers), does at the same time make it much easier for him to affect his audience by the manipulation of language.

In the establishing of standards of correctness there were many quarrels of detail, such as the dispute over the pronunciation and spelling of *serge* (*serge* or *sarge*), and the narrow escape of the conjunction *car*, which certain theorists wanted to see expelled from the Franch language. There were also, particularly at the beginning of the century, those who resisted the very principle of codification and, throughout the century, those who regretted the consequent impoverishment of French. Even Racine, annotating the *Odyssey*, noted that Greek, unlike French, could use the word 'calf' in a poetic context: 'Ces mots de veau et de vache ne sont point choquants dans le grec, comme ils le sont en notre langue, qui ne veut presque rien souffrir . . . ces délicatesses sont de véritables faiblesses.' But such regrets were rare and were not translated into action. There was widespread agreement both in theory and in practice about the standardization and classification of vocabulary and syntax. On questions of individual style a similar broad agreement united theorists who on questions of detail might be sharply opposed.

At the beginning of the century the novelist Nervèze (*c*. 1570–*c*. 1622), who was to give his name to the affected style, had written this sort of prose:

Ces ingrates lumières [eyes] qui éclairaient à vos dédains, ont refusé mes hommages, et lors que j'en ai voulu approcher se sont évanouis aux ombres de mon innocence; car vous craigniez que forçant votre cruauté (qui tenait l'empire en votre cœur) vous fussiez obligée d'y remettre mon nom, et le loger auprès de votre repentance (*Les Hasards amoureux de Palmélie et de Lirisis*).

In the middle of the century Scudéry (1601–67) was doing something similar (though more successfully) in his *précieux* verse:

> Puissant maître des sens, écoute un malheureux;
> Amour, sois alchimiste, et sers-toi de tes feux,
> A faire que son cœur prenne une autre nature;
> Comme ce cœur constant me serait un trésor,
> Je ne demande point que tu faces de l'or,
> Travaille seulement à fixer ce mercure.
>
> (*Pour une inconstante*, 1649)

In prose and in verse this metaphorical, consciously artistic style was the enemy of orthodox doctrine, particularly in the second half of the century. From Malherbe on we find denunciations of what was variously known as *le Phébus*, *le galimatias*, *le style Nervèze*, or *le style asiatique*; pedantry and ostentation were repudiated in the name of a clear and natural style. Thus Malherbe as a critic had shown an almost pathological distrust of any sort of verbal ornament (though his early *Les Larmes de Saint-Pierre* is ornamental enough in all conscience). Sorel (1597–1674) parodied the metaphorical style in his *Le Berger extravagant* (1628). La Mesnardière (1610–63) and D'Aubignac (1604–76), theorizing about the theatre, where the rule of verisimilitude made ostentation even less admissible than in other genres, were both vigorous in their condemnation of figures of speech 'qui semblent affectées par étude'. And Boileau, as everyone knows, held that 'Ce que l'on conçoit bien s'énonce clairement'.

Simplicity was fashionable in Boileau's generation. In the name of clarity, truth, or nature he conducted a constant campaign against the hyperboles, the conceits, the puns, the pompous periods of the preceding generation. Bouhours echoed the password, devoting his *La Manière de bien penser dans les ouvrages de l'esprit* to an attack on ostentation and giving in his *Entretiens d'Ariste et d'Eugène* an excellent, if unintentionally double-edged, definition of this linguistic ideal: 'le beau langage ressemble à une eau pure et nette, qui n'a point de goût.' Such is in theory the language of the *honnête homme* who, as La Rochefoucauld said, 'ne se pique de rien' and who is repelled above all by the efforts of self-conscious wits: 'le bel esprit est si fort décrié depuis la profanation qu'on en a faite en le rendant trop commun que les plus spirituels s'en défendent, et s'en cachent comme d'un crime.'

This attitude to language shows in many ways; one of the most characteristic is the seventeenth-century attitude to metaphor. This figure, which had been extolled by Aristotle, was highly spoken of by theorists throughout the period; it was considered an essential feature of the elevated style. At the same time, its use was hedged about with cautious restrictions. Metaphors must not be too remote (i.e. original), too frequent, or too prolonged, as these faults might give rise to ostentation or obscurity. Thus many of the more elaborate *précieux* metaphors fell foul of orthodox criticism and were exposed to parody such as that of Cyrano de Bergerac: 'Je vois déjà la sentinelle avancée de votre bonté paraître entre les créneaux et sur la plate-forme de vos grâces, qui crie à mes soupirs: Qui va là?' (*Le Pédant joué*). Even Théophile de Viau's charming

> Je baignerai mes mains folâtres
> Dans les ondes de tes cheveux

went beyond the limits and was condemned as *Phébus* by the generation of 1660. Bouhours and others were relentless in their mockery of such harmless expressions as 'l'apogée de la gloire' or 'le zénith de la vertu'. As a result the typical metaphor in the second half of the seventeenth century, though it may be expressive and may communicate a sense of movement or a feeling of nobility to its context, is in itself completely conventional and in many cases hardly noticeable. Where the Shakespearian metaphor seizes our attention with a vivid image, the Racinian metaphor remains discreet and colourless, though dynamic; for example:

> Depuis ce coup fatal, le pouvoir d'Agrippine
> Vers sa chute, à grands pas, chaque jour s'achemine.
> (*Britannicus*, I. i)

From the beginning of the century to the end the orthodox position condemning ostentation and pedantry remains more or less unchanged—these are rarely qualities any writer would wish to claim as his own. In practice, however, there is a fairly clear movement in the direction of greater simplicity and naturalness, with the result that many whose works seemed models of simple clarity in 1630 had become scarecrows of pretentiousness by 1670. Guez de Balzac (1594–1654) is an interesting example here. Often spoken of as the Malherbe of French prose, Balzac proclaimed the orthodox doctrine, praising the 'Attic' (i.e. simple) style above the 'Asiatic'. He knew the advantages of a 'mediocre' style, but admitted: 'Pour moi, j'ai bien plus de peine à m'arrêter dans cette médiocrité que je n'en ai à monter au genre sublime.' And later generations were all too aware of the coquettish word-spinning in his prose. Boileau, sending a parody of a Balzac letter to the Duc de Vivonne, writes of 'son style, qui ne saurait dire simplement les choses, ni descendre de sa hauteur'. In some quarters *parler Balzac* became almost as bad as *parler Nervèze*.

The same sort of disgrace overcame Antoine Lemaistre (1608–58), the Jansenist barrister. At the beginning of the century the language of the law-courts had been infested by jargon, name-dropping, irrelevant quotations, historical allusions, and pretentious figurative language. Lemaistre had cleaned out much of the rubbish, and for his time had given the example of a natural style; that he subscribed to the orthodox doctrine of naturalness can be seen from a manuscript treatise on style which once belonged to Racine. But to the young lawyer Claude Fleury, writing in 1664, Lemaistre was a venerable pioneer who 'n'a pas pu se défaire entièrement des mauvais ornements qui étaient de son temps si fort à la mode'. For those who had kept abreast of literary trends, the new oratory was that of Olivier Patru (1604–81), who demonstrated that nobility did not depend on ornament.

Just as Fleury criticized the element of ostentation in the Jansenist Lemaistre, so Bouhours drew attention to the faults of the other writers of Port-Royal, while admitting that 'ces Messieurs ont beaucoup contribué à la perfection de notre langue'. The Jansenists had a doctrinal attachment to plainness of style, but as with Balzac (who greatly influenced them), this theory accompanied a love for the grandiose which subsequent critics found it easy to ridicule.

They had had their hour of glory with the *Provinciales* (1656–7) of Pascal, which Boileau, among others, thought the masterpiece of French prose—for the sort of reason indicated by Pascal's remark: 'Quand on voit le style naturel, on est tout étonné et ravi, car on s'attendait de voir un auteur et on trouve un homme.' But no other Jansenist writers were able to match this natural, laconic style in the name of which their own ponderous works were criticized. It is Pascal's style which is adopted by Racine in his *Lettres sur les Imaginaires* (1666), when he makes fun of one of his former masters: 'Retranchez-vous donc sur le sérieux. Remplissez vos lettres de longues et doctes périodes. Citez les Pères. Jetez-vous souvent sur les injures, et presque toujours sur les antithèses. Vous êtes appelé à ce style. Il faut que chacun suive sa vocation.'

In all domains there is the same tendency towards simplicity, the same gradual rejection of metaphor and conceit, antithesis and involved sentence structure, in the name of the natural style. The drama, and in particular the tragedy, of the sixteenth century had been characterized by its display of oratorical skills; in the seventeenth-century theatre this sort of ostentation is progressively eliminated or disguised. In Corneille's early plays and the plays of his contemporaries the pattern rhetoric of antithesis, enumeration, and repetition still flourishes, while Cyrano de Bergerac in his *La Mort d'Agrippine* (1653) uses almost Shakespearian images at times:

> Il semble que ses veines
> D'une liqueur de feu sont les chaudes fontaines,
> Des serpents enlacés qui rampent sur son corps,
> Ou des chemins voûtés qui mènent chez les morts.

By 1670 both imagery and pattern rhetoric have been considerably toned down. Speeches tend to become shorter and the dialogue is brought closer to normal speech.

Such a movement may seem regrettable, but in the theatre it could be justified on the grounds of verisimilitude and dramatic effectiveness. In lyric poetry, on the other hand, very little seems to have been gained by the rejection of certain elements of what we should now call the baroque style. Although Malherbe's influence was felt throughout the century, before 1650 many poets felt free to indulge their taste for conceit, metaphor, and hyperbole; the results are sometimes puerile, but occasionally original and effective. By 1670 any such originality has virtually disappeared from French lyric poetry, which usually takes the form of a banal amplification on a set theme. It may be successful by reason of its simplicity, its music, and its oratorical construction (for example Racine's *Cantiques spirituels*), but all the flavour has gone out of it; it is Bouhours's clear and tasteless water.

Poetry's loss was prose's gain. Even in trivial matters, such as the style of literary dedications, there was a move towards a more 'natural' and thereby more effective style. Flattery was the more insidious for being apparently unaffected. It was realized that on an inscription to commemorate one of Louis XIV's most notable exploits 'le passage du Rhin' was more impressive than 'le merveilleux passage du Rhin'. But it is perhaps in the eloquence of the pulpit that this evolution is most noticeable.

In the early part of the seventeenth century French preachers seem in many cases to have regarded their sermons as opportunities for the wanton display of ingenuity and erudition—they were perhaps encouraged in this by their audiences. Sermons were divided and subdivided in the tradition of an arid scholasticism, plentifully sprinkled with reference to all conceivable branches of knowledge and embellished with numerous long-winded conceits, puns, and similar flowers of rhetoric. By the middle of the century much of the more extravagant ostentation had gone, but even in 1653 Godeau could still say in his funeral oration on Bishop Camus:

Ainsi après que Jean-Pierre Camus eut fait dans le fond de son cœur l'holocauste vivante de son fils unique à Dieu, je veux dire de sa volonté, Dieu le fit père de plusieurs enfants, le faisant évêque dans son Église et donnant à sa parole la bénédiction d'une fécondité extraordinaire.

The field was clearly ripe for reform, for reasons which were both religious and rhetorical. The main objection to all this ingenuity was that it got in the way of the real purpose of the sermon, which was to persuade. Thus St. Vincent de Paul, praising the blunt but powerful language of the New Testament, called preachers back to their duty, urging them to abandon the false rhetoric of display. Bossuet was much influenced by St. Vincent de Paul, and expounded similar theories in several of his sermons which insist that congregations in church should not expect pleasure from language, but instruction and improvement. In fact his sermons preserve the rhetoric which is needed to impress and persuade; on the whole they abandon that which merely aims to dazzle.

But of course we must not go too far in speaking of the mov towards simplicity. Any simplicity or naturalness in the sermons, poems, or plays of the 1660s is only relative; Bossuet's or Madame de La Fayette's language may be less obviously affected than that of Nervèze, but it is still a long way from 'le degré zéro de l'écriture'. A rapid glance makes it clear that words have been chosen and arranged here for the sake of beauty and persuasion—it is instructive in this respect to compare Racine's *Précis historique des campagnes de Louis Quatorze* (1684) with the bare and workmanlike notes which he made for it. Ostentation, though restricted, was still a powerful force in the age of Versailles. It was simply that earlier forms of display, like earlier styles of clothing, came to look ridiculous; new and subtler forms had to be found. Guarding himself carefully against accusations of affectation, every writer got away with as much fine writing as he could. For a time the new art might conceal art, but it eventually became apparent that this new art was in reality no more natural than that which preceded it. Thus Bouhours, whom we have seen attacking gratuitous and over-elaborate wit, was an apostle and a practitioner of a flowery and elegant style, so that it was not difficult for Barbier d'Aucour, defending the Jansenists, to cast his charges of ostentation back in his face.

In all great writers of the classical period we can see the same tensions between the Attic and the Asiatic, between functional simplicity and decorative ostentation, but in all cases it is the former which is the official favourite. Towards the end of the century, however, there are interesting signs that the ideals of correctness and naturalness might not always be enough. Without in any way wanting a return to *le style Nervèze* several writers seem to have felt that the way in which the language had developed was perhaps harmful to poetry. These writers include Boileau, Bossuet, le Père

Rapin, Racine, and, above all, Claude Fleury; they met at the Hôtel de Lamoignon and formed the nucleus of the camp of the Ancients. Against the elegance of the Moderns they set the sublimity of Greek and Hebrew literature. The Old Testament in particular, while on the one hand it provided the classic example of simple sublimity, 'Fiat Lux', also contained poetry which was not afraid of obscurity, hyperbole, metaphor, and metonymy, combining to create effects of powerful sublimity in comparison with which, as Fleury said, 'toute notre poésie moderne est fort misérable'. In practice, the 'Messieurs du Sublime' made only the tiniest of breaches in the wall of classical linguistic conformity, but their criticisms look forward timidly to Diderot's 'La poésie veut quelque chose d'énorme, de barbare et de sauvage' and to the renaissance of French poetry in the nineteenth century.

NOTE

There is one essential work: F. Brunot, *Histoire de la langue française* (vols. iii–iv, 1930–9). Two shorter works provide an introduction: C. Bruneau, *Petite Histoire de la langue française* (1955–8), vol. i, and A. François, *Histoire de la langue française cultivée* (1959), vol. i. Littré's dictionary is invaluable, and there are also two handy modern dictionaries: G. Cayrou, *Le Français classique* (1948), and J. Dubois and R. Lagane, *Dictionnaire de la langue française classique* (1960). Some aspects of the subject are treated in D. Mornet, *Histoire de la clarté française* (1929); Y. Le Hir, *Rhétorique et stylistique de la Pléiade au Parnasse* (1960); M. Magendie, *La Politesse mondaine* (1925); H. M. Davidson, *Audience, Words and Art: Studies in Seventeenth-Century French Rhetoric* (1965); T. Rosset, *Le Père Bouhours, critique de la langue des écrivains jansénistes* (1908); and P. France, *Racine's Rhetoric* (1965), ch. i.

Among theoretical works of the period, see in particular C. Vaugelas, *Remarques sur la langue française* (1647; ed. Streicher, 1934); N. Boileau, *Art poétique* (1674), *Traité du sublime* (1674), and *Réflexions sur Longin* (1694–1709); Père D. Bouhours, *Entretiens d'Ariste et d'Eugène* (1671; re-ed., Bibliothèque de Cluny, 1962) and *La Manière de bien penser dans les ouvrages de l'esprit* (1687); Abbé C. Fleury, *Dialogues sur l'éloquence judiciaire* (1664; ed. Gaquère, 1925); Père B. Lamy, *L'Art de parler* (1675) and the *Grammaire générale et raisonnée* of Port-Royal (1660).

For the practice of eloquence a brief selection must suffice. There are several anthologies of seventeenth-century verse, among them *An Anthology of French Seventeenth-Century Lyric Poetry* (ed. O. de Mourgues, 1966); *La Poésie française de 1640 à 1680* (ed. R. Picard, 1964); and *Anthologie de la poésie baroque française* (ed. J. Rousset, 2 vols., 1961). The speeches of Lemaistre and Patru have to be read in seventeenth-century editions, but there are modern editions of many of the preachers, for example Bourdaloue, *Sermons choisis* (ed. Dimier, 1936), and Bossuet, *Oraisons funèbres* (ed. Truchet, 1961). Also of interest for the development of prose style are the works of J. L. Guez de Balzac (*Œuvres*, ed. Moreau, 2 vols., 1854) and various novels, for example H. d'Urfé, *L'Astrée* (selections, ed. Magendie, 1928), Abbé de Pure, *La Précieuse* (ed. Magne, 2 vols., 1938), and *Romanciers du XVIIᵉ siècle: Sorel, Scarron, Furetière, Madame de La Fayette* (ed. Adam, Bibliothèque de la Pléiade, 1958). A useful wide view is given in G. Lanson's *Choix de lettres du XVIIᵉ siècle*.

2. Corneille

LOOKING back some twenty years later to the first production of
Le Cid, Corneille writes of the scenes in which Rodrigue, fresh
from killing the Count, visits the Count's daughter Chimène:

> J'ai remarqué aux premières représentations, qu'alors que ce malheureux
> amant se présentait devant elle, il s'élevait un certain frémissement dans
> l'assemblée, qui marquait une curiosité merveilleuse, et un redouble-
> ment d'attention pour ce qu'ils avaient à se dire dans un état si pitoyable.
> Aristote dit qu'il y a des absurdités qu'il faut laisser dans un poème, quand
> on peut espérer qu'elles seront bien reçues; et il est du devoir du poète,
> en ce cas, de les couvrir de tant de brillants, qu'elles puissent éblouir.
> (*Examen du Cid*.)

As we read this passage, we have a picture of Corneille the impresario
watching the audience react to the situations, characters, and words
he has created to dazzle them (note 'éblouir', a key word in Corneille's
theatre). The 'curiosité merveilleuse' of the audience as they wonder
how the two lovers will react to their desperate situation reminds one
of the 'admiration' which Corneille in the *Examen de Nicomède*
substitutes as a tragic emotion for Aristotle's pity and terror. He sees
his audience as fascinated spectators of great actions, strange meet-
ings, impossible dilemmas, and unbelievable solutions.

At the same time, of course, he is anxious to win the approval of
the knowledgeable; he will not want to be caught breaking the rules
of the theatre and will quote Aristotle whenever Aristotle helps his
case—though he deals high-handedly enough with the philosopher
at other times. In particular he will defend the *vraisemblance* (verisimilitude) of scenes which might shock an audience—as we know *Le
Cid* shocked its first audiences. But his aim is clearly to get away with
as much as he can. From the point of view of *vraisemblance* Rodrigue's
visits may have seemed 'des absurdités', but they are marvellously

effective on an audience, and this is what matters to Corneille.

In almost all the *Épîtres* and *Examens* which he printed with his plays we find the same charming pride, the same satisfaction at the effectiveness of his writings and the variety of his achievement. In the *Examen de Pompée* he admires the nobility of his language: 'Pour le style, il est plus élevé en ce poème qu'en aucun des miens, et ce sont, sans contredit, les vers les plus pompeux que j'aie faits.' In the *Épître* to his next play, *Le Menteur*, he congratulates himself on his virtuosity: 'Dans le premier [*Pompée*], j'ai voulu faire un essai de ce que pouvaient la majesté du raisonnement, et la force des vers dénués de l'agrément du sujet; dans celui-ci, j'ai voulu tenter ce que pourrait l'agrément du sujet, dénué de la force des vers.' And in his *pièce à machines*, *Andromède* (1649), it is no longer the language or the plot which dazzles the spectator but the music and the visual effects of Torelli, who has introduced a flying Venus 'avec tant d'art et tant de pompe qu'elle remplit tout le monde d'étonnement et d'admiration'. 'Pompe', 'étonnement', 'admiration', 'éclat', 'éblouissement'—these are the words which spring to Corneille's mind as he meditates on his theatre.

The modern reader or spectator will similarly be struck by the 'pompe' of Corneille's plays, though the change of taste indicated by the pejorative meaning now attached to 'pompe' may make him less receptive to Corneille's effects than he might be. First, if he is to appreciate Corneille's plays at all, he will admire in him a master technician of the word. Nor will what he admires necessarily be the art which conceals art; Corneille's verbal art, like the eloquence of the barristers with whom he was trained, stands forth and seeks our applause. This is not to say that it is purely the art of the word-spinner. Corneille himself insisted that

il y a cette différence pour ce regard entre le poète dramatique et l'orateur, que celui-ci peut étaler son art, et le rendre remarquable avec pleine liberté, et que l'autre doit le cacher avec soin, parce que ce n'est jamais lui qui parle, et ceux qu'il fait parler ne sont pas des orateurs. (*Discours du poeme dramatique*, 1660)

The language he puts into his characters' mouths is often excellent dramatic language, particularly when it is ironic or combative—thus the scene in *Le Cid* where Rodrigue challenges the Count:

DON RODRIGUE

A moi, Comte, deux mots.

LE COMTE

Parle.

DON RODRIGUE

Ôte-moi d'un doute.
Connais-tu bien don Diègue ?

LE COMTE

Oui.

DON RODRIGUE

Parlons bas ; écoute.
Sais-tu que ce vieillard fut la même vertu,
La vaillance et l'honneur de son temps ? le sais-tu ?

LE COMTE

Peut-être.

DON RODRIGUE

Cette ardeur que dans les yeux je porte,
Sais-tu que c'est son sang ? le sais-tu ?

LE COMTE

Que m'importe ?

DON RODRIGUE

A quatre pas d'ici je te le fais savoir.   (II, ii)

Here the dialogue gives perfect expression to Rodrigue's cool impetuosity and the Count's superciliousness and grips the audience with its masterly suggestion of muttered quarrel and its rapid crescendo.

But often it is not like this. *Pompée* (*c.* 1642) opens with a grandiloquent tirade in which the Egyptian king Ptolomée outlines the political situation to his court, beginning with an account of the battle of Pharsalus:

Ses fleuves teints de sang, et rendus plus rapides
Par le débordement de tant de parricides,

> Cet horrible débris d'aigles, d'armes, de chars,
> Sur ses champs empestés confusément épars,
> Ces montagnes de morts privés d'honneurs suprêmes,
> Que la nature force à se venger eux-mêmes,
> Et dont les troncs pourris exhalent dans les vents
> De quoi faire la guerre au reste des vivants,
> Sont les titres affreux dont le droit de l'épée,
> Justifiant César, a condamné Pompée. (I, i)

This single sentence, with its cumulative effects, its strong visual appeal, its strangely elaborate way of describing the plague spread by the corpses, and its resounding antithetical conclusion, is designed above all to impress. These are words to be enjoyed and savoured for their own sake. It seems also that they are words which Corneille enjoyed writing, just as he enjoyed experimenting with *vers libres* in *Andromède* and with different strophic forms in his translation of *The Imitation of Christ*.

As often as not then, when one reads or hears Corneille's language, one admires the virtuosity of the writer, the effectiveness with which he plays on our emotions, the force, splendour, elegance, or novelty of his style. One's admiration is similarly aroused with the situations he puts before us, the plots he weaves for our amazement. His early comedies are full of disguises, mistaken identities, unexpected twists and turns of intrigue. And later, when examining *Héraclius* (1646), Corneille says: 'Le poème est si embarrassé qu'il demande une merveilleuse attention. J'ai vu de fort bons esprits, et des personnes des plus qualifiées de la cour, se plaindre de ce que sa représentation fatiguait autant l'esprit qu'une étude sérieuse. Elle n'a pas laissé de plaire'. So indeed it might, since the whole point of this fascinating play lies in its complicated plot and its uncertain identities; we read in the *dramatis personae*:

> HÉRACLIUS, Fils de l'empereur Maurice, cru Martian, fils de Phocas, amant d'Eudoxe.
>
> MARTIAN, Fils de Phocas, cru Léonce, fils de Léontine, amant de Pulchérie.

and this is only the beginning. Corneille is similarly (and rightly) pleased with *Othon*, one of his tragedies of matrimonial bargaining:

'je puis dire qu'on n'a point encore vu de pièce où il se propose tant de mariages pour n'en conclure aucun.'

With intricacy of plot Corneille plays on his audience's wits, but above all he loves to play on their emotions through singularity of situations, sudden surprises and reversals, unexpected confrontations. Just as his whole dramatic output shows a concern to be constantly changing, so inside the plays we find variety of tempo and skilfully contrived effects of contrast and crescendo. *Horace* is a typical example. The situation is as extraordinary as could be imagined: the three brothers Horace do battle for Rome against their relations by marriage, the three brothers Curiace, champions of Alba. But besides this formidable and nerve-racking symmetry, Corneille screws every possible emotion out of the situation, keeping us guessing with an oracle, starting, stopping, and restarting the hostilities, showing us the moments of decision, telling us the result of the tournament in two contradictory stages, and following the triumphant return of Horace with his murder of his own sister. As one of the characters puts it, blaming the gods (we should rather attribute it to Corneille):

> Vit-on jamais une âme en un jour plus atteinte
> De joie et de douleur, d'espérance et de crainte,
> Asservie en esclave à plus d'événements,
> Et le piteux jouet de plus de changements?
> Un oracle m'assure, un songe me travaille;
> La paix calme l'effroi que me fait la bataille;
> Mon hymen se prépare, et presque en un moment
> Pour combattre mon frère on choisit mon amant;
> Ce choix me désespère, et tous le désavouent;
> La partie est rompue, et les Dieux la renouent. (IV, iv)

The audience shares Camille's oscillation between hope and fear, joy and despair.

Thus we have impressive language, elaborate plots, and extraordinary situations—and with them striking extremes of character, action, and emotion. Our 'admiration' is asked not only for the flawless grandeur of Nicomède, but also for the extreme and demented ambition of Cléopatre in *Rodogune*. This queen, who controls her twin sons' destinies by being able to reveal which of them was born first, offers the throne to whichever of them will kill her enemy, princess Rodogune, whom they both love (Rodogune makes them a similar offer). Somewhat melodramatically—and this is the reproach which constantly lies in wait for Corneille, who never does things by halves—she proclaims her absolute love of power:

> Dût le ciel égaler le supplice à l'offense,
> Trône, à t'abandonner je ne puis consentir:
> Par un coup de tonnerre il vaut mieux en sortir;
> Il vaut mieux mériter le sort le plus étrange.
> Tombe sur moi le ciel, pourvu que je me venge! (V, i)

Corneille says of her: 'tous ses crimes sont accompagnés d'une grandeur d'âme qui a quelque chose de si haut, qu'en même temps qu'on déteste ses actions, on admire la source dont elles partent' (*Discours du poème dramatique*). Once again it is the admiration of the audience which is sought, this time for a character larger than life. In a different way, Cléopâtre should provoke the same gasp of wonder as does Auguste when he makes his magnanimous decision in *Cinna*, or Pulchérie when she resolves to contract an unconsummated marriage with the aged Martian, sacrificing her love to preserve the empire.

In short, Corneille's theatre aims largely to astonish us. It is partly for this reason that he took many of his subjects from little-known corners of Roman history. For one thing these subjects, being unfamiliar to the audience, would be the more likely to create surprise effects—there are comparatively few of Corneille's plays in which a spectator coming to the play for the first time can easily foresee the denouement. Secondly, these unknown territories gave Corneille more scope for the invention of striking episodes and characters than did better-known subjects. But at the same time, paradoxically, being history, or what seemed to be history, they could be defended from the attacks of critics.

Probably the most important principle of seventeenth-century dramatic theory (as expounded for instance in the Abbé d'Aubignac's *Pratique du théâtre*, 1657) was *vraisemblance*. Whatever else a play's merits, it was argued that it could make no impact on an audience if they could not believe in it as a representation of life. Corneille was one of the few writers of the time who in theory, as well as in practice, challenged this 'rule', preferring in many cases *le vrai* (i.e. facts attested by history) to *le vraisemblable*. The Roman historians offered him a wealth of subjects which would be difficult to believe unless we had some sort of proof of them (the conversions in *Polyeucte*, for instance); Corneille did not see why a craven respect for *vraisemblance* should rob him of them. More than this, he was prepared to allow offences against *le vrai* as well as *le vraisemblable* if they helped the poet to achieve his aim:

Le but du poète est de plaire selon les règles de son art. Pour plaire, il a besoin quelquefois de rehausser l'éclat des belles actions et d'exténuer l'horreur des funestes. Ce sont des nécessités d'embellissement où il peut bien choquer la vraisemblance particulière par quelque altération de l'histoire, mais non pas se dispenser de la générale, que rarement, et pour des choses qui soient de la dernière beauté, et si brillantes, qu'elles éblouissent. (*Discours de la tragédie*)

It is as with *Le Cid*; everything gives way to *éblouissement*.

Éblouissement and *éclat*; the spectator is dazzled, perhaps even tricked, by the master magician. A man of the theatre, Corneille was very conscious of this aspect of his art. The two comedies which stand at either end of his greatest tragic period are entitled *L'Illusion comique* and *Le Menteur*. In the second of these the theme of illusion is strong, even in such inessential points as the conversation between Dorante and Géronte on the miraculous renewal of Paris:

Paris semble à mes yeux un pays de romans.
J'y croyais ce matin voir une île enchantée:
Je la laissai déserte, et la trouve habitée;
Quelque Amphion nouveau, sans l'aide des maçons,
En superbes palais a changé ses buissons.   (II, v)

The magician who has created this fairy-tale world is akin to the magician of the theatre.

Dorante, the hero of *Le Menteur*, excels in changing bushes into palaces, using language to transform his years as a law student into years of glamorous military service, inventing on the spur of the moment extravagant entertainments and adventures which he sets forth in *récits* which are like parodies of the narrations of tragedy.

The self-parody is carried further in scenes between father and son which echo Act I, scenes 4–5 of *Le Cid*:

GÉRONTE

Ô vieillesse facile! o jeunesse impudente!
Ô de mes cheveux gris honte trop évidente!...
(enter DORANTE)
Êtes-vous gentilhomme?

DORANTE

Ah! rencontre fâcheuse!
Étant sorti de vous, al chose est peu douteuse. (V, ii–iii)

Parody figures too in *L'Illusion comique*, where Corneille, who had previously excluded from his comedies the stock types of earlier comedy, gives us a Matamore who puts all previous *faux braves* in the shade. The *faux brave* is essentially a by-product of a heroic military age. The fragility of the heroic figures of tragedy can be measured in the appearance of this posturing puppet whose speeches read like anticipations of the grandiloquence of *Le Cid*:

Le seul bruit de mon nom renverse les murailles,
Défait les escadrons, et gagne les batailles.
Mon courage invaincu contre les empereurs
N'arme que la moitié de ses moindres fureurs. (II, ii)

But more important than Matamore is Alcandre, the magician. Pridamant has lost his son and goes to the magician for help. Like a playwright (and like Shakespeare's Prospero) Alcandre sets before the wondering and credulous father's eyes figures who play out the adventures of the missing son. These adventures appear to reach exalted and tragic dimensions in Act V, when suddenly Alcandre draws back a curtain and, to the surprise of the father and the audience, reveals actors counting their takings. Pridamant's son has gone on to the stage. And, as the play-within-a-play-within-a-play ends, the magician, satisfied at having played on Pridamant's feelings, expounds to us the theatrical fraud:

L'un tue, et l'autre meurt, l'autre vous fait pitié;
Mais la scène préside à leur inimitié.
Leurs vers font leurs combats, leur mort suit leurs paroles,
Et sans prendre intérêt en pas un de leurs rôles,

> Le traître et le trahi, le mort et le vivant,
> Se trouvent à la fin amis comme devant. (V, v)

What really matters is the money: 'Le théâtre est un fief dont les rentes sont bonnes.'

Exposing in this way the theatrical illusion, Corneille was very much aware of the vulnerability of any serious theatre—let alone the theatre of admiration. He was capable of seeing tragic drama as nothing but a set of dazzling images, heroic figures, extraordinary situations, high-sounding speeches—and this is how his plays appear to many of his audiences. Splendid fairy-tales which excite or amuse us with visions of the extraordinary and the impossible—is this all that Corneille offers us? Can he be taken seriously?

Certainly an understanding of Corneille is not helped by the attempt to ignore the ostentation and glamour of his plays, regarding him simply as a stern moralist, propagator of the doctrine of duty before love, honour before passion. He was a moralist of course and, as he says in his *Discours du poème dramatique*, was not averse to using the theatre for the inculcation of virtue. In particular his theatre dwells indefatigably on the possibilities and various forms of heroic action. The important thing to remember, however, is that, in spite of the many quotable *sententiae* of the 'Qui veut mourir ou vaincre est vaincu rarement' type, these plays do not simply provide moral lessons through easy successes. Rather do they show us the strivings, occasional successes, and far more frequent failures of the attempt of man to be more than man, to cut himself free from the humiliating normality of natural life, to be master of his destiny and creator of himself. In placing before his audiences such dazzling figures of aspiration as Rodrigue, Corneille was mirroring the moral preoccupations of many men of his time, preoccupations fed by many sources, among them the Stoic revival of the late sixteenth century and the military values of a declining feudal aristocracy. In the seventeenth century, as always, the heroic enterprise faced daunting odds in the shape of time, the emotions, and the realities of politics. In many of Corneille's tragedies we are made poignantly aware of the contrast between the noble expression of heroic aspirations and the reality to which the hero remains ultimately vulnerable.

This central theme of Corneille's theatre is brought out more strongly by an awareness of the 'magician' aspect of his dramatic technique. The attempt of the hero to establish himself above the world of ordinary men is as splendid and fragile as Corneille's creation of a magical world. The hero, like the playwright, may astonish, and even convince, the characters on stage and the audience in the theatre, but dazzlement cannot last for ever. More than is often thought, Corneille should be read in the light of Pascal's sombre *pensée*: 'Le dernier acte est sanglant, quelque belle que soit la comédie en tout le reste.' With this in mind, let us now look at some of Corneille's heroes, not forgetting that such a thematic approach, especially when briefly sketched, inevitably does violence to Corneille's many-sided genius.

First Alidor: Corneille's early comedies do not differ essentially from many of his tragedies, except that they deal with affairs which are private, not public. The world of the comedies is one of bewildering change, in which the only solid values appear to be those of money. But in this world some men and women attempt in one way or another to elevate themselves above the flux of ordinary life. The most significant of these is Alidor of *La Place Royale*. Realizing that his love for Angélique endangers his personal independence, he takes the 'heroic' decision to cut himself off from her:

> Je veux la liberté dans le milieu des fers.
> Il ne faut point servir d'objet qui nous possède;
> Il ne faut point nourrir d'amour qui ne nous cède:
> Je le hais, s'il me force; et quand j'aime, je veux
> Que mon feu m'obéisse au lieu de me contraindre. (I, iv)

Corneille seems to approve of this stand; he says in his dedication: 'C'est de vous que j'ai appris que l'amour d'un honnête homme doit être toujours volontaire; qu'on ne doit jamais aimer en un point qu'on ne puisse n'aimer pas; que si on en vient jusque-là, c'est une tyrannie dont il faut secouer le joug.' Nevertheless Alidor's attempt to rebel against nature is unsuccessful.

It is not just that his action, unlike that of many of the heroes of the tragedies, leads nowhere and has no purpose outside himself. Much worse, he fails to be master of himself and, for all his boasting, remains a slave to Angélique. In an attempt to win both ways,

Alidor tries to keep Angélique by proxy, 'giving' her to his friend
Cléandre—this solution will be adopted again and again by Corneille's heroes and heroines (from the Infanta in *Le Cid* to Bérénice
in *Tite et Bérénice*). But in Alidor's case the attempt is a miserable
failure; not only does he remain in love with Angélique, but she
does not marry the man to whom he destines her. He tries to carry
her off for his friend and carries off the wrong woman in a nocturnal
scene of confusion which brings to a head Fate's mockery of this
would-be superman. Finally he repents, but too late; Angélique
refuses him and goes off to a convent, leaving him to make a virtue
of necessity, hero in spite of himself:

> Je cesse d'espérer et commence de vivre;
> Je vis dorénavant, puisque je vis à moi. (V, viii)

This could be triumphant, but in the circumstances it has a hollow
ring, like so many of Corneille's apparently happy endings.

The heroes of what are usually considered the great tragedies,
Rodrigue, Horace, Auguste, and Polyeucte, all have aspirations
which in some way resemble those of Alidor. Their aim is to be
masters of themselves and their destiny, members of a heroic élite.
But unlike his, their action is set in a political or religious context
which gives it greater seriousness and seems to guarantee it the
permanence and solidity to which a comic hero could never attain.
On the whole they succeed in establishing their heroic status through
an action which also establishes or confirms a religious or political
order. All these plays look forward to a conquering, triumphant
future; *Cinna*, for instance, in spite of possible doubts about the
motives behind Auguste's clemency and the permanence of his
solution, ends with a confident prediction of the future greatness of
the emperor and Rome. This is the period when what has been
called Corneille's 'mensonge héroïque' looks least illusory, when the
'mensonge' of the heroic posture leads to the 'vérité' of a new order.
But both hero and order are still fragile; in no play is this clearer—
as far as the hero is concerned—than in the problematic *Horace*.

Horace is Corneille's first Roman play. He was to use some fifteen
subjects from Roman history, ranging from the seventh century
B.C. (*Horace*) to the seventh century A.D. (*Héraclius*). Like many

men of his time he naturally thought out political and moral issues by way of Roman examples; French and Roman history were seen as reflecting one another, French kings were compared to the emperors and heroes of Rome, and Corneille, dedicating *Horace* to Cardinal Richelieu, says with a typical oratorical flourish: 'Ce généreux Romain, que je mets aux pieds de Votre Éminence, eût pu paraître devant elle avec moins de honte, si les forces de l'artisan eussent répondu à la dignité de la matière.' In view of the readiness of such parallels, commentators have rightly shown that Corneille in many of his plays used Roman history to discuss precise topical questions. Thus in *Horace* the fratricidal war of Rome and Alba can be read as the war between France and Spain, and the apparent justification of Horace's action as a defence of Richelieu's firm policy. Such 'allegory' is constantly present in Corneille's theatre, which is much closer to contemporary currents of thought and contemporary issues than is sometimes believed.

But it is in its view of the hero that *Horace* is of most interest. The play is set near the beginning of Roman history, so that the audience can look forward over the centuries of conquest and greatness which are foreseen by Sabine in the first scene of the play. We are at a crucial point in this development; in the course of the play the valorous Horace, well-nigh single-handed, defeats the brothers Curiace of Alba and so lays the foundation for this future greatness. There can be no question, then, of the importance of Horace's achievement, the integration of his heroic action into a greater whole; no question either of his success in conquering his nature and using his misfortune to make himself into a sort of superman. This is how he expounds the code of the heroic élite:

> Mourir pour le pays est un si digne sort,
> Qu'on briguerait en foule une si belle mort;
> Mais vouloir au public immoler ce qu'on aime,
> S'attacher au combat contre un autre soi-même,
> Attaquer un parti qui prend pour défenseur
> Le frère d'une femme et l'amant d'une sœur,
> Et rompant tous ces nœuds, s'armer pour la patrie
> Contre un sang qu'on voudrait racheter de sa vie,
> Une telle vertu n'appartenait qu'à nous.   (II, iii)

Indeed Horace is far too successful for the taste of many critics who, attributing their reaction to Corneille's intention, see in *Horace* a denunciation of the hero's fierce anti-natural heroism and a defence of the more humane attitude of Curiace. However we may feel about it, it is very doubtful if this was Corneille's view of the matter; nothing suggests that he intended his play specifically as a plea for or against the kind of attitude represented by Horace—though there is no doubt that he was fascinated by it. While all his plays reflect ideas which were currently being debated, it would be a mistake to read them as expositions of clearly defined opinions.

But even if the debate of *Horace* is inconclusive, we must surely admire Horace's firmness ('ce généreux Romain'), while pitying him in that the height of his glory is so immediately followed by his degeneration. No sooner has he won himself the position of supreme national hero at great personal cost than he meets his match in his sister Camille, who is so opposed to his heroic values that she provokes him into sullying his reputation by murdering her. In the final act, where he is brought to trial for this murder, he is declared to be above the laws because of his exceptional usefulness to Rome. Thus the hero is made to serve the State, but this is achieved at the expense of his personal honour, for Horace's only wish is to die, so aware is he of the fragility of reputation in the face of time and the ignorant populace. A triumph for Rome, the end is a defeat for Horace; the play, beginning with his noble sacrifice at the altar of heroism, ends on an imperfect compromise—Horace's verdict is: 'Pour mon honneur, j'ai déjà trop vécu.'

In the tragedies following *Polyeucte* the victorious but precarious equilibrium of the early tragedies is shattered (this by no means implies that the plays themselves are less successful). Nowhere is this more clear than in *Nicomède*, a play apparently largely inspired by the struggles of the Fronde, the civil war which then divided France. The difference between this play and, for instance, *Le Cid* is at once very clear. *Le Cid* shows us a man creating himself as hero and at the same time strengthening the State. Nicomède, on the other hand, is already the perfect hero when the play begins and is at odds with the heads of the state, the weak king Prusias, his father, the scheming Arsinoe, his stepmother, and his half-brother Attale, protégé of

Rome. Rome, incidentally, appears now not as a young and conquering nation, but as an imperialist power; it is fascinating to trace in Corneille's theatre the changing image of Rome, which never again recovers the integrity of *Horace* and *Cinna*.

In the course of the play Nicomède does almost nothing; his role is to stand unmoved and uncompromising, flaying his opponents with the haughty and aggressive eloquence of which Corneille is such a master. Meanwhile the initiative has passed into the hands of the mean-minded Machiavellian politicians whom we see at work in Corneille's theatre from *Pompée* onwards (and even in the Félix of *Polyeucte*). They set against the nobility of the hero the unvarying 'règle de la vraie et saine politique':

> Aussitôt qu'un sujet s'est rendu trop puissant,
> Encor qu'il soit sans crime, il n'est pas innocent:
> On n'attend point alors qu'il s'ose tout permettre;
> C'est un crime d'État que d'en pouvoir commettre;
> Et qui sait bien régner l'empêche prudemment
> De mériter un juste et plus grand châtiment.   (*Nicomède*, II, i)

The gulf between hero and state seems to be unbridgeable. The hero's virtue, though undoubted, appears to lead nowhere but to the grave—the whole play is acted out in the shadow of the treacherous murder of Nicomède's master, Hannibal, at the instigation of the Roman ambassador Flaminius. Yet in spite of all this we have a surprise happy ending, thanks to a hardly credible change of heart on the part of the Machiavellians. Superficially the wicked stepmother's conversion reminds one of those of Félix in *Polyeucte* and Émilie in *Cinna*: 'Contre tant de vertu je ne puis le [mon cœur] défendre', but in fact Nicomède has done nothing new to deserve this, other than exercising an easy clemency. The fairy-tale ending is unconvincing and the sinister words of the evil counsellor remain in our ears as a constant threat to the hero.

The 'false happy ending', which half masks the decline or the impasse of heroism, is a constant in Corneille's later plays. After *Sertorius* (1662) and *Sophonisbe* (1663), which show the downfall of heroes and kings without any façade of happy ending, we witness in *Othon* (1664), *Agésilas* (1666), *Attila* (1667), *Tite et Bérénice* (1670), and *Pulchérie* (1672) a series of apparent solutions to

hopelessly entangled situations. These tragedies of matrimonial bargaining resemble nothing so much as Corneille's early comedies, but
whereas in a comedy a conventional ending is expected, in a serious
'comédie héroïque' (as Corneille calls some of his later plays) such
an ending is more obviously a screen. *Tite et Bérénice* and *Pulchérie*
in particular end on a note of sterility disguised as victory.

The two male characters in *Tite et Bérénice* are both feeble figures
in comparison with the heroes of Corneille's early tragedies. Tite,
the emperor, has no will left in him; his tiredness is poignantly
expressed:

> Oui, Flavian, c'est à faire à mourir.
> La vie est peu de chose; et tôt ou tard, qu'importe
> Qu'un traître me l'arrache, ou que l'âge l'emporte?
> Nous mourons à toute heure; et dans le plus doux sort
> Chaque instant de la vie est un pas vers la mort. (V, i)

His brother Domitian is ready to go to almost any lengths to win
the woman he loves, Domitie.

It is left to the women, Domitie and Bérénice, to show the men
the way—this reversal of roles is frequent in late Corneille. But the
women by themselves can achieve nothing solid. Their actions,
though noble, lead nowhere. Bérénice seems to achieve a victory
comparable to that of Auguste in *Cinna* as she voluntarily renounces
Tite and the empire:

> Ma gloire ne peut croître, et peut se démentir.
> Elle passe aujourd'hui celle du plus grand homme,
> Puisque enfin je triomphe et dans Rome et de Rome:
> J'y vois à mes genoux le peuple et le sénat;
> Plus j'y craignais de honte, et plus j'y prends d'éclat;
> J'y tremblais sous sa haine, et la laisse impuissante;
> J'y rentrais exilée, et j'en sort triomphante.   (V, v)

But this victory founds no new order and produces only a hollow
reputation. Where Auguste and Rodrigue had found something
approaching immortality through actions which changed the world,
Bérénice's form of immortality is merely narcissistic. It is no accident that the play contains a *raissonneur*, Albin, who propounds the
gospel of La Rochefoucauld:

> L'amour propre est la source en nous de tous les autres:
> C'en est le sentiment qui forme tous les nôtres.   (I, iii)

This is true of Bérénice as it had been many years earlier of
Alidor.

Still, at least these noble women do mask their sorrows, saying
bravely (in Domitie's case) 'A l'amour vraiment noble il suffit du
dehors'. But in Corneille's last and beautiful play, *Suréna*, the mask
is off; 'les dehors' are not enough and there is no face-saving
triumph. It is Pascal's 'dernier acte . . . sanglant'. We are back with
the situation of *Nicomède*; Suréna, the perfectly virtuous, perfectly
handsome hero, saviour of his country, is at odds with his king
because his love runs counter to the national interest and because
his reputation is too great. Suréna, like Nicomède, will not compromise, but for him there will be no fairy-tale ending. There is no
room for the hero—and particularly the hero in love—in a state
where the Machiavellian counsellors have taken over. From the
first scene the action moves inexorably to a brutal ending which
is recounted with a striking lack of heroic adornment:

> A peine du palais il sortait dans la rue,
> Qu'une flèche a parti d'une main inconnue;
> Deux autres l'ont suivie; et j'ai vu ce vainqueur,
> Comme si toutes trois l'avaient atteint au cœur,
> Dans un ruisseau de sang tomber mort sur la place. (V, v)

This is the end for a stoical hero, who has virtually abandoned all
the hopes (political, religious, or personal) which spurred on Corneille's earlier heroes—even that last comfort, faith in posterity:

> Quand nous avons perdu le jour qui nous éclaire,
> Cette sorte de vie est bien imaginaire,
> Et le moindre moment d'un bonheur souhaité
> Vaut mieux qu'une si froide et vaine éternité. (I, iii)

These are only a few of the steps in what (to speak untheatrically)
we may call Corneille's forty-year-long meditation on heroism. His
theatre is rich in other themes, but this one is central. It is no good
going to Corneille for a natural, reasonable view of human life; one
may regret this, but Corneille remains fascinated by heroes of the
all-or-nothing. He offers us a vast series of variations on a single
theme, the possibility of creating (against nature) a new man and a
new order. His theatre evokes the splendour of this enterprise, but
also its fragility. Just as behind the clashing swords and clashing

words of the stage play there are the actors counting their money, so behind the glories of heroism lurk a mediocre reality and a great sadness.

NOTE

PIERRE CORNEILLE, 1606–84, belonged to a family of Rouen lawyers. He was educated at a Jesuit college, studied as a barrister, and for much of his life held a sinecure in the Rouen *parlement*, though he was eventually able to live by his pen. The main events of his life were literary publications and literary quarrels, particularly the dispute with Cardinal Richelieu and many fellow writers over his play *Le Cid*. Otherwise his life was uneventful. He lived in Rouen and Paris, married in 1641, and became a member of the Académie Française in 1647.

Works. Corneille's earliest play, the comedy *Mélite*, was first performed in 1629.[1] It was followed by a series of comedies of which the best known are *La Place Royale* (1634) and *L'Illusion comique* (1636). In 1637 Corneille entered on his greatest period, in which were performed the four tragedies *Le Cid* (1637), *Horace* (1640), *Cinna* (1641), and *Polyeucte* (1643). Over the next thirty years there followed twenty more plays; among the best of these are the comedy *Le Menteur* (1644), and the tragedies *Rodogune* (1645), *Nicomède* (1651), *Sertorius* (1662), *Othon* (1664), and *Suréna* (1674—his last play). From 1651 to 1656 Corneille devoted himself mainly to a verse translation of *The Imitation of Christ*.

Editions. The standard edition of Corneille's complete works is that of C. Marty-Laveaux (12 vols., 1862–8). More portable recent editions include that published in the Integrale series edited by A. Stegmann (1963), and (for the plays only) the two Pléiade volumes edited by P. Lièvre and the three Garnier volumes edited by M. Rat. Garnier have also published a useful *Théâtre choisi*. For Corneille's dramatic theory see his *Writings on the Theatre*, edited by H. T. Barnwell (1965).

Criticism. There are two general studies in English: P. J. Yarrow, *Corneille* (1963), and R. J. Nelson, *Corneille, his heroes and their worlds* (1963). Over the last twenty years valuable work has been done in relating the themes of Corneille's theatre to contemporary intellectual and political history by P. Bénichou, *Morales du Grand Siècle* (1948), O. Nadal, *Le Sentiment de l'amour dans l'œuvre de Pierre Corneille* (1948), B. Dort, *Pierre Corneille, dramaturge* (1957), G. Couton, *Corneille* (1958), and J. Maurens, *La Tragédie sans tragique* (1966). J. Boorsch, 'Remarques sur la technique dramatique de Corneille', *Yale Romanic Studies* (1941), and G. May, *Tragédie cornélienne, tragédie racinienne* (1948), illuminate Corneille's mastery of the theatre. There are suggestive chapters in E. B. O. Borgerhoff, *The Freedom of French Classicism* (1950), A. Rousseaux, *Le Monde classique* (vol. iii, 1951), and J. Rousset, *La Littérature de l'âge baroque en France* (1953). An important contribution is S. Doubrovsky, *Corneille et la dialectique du héros* (1963).

[1] The dates of first performance of most of Corneille's earlier plays are uncertain.

3. Religion and Society

THE religious history of France in the seventeenth century revolves largely around the progress of the counter-Reformation. Almost every issue which came up during the century may be related to this central fact. Its influence is to be seen in the foundation of new religious orders and the expansion of old ones, in the growing influence of the Jesuits, in the phenomenon of Jansenism, in the provision of seminaries for the secular clergy, and in the reaction of Gallican traditionalists to 'Papal Aggression'. Not least, the effect of the counter-Reformation may be seen in the Revocation of the Edict of Nantes (1685), which, by removing the last vestiges of toleration for the French Protestants, seemed to round off the victory of the forces of righteousness. And, if we seek a postscript, we may find it in Louis XIV's destruction of the Jansenist religious centre of Port-Royal-des-Champs in 1709. He made it a desert and called it peace.

The essential background to all these issues may be found in events which took place in the middle of the sixteenth century in the remote Italian town of Trento. The Council of Trent, an assembly of mainly Italian bishops under Papal leadership, provided general lines for the defence and renewal of the Roman Church—a task which had taken nearly twenty years (1545–63). The fathers of the Council defined doctrine more clearly in order to emphasize the gap between orthodoxy and the heresies of Luther and Calvin. They also laid down measures for the tightening of church discipline, in order to answer the charge that the Church of Rome was degenerate. In particular, the Council strengthened the authority of the local bishops over the clergy of their dioceses and authorized them to set up seminaries for the education of the clergy. The Jesuits, a new religious order founded in 1540, had dominated the Council in its later stages, and it was their view which prevailed in most areas of theology. The age of Erasmus was over. It was succeeded by one in which the scholasticism of the Middle Ages, a synthesis of Aristotle and Christianity, enjoyed an astonishing revival. In a sense the 'moderns' of 1600 were the Jesuit schoolmen, Bellarmine and Suarez.

The impact of Trent upon France was to be immense, but the most decisive changes were delayed for fully half a century. In many areas of Europe, reorganization of the Roman Church had already begun in the decades following the Council. In France, however, the Wars of Religion left open several possibilities. There was always the chance of a Catholic defeat or of a compromise settlement with Calvinism. Catholic fortunes turned for the better with the Massacre of St. Bartholomew's Day in 1572, but it was not until Henri de Navarre accepted the Mass in 1593 that the future took shape. From then on the missionary forces of the counter-Reformation were able to rely upon Crown tolerance and, after Henri IV's death in 1610, upon Crown support.

Thus, we may take as part of the story the ways in which the measures of Trent changed the outlook of the French Church. But the tale was not a simple one. In fact Trent was not formally received in France. In 1614, at the last meeting of the Estates General before the French Revolution, the clerical estate pressed for the acceptance of the Tridentine decrees, but its proposals were rejected by the nobility and the bourgeoisie. The work of Trent went forward, but often in the teeth of local opposition. The counter-Reformation with its emphasis upon uniformity and episcopal power did not appear as an unmixed blessing to all Frenchmen. Indeed the 1614 episode should be seen as setting the disturbed tone of much of the religious history of France during the century. Reform in the eyes of one group appeared as reaction in the opinion of another.

If our theme is the impact of the Council of Trent in France, we are led to discuss the role of the French clergy. We will begin by discussing the role of the parish priests and the bishops, that is, the secular clergy, and then go on to deal with the regular clergy, namely the priests who lived according to a strict rule (*regula*) of life and were organized into communities or societies. This second class of clergy included monks and nuns living permanently in a fixed place as well as more mobile (though centralized) orders like the Friars and the Jesuits.

The French secular clergy numbered about 150,000 at this period, or about one in 100 of the population. We may think of them in the main as being drawn from the comfortably-off members of the French middle class. There was indeed a wide social gap between the clergy and most of their parishioners. Of nearly 150 seminary students at Beauvais in the second half of the century, none were sons of artisans or of the middle and lower peasantry. The Church was on the side of property. In fact the establishment of seminaries may have widened the social gap between priest and people still further, since it took an income of 50 *livres* a year (the net annual income of an average peasant family) to maintain a student at the seminary, and this was beyond the reach of the vast majority. Even within the clerical groups there were social distinctions. Those who came from well-to-do merchant families or from the class of royal administrators (*officiers*) often ended up as comfortable canons in the local cathedral, whereas the less prosperous students were more likely to pass their days in a rural parish, frequently the one in which they had been born.

During the course of the seventeenth century, bishop after bishop set up a seminary in his diocese, usually with the assistance of regular clergy, especially the Jesuits. As a result, by the end of the century the character of the secular clergy had changed. Seminary education raised the educational standard of the clergy, and with it, we may assume, their social status. In 1600 many local *curés* led a life scarcely different from that of their peasant flock. By 1700 seminary training had separated them socially and intellectually. We may see the effects of this change in the rise of the Richerist movement of the eighteenth century, which seems to have been a movement of protest by a more highly educated clerical body. The ultimate effects of higher educational standards were to be evident in the unrest of many of the lower clergy during the early stages of the French Revolution.

But seminary education was not perfect. It often consisted of a year or two's instruction at an elementary level, with a great emphasis on intellectual conformity. The seminaries of the Sulpicians laid particular stress upon piety rather than learning. So there is perhaps a sense in which the seminary had an unfortunate influence upon many of the clergy, in forcing them into a particular intellectual mould. From the Crown's point of view, however, a seminary-trained clergy was an additional social bulwark against rural disorder. The seminary instilled into the clergy acceptance of the values of a deferential society which could then be propagated from the pulpit.

Further social divisions within the secular clergy reflected the divisions of society at large. There was a wide social gap between the parish clergy and the episcopate, whose membership was over-whelmingly aristocratic. Of the total number of 194 bishops for the period 1683–1700, no less than 170 (88 per cent) were men of noble birth, and about half of these had been born into the *noblesse d'épée*. It can be argued from this that the reforms of the Council of Trent, which aimed at reinforcing the authority of the bishops in their dioceses, led indirectly to strengthening the power of the aristocracy in seventeenth-century France. Religious authority and social status became so intermingled that it is easy to understand how social unrest was later to be associated almost inevitably with anti-clericalism. The roots, or some of them, of the French Revolution are to be found in the Council of Trent.

The bishops were also linked directly with the government. They were appointed by the Crown and often used as royal servants. Pierre de Bonzy, for example, Archbishop of Toulouse and later a cardinal, served as a French ambassador overseas. At every level the bishops were exposed to royal pressure. They corresponded directly with Colbert, as local agents of the government, to provide him with information which ensured the smooth running of the provincial estates. They were also expected to vote with the government on contentious matters, much as the English bishops were expected to do in the House of Lords during the eighteenth century. (When the bishops voted against him on one occasion, the Duke of Newcastle remarked 'They have forgotten their Maker'.) When ecclesiastical politics were important, as during the crisis with the Papacy in 1682, the Crown had no difficulty in packing the Clerical Assembly with pliant bishops. Louis XIV might have said of himself: 'L'Église, c'est Moi'!

Behind this administrative and political picture there was a complex system of interlocking family relationships by which a strong tradition of clerical careerism was maintained in particular familes. The De Bonzy family controlled the see of Béziers for nearly a century. The Bishop of Beauvais in the 1640s, Auguste Potier, had succeeded his uncle in the see. Cardinal de Retz, Archbishop of Paris, was a member of the Gondi family which had held the see for several generations. It is doubtful whether the Tridentine reforms made much difference to this kind of family vested interest.

When we turn to the regulars, 100,000 strong, we enter a world of somewhat greater complexity. In general, the regulars came from higher social groups than the seculars and tended to reach a higher intellectual standard. This in itself would be enough to account for the rivalry, indeed hostility, which often existed between the seculars and the regulars. In addition, the regulars were better off financially, often at the expense of the secular clergy, and, since they belonged to centralized bodies within the Church, they enjoyed the advantage of sharing in corporate power. Indeed the social division between regular and secular clergy is as significant in its own way as the split between the *curé* and his bishop.

At the top of the social scale among the religious orders were the Benedictines. The greatest monasteries of France, in many cases dating back to the early Middle Ages, were Benedictine. They were strongest in areas which were most traditional, socially and economically. In Lorraine, for example, as M. Taveneaux has shown,[1] the Benedictine monasteries dominated the aristocratic countryside of the diocese of Verdun, but they were not nearly so strong in the more urbanized Alsace.

The Tridentine reform which affected the monks most closely was a regrouping of their traditionally independent houses into loose federations. In France the new monastic association was known as the Congregation of St. Maur, from the name of the mother house in Paris. By the end of the century this association numbered well over a hundred monasteries, divided into five provinces. But the traditional independence of so many monasteries was not surrendered without resistance. At La Daurade, near Toulouse, the first Maurists ran into serious difficulties before they

[1] See R. Taveneaux, *Le Jansénisme en Lorraine, 1640–1789*, Paris, 1960.

succeeded in reforming the monastery. The open support of Richelieu was necessary before the expansion of the Congregation could achieve the momentum aimed at. But this success was obviously bought at a price. It seemed on occasion as if Tridentine reform was an instrument of absolutism under another name. The advantage from Richelieu's point of view was that local aristocratic resistance could be denounced as hostility to the true interests of the reforming Church. (A similar method was used in the Netherlands under Philip II and in Germany under the Habsburgs.)

This revival of monasticism—the number of Maurists increased fourfold during the century—was a remarkable reversal of fortune after the hammer blows of the Erasmians against the monastic way of life, and it is not to be explained entirely in terms of state support. Some form of social explanation is called for. The wish to enter a monastery indicated a considerable degree of alienation from the world. And perhaps we should seek the origins of so substantial a trend against the pressures of the world not merely in the revival of the true spirit of religion, but also in the anxieties of the declining minor aristocracy. To enter a monastery was an acceptable form of migration for a gentleman at a time when no other alternative existed. The Maurist innovations in the monastic life included the provision of a separate room for each monk, and a strong emphasis on scholarly work as distinct from the manual labour of more traditional monasticism—both of them changes acceptable to gentlemen. By the eighteenth century, the tradition of gentility had come to dominate some houses, as the following description by J. McManners shows us:

On the other hand, life was undoubtedly comfortable. Monks no longer wore their habit as a badge of separation from the world: their tonsure was nominal, their frocks were cut to resemble the cassocks of secular priests and beneath appeared elegant shoes and black silk stockings. Pleasant social occasions relieved the tedium of Benedictine life—a hand at cards, a musical concert on Sunday evenings after vespers. Meat was banished from the common table, but the best sea and river fish, ducks, teal, hares, and woodcocks were lavishly supplied, and the 'infirmary table', where the prior himself habitually dined, was free from restrictions. Each monk received 120 *l.* a year as pocket-money, and was allowed to take a month's holiday, on condition of attending offices at a house of the order if one were conveniently near. The abbey provided a horse, or, for older monks, a two-horse cabriolet with grooms, so that once every year the comfortable boredom of existence was broken by a pleasant excursion, with relaxation in the company of relatives at Tours, Brest, Rennes, or even as far afield as Cambrai.

The counter-Reformation saw the establishment of many other religious orders in France, each of them tending to have a particular social allegiance. The French Oratory catered in the main for the higher social groups. Its founder, Pierre Bérulle (1575–1629), took as his model the Oratory of Saint Philip Neri (1515–95), one of the dominating figures of the Italian counter-Reformation. The order increased rapidly in numbers and became particularly important in the field of education, where the success of its schools rivalled that of the Jesuits. The order produced its share of intellectuals, among them Malebranche. In contrast, the Lazarists founded by St. Vincent de Paul (1580–1660) and the Brothers of the Christian Schools founded by Jean-Baptiste de La Salle (1651–1719) drew their membership from lower social ranks and sought to deal with the social and educational problems of the deprived. There were similar social differences among the women's religious orders. Indeed, in a society so sharply stratified socially as seventeenth-century France, it could hardly have been otherwise. The social differences were evident in the largely intellectual orientation of the Oratorians as compared with the practical approach of the Lazarists and the Christian Brothers. It is not surprising that St. Vincent de Paul should have had no sympathy at all with intellectuals, who seemed to be impeding the work of Christ by creating a mist of verbal subtleties.

However, the most important of the religious orders was the Society of Jesus, whose influence by and large was thrown on the practical side. Socially, and in many other ways, the Jesuits stood in marked contrast to the monks. They were very much an urban phenomenon. Their churches and colleges were to be found in the towns, rarely in the countryside. In its social origins the order was broadly middle class, and the same seems to have been true of those whose ear it hoped to catch. P. Dainville has shown that in the

Jesuit seminary at Toulouse only six of the list of fifty-three names were noble. The majority came from upper-middle-class families, *officier* or merchant in origin. This placed the order socially on much the same level as the Oratorians, with whom it came into direct competition.

The Jesuits more than most religious orders reflected the centralizing aspect of Tridentine reform. If the Benedictine ideal was that of a religious family, the Jesuit ideal envisaged a missionary army. The Jesuits brought into the Roman Church the bureaucratic spirit which Max Weber has described (for example in *Wirtschaft und Gesellschaft*) as the source of modernity. They distrusted the forming of links with local society. They took their members away from their families and by means of a very long and severe training inculcated a different set of values in which obedience to the organization played a dominant role. They were liable to be moved at a moment's notice and had to accept this without question. If many of their members were learned men, they were orientated towards learned polemic rather than genuine scholarship. This was the religious order which came to dominate the religious life of France. In fact it is hardly an exaggeration to describe the seventeenth century as the century of the Jesuits. The eighteenth century, in contrast, saw their decline and collapse.

The link between Tridentine reform and royal absolutism is illustrated most clearly in the use to which the Jesuits were put by successive ministers. The mobility of the Jesuits meant that the Crown could bring them into troubled areas in order to create or restore an atmosphere of orthodoxy. The foothold established in Huguenot parts of France by Jesuit missionaries was often enlarged and made permanent by the setting up of a Jesuit college. In the 1620s Jesuit houses were established in the Huguenot towns of Montpellier, Albi, and Carcassonne. In 1630 Richelieu's successful campaign against the Huguenots was followed up by the establishment of a Jesuit house at La Rochelle. In 1633 the Huguenot colleges at Castres, Montauban, and Nîmes were converted into *mi-partie* colleges by a decree of Louis XIII (i.e. the administration was divided between Protestants and Jesuits). In 1622 the colleges were taken over completely after a show of force by the Lieutenant of Guienne.

The Jesuits were prominent in more obviously political enterprises. In 1654/5, following the acquisition of Roussillon from Spain, a Jesuit house was set up at Sedan. In 1640, when Arras was taken by the French, the Jesuits were brought in to establish a college. In 1682 the Jesuits moved into Strasbourg in the wake of the armies of Louis XIV. It is clear from these examples that there was a working alliance between the Jesuits and the Crown. It is also clear why criticism of the Jesuits was resented by Louis XIV.

In spite of their ties with the Crown, there was a good deal of local opposition to the Jesuits. At Caen there was resistance from the mayor and the upper bourgeoisie before the governor, acting with Crown support, succeeded in introducing the Jesuits in 1609. At Bayonne the Jesuits never succeeded in overcoming local prejudices against them (it was, after all, the birthplace of Saint-Cyran). At Auxerre the local clergy were hostile to the order, and at Bordeaux, where the Jesuits had been brought in to set up an orthodox alternative to the College of Guienne, resistance to the Jesuits remained a live issue (it was the *Parlement* of Bordeaux which refused to condemn Pascal's *Lettres provinciales*). At Reims the hostility of the archbishop was a factor in explaining the decline of the Jesuit college there.

Behind all the hostility to the Jesuits lay, no doubt, the conservatism of many vested interests. But there was also an intellectual basis for opposition to the order, and this provided a thread of unity among its critics. This opposition, which can loosely be called the Gallican tradition though its influence was not confined to France, maintained that the language of theology should be based upon a return to the tradition of the early Church from the Bible to St. Augustine. This outlook in theology stretched back, as far as France was concerned, to the dominating figure of Jean Gerson, chancellor of the University of Paris in the fifteenth century. Its twin capitals were the universities of Paris and Louvain, both of which had been influenced by the revival of classical studies in the sixteenth century. The Gallican tradition was especially strong among the secular clergy, but in the seventeenth century its influence was to be found in religious orders like the Oratorians and the Benedictines. Its central figure was Jacques-Bénigne Bossuet (1627-1704), Bishop of Meaux, but it could also claim to include men like St. François de Sales (1567–1622), Bérulle, and Saint-Cyran. At a lower level, we may see the influence of Gallicanism in the choice of reading for seminary students at Beauvais. At the level of scholarship it is clear in the Maurist edition of Augustine, and at the level of polemic in the work of Ellies du Pin (1657–1719).

In contrast, the Jesuits stood for the revived scholasticism of Trent. The great schoolmen of the order were Robert Bellarmine (1542–1621) and Francisco Suarez (1548–1617), but it also produced a whole host of minor figures stretching well into the late seventeenth century, with Arriaga (1592–1667) as the most significant. Their critics maintained that they used an unsuitable technical vocabulary in their approach to theology, but the Jesuits claimed to incorporate all knowledge, whether derived from reason or revelation, within one synthesis. It is easy to understand the attraction which this claim might have for many minds, not the least being the notion that theology was a 'science'. The Jesuit approach was to crumble under the impact of the scientific discoveries of the seventeenth century, but it was an unconscionable time a-dying.

The clash between the Jesuit and Gallican traditions, neither of them more 'modern' than the other, forms an essential part of the religious history of France in the seventeenth century. It explains, for example, the tension between the French Oratory and the Jesuits, which was so marked a feature of the period. Pierre Bérulle was a theologian formed essentially in the Gallican tradition. He was critical of the Jesuits for being too aggressive in their missionary activity at the expense of the Oratorians, and he attacked them in print for this. But part of the antipathy may be explained by the anti-scholastic, Augustinian cast of Bérulle's mind which was part of his legacy to the Oratory. The Jesuit–Gallican clash also forms the background to the best known of all the religious controversies of seventeenth-century France—the conflict between the Jesuits and the Jansenists.

Cornelius Jansen (1585–1638) and his associate, Jean Duvergier de Hauranne, abbé de Saint-Cyran (1581–1643), were two secular priests who aimed at a drastic religious reform in accordance with the spirit of the early Church. They both set their faces against the idea of establishing a religious order, but by the 1640s their followers established a centre at the former monastery of Port-Royal in the valley of the Chevreuse, forty miles from Paris (there was also another Port-Royal in Paris, catering for women). Port-Royal provided a place of retreat for its 'solitaries', and there was little in the idea to suggest that it would develop in any way differently from other centres of religious reform. Indeed, Saint-Cyran had been greatly influenced by Bérulle, and he and Jansen planned to introduce the Oratorians into Holland as soon as the Spanish offensive against the United Provinces was successful.

Where Port-Royal differed from other groups was in its devotion to the teaching of Saint Augustine, as explained by Jansen and Saint-Cyran. Jansen himself was an unusual combination of saint and theologian, but it was his posthumous book, the *Augustinus*, published in 1640, which provided his followers with a rallying-point. In this book Jansen intended to do what Augustine himself had been unable to do—to draw out the implications of Augustinian theology and set them out in a comprehensive pattern. What the *Summa Theologica*, as interpreted by Suarez, was to the Jesuits, Augustine, as interpreted by Jansen, was to the Jansenists. Behind all the controversies which were later to develop lay the simple fact that the Jansenists regarded themselves as the faithful exponents of the teaching of Augustine, doctor of Grace and, they maintained, the most important theologian in the history of the Church.

Tension between Jansen and the Jesuits already existed in the 1620s, but 'Jansenism' at this date was very much a Flemish phenomenon, largely associated with the resistance of the University of Louvain, that centre of Augustinian theology, against the infiltration of the Jesuits. It was also connected with the opposition of the Flemish provinces to centralization, in which two prominent bishops, Van Boonen of Malines and Triest of Ghent, were spokesmen for Flemish liberties. In fact, the publication of the *Augustinus* in 1640 was more an episode in Flemish than in French history, and the chief opposition to its condemnation in Rome came from the archbishop of Malines and the bishop of Ghent, backed by great numbers of their clergy.

The central position which Jansenism came to occupy in French politics and religion began to develop almost accidentally, and was related to the plans which Jansen, Dutch by birth, and Saint-Cyran had developed for the counter-Reformation in Holland. The success of the Spanish forces, operating from their bases in the southern Netherlands, was an essential prerequisite for this enterprise. On the other hand, Richelieu saw the situation from an opposite point of view. His aim was to destroy Habsburg power, preferably by fighting to the last Protestant but, if this failed, by open war. In 1635, following upon the death of Gustavus Adolphus in 1632 and a subsequent Spanish resurgence, Richelieu reluctantly declared war against Spain and in alliance with the Dutch marched against the Spanish Netherlands. Jansen and Saint-Cyran saw this as the Machiavellian death-blow to their hopes for a Catholic Holland, and in the same year they openly criticized Richelieu in a pamphlet *Mars Gallicus*. The characteristic Jansenist mistrust of the Court thus had its origins in the split with Richelieu over foreign policy.

The later history of Jansenism was a tale of strategic retreat in the face of papal condemnation. In 1643 the *Augustinus* was condemned, but as the papal bull was not formally received in France, it was possible for French Jansenists tacitly to ignore it. The next step taken by their opponents was to arrange for certain 'Jansenist' propositions, eventually five in number, to be condemned by the Sorbonne, with the backing of Mazarin. The Jansenist reply to this was to deny that the propositions were in the *Augustinus*. When further papal condemnation followed, the Jansenists were forced to adopt a position by which they accepted the Pope's right to decide in doctrine but denied that his knowledge of the facts of a particular situation was necessarily correct. (This was the famous distinction between *droit* and *fait*.) For the next ten years Mazarin and Louis XIV tried to force the Jansenists to accept a formulary which condemned Jansen. In 1668 a compromise was agreed upon which led to peace for a decade but, from 1679, the struggle flared up once more until it became a major issue of Church–State relations.

There is a barren air about this catalogue of facts, but it dissolves when we look more closely at the political background. Throughout the history of Jansenism politics played a substantial part, not merely the politics of Mazarin about which we know something, but also the ecclesiastical politics of Rome about which we know all too little. It is clear that the Jesuits were in a position to play 'the Roman card' during the middle decades of the century. Their influence was particularly strong in the Holy Office, where the pro-Jesuit Albizzi was secretary. The two popes of the mid century, Innocent X and Alexander VII, were also favourably disposed towards the Jesuits. Against this the Jansenists had little to rely upon but the assistance of the Flemish hierarchy, the support of anti-Jesuit circles in Rome among orders like the Franciscans, and the Gallican tradition at home. In Rome, when it came to the test, they could not match the power of the Jesuits, while at home Mazarin's fanatically anti-Jansenist outlook made it difficult for anyone to support them openly. Mazarin saw the Jansenists as a major factor behind the unrest of the Fronde. He even regarded the wayward archbishop of Paris, Paul de Gondi, as a Jansenist. In the face of Mazarin's enmity, which stretched to an unprecedented show of force in the precincts of the university, the Jansenists' attempt to build up support in the Sorbonne failed completely. Sixty Jansenist sympathizers among the Sorbonne professors were simply weeded out and punished for their disobedience. The young Bossuet kept his peace and earned his reward later. But no openly Jansenist sympathizer could hope for promotion in the Church.

If we seek a more general social background to Jansenism, we may find it perhaps in the decline of the aristocracy in the first part of the century. It does not seem an accident that Jansenism should find a home in provinces whose tradition, liberties, and culture were most severely threatened by the advance of absolute monarchy. In the south-west (the home of Saint-Cyran), in Brittany, in parts of Normandy, and in Lorraine, Jansenism was taken up by a declining aristocracy and its intellectuals, the clergy. The situation was parallelled in the Spanish Netherlands and in Holland where the Flemish aristocracy on both sides of the frontier was threatened with extinction. Perhaps it was for this reason that Jansenism was not merely a matter for the theologians, but became a statement of pessimism which someone like Mme de Sévigné could appreciate. It also seems no accident that the Irish theologians, Florence McConry and John Sinnich, representatives of a dying Gaelic culture, should have turned to Augustinianism and helped Jansen to formulate his ideas.

It would be wrong to assume that Jansenism was the only religious issue in France in the middle and later decades of the seventeenth century. After all, Jansenists were few in number and élitist in outlook, and they believed that grace was given only to the chosen minority. Many of them were also intellectuals, which limited the appeal of their movement. But Jansenism did have the effect of raising the emotional temperature and forcing people to take sides. St. Vincent de Paul, for example, was violently anti-Jansenist and we may detect perhaps in his outlook, and in the standpoint of the Christian Brothers and the Sulpicians, the anti-intellectualism of the practically minded. The same also applies to the Trappists who, as one writer has put it, sought grace by spiritual athletics. Only among the intellectual orders did the Jansenists find support. It is significant that the Maurists produced a critical edition of Augustine in 1680, which was attacked by the Jesuits for being pro-Jansenist. Many of the Oratorians also showed sympathy for the Jansenist cause, and it was no accident that their order produced the best-known Jansenist of the second generation, Quesnel. Among the secular clergy Jansenism had its spokesmen, notably Antoine Arnauld and Pierre Nicole, but the full extent of clerical support was not revealed until after the death of Louis XIV when the Jesuit control of church appointments was removed.

There is a great deal that we have not touched upon in this brief survey. Another account might well have paid more attention to the phenomenon of religious 'conversion' among the laity, to the spirituality of St. François de Sales, the humanitarianism of St. Vincent de Paul, or the devious ideals of the Compagnie du Saint-Sacrement. We have chosen to stress here the impact of the counter-Reformation and the many-sided character of its fortunes in France, from Richelieu to Saint-Cyran. In doing so, however, we have ignored completely a most interesting feature of religion in seventeenth-century French life, namely the religion of the peasantry. In this area, the field of popular religion, scarcely any work has been done. Local studies might well show that the medieval religious outlook of the French peasant changed during the century, the rural counterpart of a process by which, under the impact of the counter-Reformation, the France of Rabelais changed into the France of Bossuet—and Voltaire.

NOTE

FRANÇOIS DE SALES, 1567–1622, was Bishop of Geneva from 1602. Much of his life was spent preaching the cause of the counter-Reformation in his native Savoie. In 1610, in conjunction with Jeanne de Chantal, he founded the Visitandines. François de Sales's most famous work, *Introduction à la vie dévote* (1609), showed his views to be at an opposite pole from Bérulle's form of spirituality.

PIERRE BÉRULLE, 1575–1629, came into conflict with the Jesuits when he founded the French Congregation of St. Philip Neri's oratory (the Oratorians) in 1611. He was a theologian of wide influence and laid particular stress on the omnipotence of God.

VINCENT DE PAUL, 1576–1660, was the founder of the Congrégation de la Mission, usually called the Lazarists, in 1625. Eight years later he founded the Sisters of Charity in association with Louise de Marillac. He was noted for his benevolence, simplicity, and work on behalf of the aged and the oppressed.

FRANÇOIS D'AIX DE LA CHAISE, 1624–1709, was Jesuit confessor to Louis XIV from 1675 until his death.

CORNELIUS JANSEN, 1585–1638, was born in Holland and studied at Louvain, Paris, and Bayonne. He was appointed professor at Louvain and became Bishop of Ypres in 1636. His massive work, the *Augustinus*, was published posthumously in 1640 and became the central point of controversy between the Jesuits and his own followers.

SAINT-CYRAN (JEAN DUVERGIER DE HAURANNE), 1581–1643, was a fellow-student of Jansen's in Paris and Bayonne where he studied Augustinian theology. He became spiritual director of the convent of Port-Royal in 1633. In 1638 he was imprisoned by Richelieu at Vincennes and was released shortly before his death.

ANTOINE ARNAULD, 1612–94, took clerical orders in 1638 and was ordained in 1641 when he retired to Port-Royal. He is 'le Grand Arnauld' of Jansenism who came into conflict with the Jesuits from 1643 when he published *La Fréquente Communion*. Censored by the Sorbonne in 1656, he remained in retirement until the 'paix de l'Église' in 1668.

PIERRE NICOLE, 1625–95, taught at Port-Royal with his close friend Antoine Arnauld. In 1658 he published a Latin version of Pascal's *Lettres provinciales*. His principal work, *Essais de morale*, appeared from 1671 to 1678. In 1679 he went into exile with Arnauld, but returned to France in 1683 after making his peace with the authorities.

Further Reading. Little has been written on the Jesuits apart from the massive work of P. Delattre, *Les Établissements jésuites en France* (1940–57), and the stimulating articles by P. Dainville published in the periodical *Populations* (1955). We need a study of popular religion that goes further than the somewhat orthodox though valuable pages of G. Le Bras, *Études de sociologie religieuse* (1955–6). J. McManners, *French Ecclesiastical Society under the Ancien Régime* (1960), offers a fascinating picture of clerical life in the provinces at a somewhat later date than is dealt with in this chapter. There is also a valuable section in P. Goubert, *Beauvais et le Beauvaisis de 1600 à 1730* (1960), pp. 197–206.

Jansenism has attracted a great deal of attention. Two sharply contrasting works of reference are Sainte-Beuve's *Port-Royal* (available in three Pléiade vols.) and the relevant articles in the *Dictionnaire de théologie catholique* (1903–50). Modern studies are discussed in an imaginative article by P. Chaunu, 'Jansénisme et frontière de catholicité', in *La Revue historique* (Jan. 1962). On the sociological side, L. Goldmann, *Le Dieu caché* (1955), is a provocative work, and R. Taveneaux, *Le Jansénisme en Lorraine* (1960), is a penetrating sociological study with wide implications. Taveneaux's shorter book, *Jansénisme et politique* (1965), is also important. The acknowledged master of Jansenist studies in France is J. Orcibal. His series, *Les Origines du jansénisme*, is still in progress, five volumes having been published between 1947 and 1962. Vol. i is an edition of Jansen's letters and vol. iv, edited by Annie Barnes, is devoted to the correspondence of Saint-Cyran. The letters of another Jansenist, Martin de Barcos, were edited by L. Goldmann (1956). Mention should also be made of a Franciscan scholar, L. Ceyssens, whose many informative articles include 'Jansénisme et antijansénisme en Belgique au XVIIᵉ siècle', *Revue d'histoire ecclésiastique* (1956). Among many general accounts of Jansenism are A. Gazier, *Histoire générale du mouvement janséniste* (1922, 2 vols.) and L. Cognet, *Le Jansénisme* (1964). Finally, there is much of relevance in R. A. Knox, *Enthusiasm* (1950), though the author makes the strange assumption that enthusiasm is only found outside the Church of Rome, never within it.

4. Pascal

PRACTICALITY and concreteness were fundamental features of Pascal's mind. They emerge with particular clarity in his scientific and mathematical studies. Where science was concerned, he insisted on the need for experimentation and distrusted the assertions of traditional authority. He also found useful ways in which to apply various aspects of his theoretical work. This last point is emphasized in most accounts of his life, and many readers will be familiar both with the *pascaline* and the *carrosses à cinq sols*. The *pascaline* is the name given to the calculating machine which Pascal devised at the age of nineteen. Its original purpose was to help his father's work as *commissaire pour l'impôt* in upper Normandy, and the machine was finally constructed, with the aid of a mechanic from Rouen, in 1644. As regards the *carrosses à cinq sols*, these are the carriages which he invented towards the end of his life to provide a cheap form of public transport in Paris. Letters-patent were granted in 1662 and the first route linked the Luxembourg with the Porte Saint-Antoine. In the field of mathematics, Pascal made important contributions with his work on probability and conic sections. His gifts were more geometric than algebraic (in contrast to Descartes) and his practical bent emerges clearly—if negatively—in a letter of 1660 to the mathematician Fermat when he writes: '. . . je l'appelle [i.e. la géométrie] le plus beau métier du monde; mais enfin ce n'est qu'un métier; et j'ai dit souvent qu'elle est bonne pour faire l'essai, mais non pas l'emploi de notre force' (282).[1]

Pascal's insistence on a sound experimental method is particularly evident in his work on the vacuum and on atmospheric pressure.

---

[1] All quotations from Pascal, apart from the *Pensées*, are followed by a page reference to the Intégrale edition of the *Œuvres complètes*. Quotations from the *Pensées* are followed by two numbers, preceded by the letters L and B respectively, indicating the order of the Lafuma and Brunschvicg arrangements.

The latter question, for example, prompted him to mount the Tour Saint-Jacques in Paris in order to test his theories. His having done so is not in itself remarkable, but it has to be set against the fact that Aristotelianism still dominated traditional seventeenth-century science especially strongly because of the extent to which Aristotle's ideas had been adapted and absorbed by the Church. This is why we find Pascal, in his correspondence about the vacuum with the Jesuit Père Noël, arguing that to cite the opinions of the ancients in scientific matters is not to prove anything. He attacks the Aristotelian approach which 'ne met point de différence entre définir une chose et assurer son existence' (210) and adds the warning: '. . . pour faire qu'une hypothèse soit évidente, il ne suffit pas que tous les phénomènes s'en ensuivent, au lieu que, s'il s'ensuit quelque chose de contraire à un seul des phénomènes, cela suffit pour assurer de sa fausseté' (202). The need for repeated practical experiments, which he deduces from these ideas, is put succinctly in his conclusion to the posthumously published *Traités de l'équilibre des liqueurs et de la pesanteur de la masse de l'air*: '. . . les expériences sont les véritables maîtres qu'il faut suivre dans la physique' (259).

Pascal's practical turn of mind shows itself with equal clarity and insistence in his attitudes to philosophy, morals, and theology. In these areas, however, practicality takes the form of relating ideas to human realities and human needs. As regards philosophy, Pascal was dissatisfied with that branch of it which used to be called 'natural philosophy' (speculation on the nature of the physical world). In the *Pensées*, referring to natural philosophy as practised by Descartes (whose science, in any case, he considered too abstract and lacking a sound experimental basis), he writes: '. . . nous n'estimons pas que toute la philosophie vaille une heure de peine' (L. 84, B. 79). Another fragment emphasizes the need which he felt to study man first and foremost:

J'avais passé longtemps dans l'étude des sciences abstraites et le peu de communication qu'on en peut avoir m'en avait dégoûté. Quand j'ai commencé l'étude de l'homme, j'ai vu que ces sciences abstraites ne sont pas propres à l'homme, et que je m'égarais plus de ma condition en y pénétrant que les autres en l'ignorant. J'ai pardonné aux autres d'y peu savoir, mais j'ai cru trouver au moins bien des compagnons en l'étude de

l'homme et que c'est la vraie étude qui lui est propre. J'ai été trompé.
Il y en a encore moins qui l'étudient que la géométrie (L. 687, B. 144).

A phrase from another fragment—'la science des mœurs me consolera
toujours de l'ignorance des sciences extérieures' (L. 23, B. 67)—is
consistent with these ideas and also indicates Pascal's deep interest
in the analysis of human behaviour. In fact, his 'humanism' takes
the form of regarding man himself as the most puzzling and revealing of all objects of study. We shall see later something of the way
in which he uses the study of the natural world specifically to shed
light on man's nature and then, by scrutinizing this human nature
more closely, uses man to illuminate and confirm the truths of the
Christian religion.

If it is true that Pascal placed moral philosophy above scientific
speculation because, at least in his own day, it seemed more directly
concerned with the nature of man and with the question of how
he should live his life, it is also true that he opposed the tendency to
abstraction that can be present even in the sphere of moral philosophy. One of his main objections to Cartesianism arises from his
insistence that so-called 'objective' knowledge is a false ideal. He is
aware that there is always a personal contribution which shapes and
affects the knower's own knowledge—in a word, that the act of
knowing is a concrete, human act. Having pointed out, in the long
and fascinating fragment headed 'Disproportion de l'homme', that
anthropomorphism, often unconscious, causes natural philosophers
to speak of the physical world in terms of 'des inclinations, des
sympathies, des antipathies', he adds: 'Au lieu de recevoir les idées
de ces choses pures, nous les teignons de nos qualités . . .' (L. 199,
B. 72). This is a fundamental aspect of Pascal's epistemology. He is
sharply aware that those acts of understanding and knowing with
which philosophy concerns itself involve some element of personal
participation and therefore some element also of prior assumption
or belief. Furthermore, when he makes this point, Pascal is not only
saying that all knowledge is rooted in a measure of subjectivity. He
is preparing the ground for what he will wish to argue, in a religious
context, about the relationship between knowledge and belief. His
attitude also shows us, incidentally, that he stands in a tradition
going back beyond Saint Augustine and reaching forward through

Maine de Biran and Kierkegaard to present-day phenomenological and existential thinkers, which focuses philosophical speculation on the initial fact of human experience of the world. This is a tradition which may be conveniently summed up in the formulation of Karl Jaspers: 'In the world _man_ alone is the reality which is accessible to me. Here is presence, nearness, fullness, life. Man is the place at which and through which everything that is real exists for us at all.'

This emphasis on man as the starting-point of all 'realistic' thinking would have been endorsed by Pascal as it has been by various modern 'Christian existentialists'. It also renders more or less inevitable Pascal's strong concern with human behaviour, particularly in its moral aspects, in his two major works: the eighteen _Lettres provinciales_ of 1656–7 and the posthumously published _Pensées_ (1670). At first sight, however, the _Lettres provinciales_ might seem to be an exception to this 'man-centred' approach. After all they were written to confound, among other things, the Jesuit tendency to adapt moral laws to limited human capacities. In fact, the Jesuits appear to have the more human, and humane, attitude. It should be remembered, too, that the initial purpose of casuistry (the object of some of Pascal's most searing attacks) was to produce a practical ethics. The aim was to offer guidance on moral conduct in specific cases where no general moral law seems to offer a clear pronouncement that will meet the human particularity of the problem. Nevertheless, in his demonstration of the gap which he finds between the theory and the practice of certain Jesuits, Pascal shows himself to be both practically minded and acutely sensitive to human reality. He makes it clear that a practical ethics can become so befogged by fine verbal distinctions and ultimately meaningless definitions that it ceases to be an ethics of any kind, either practical or theoretical. Similarly, Pascal repeatedly measures theory against actual human practice. He points out the way in which human beings are encouraged to behave under the influence of a _morale relâchée_. He is both practical and 'man-centred' in the sense that he holds religion to be a call to certain modes of action and not simply a set of ideas whose human consequences can be ignored. No doubt it has to be admitted that his insistence on certain forms of behaviour and his attack on moral laxity arise in some measure from a fundamental moral absolutism. But they also derive in at least as great a degree from his concern that men should live up to their highest potential as human beings.

The debate to which the *Lettres provinciales* made a significant and memorable contribution requires some explanation. The issues which Pascal discusses with such polemical skill and satiric verve will at first seem remote because they are couched in the theological jargon of the period. This jargon itself, however, is one of the targets of his wit, and a number of the questions which he raises are still very much alive. The origins of the debate are to be found in the previous century, in the twin facts of the Reformation and counter-Reformation. In France the Protestant Reformation, reacting in large measure to abuses within the Catholic Church, took the form of Calvinism with a theological insistence on innate human sinfulness and a rigorous moral code. The Jesuits, on the other hand, who had grown greatly in numbers and influence since their foundation in 1534, became the spokesmen of the more militant element in the counter-Reformation movement. They naturally attacked Protestant theology, but they also opposed the standards of piety and moral rigorism derived from this theology. Where the Calvinists insisted on the natural corruption of man and on his utter dependence on God, the Jesuits emphasized the potentialities of human free will, thereby liberating man from entire reliance on divine grace. This doctrine eventually became known as Molinism following the publication, in 1588, of a work in Latin by the Spanish Jesuit Luis Molina: *Concordia liberi arbitrii cum gratiae donis*. Molina elaborated a theory of 'sufficient grace' which comes from God and which, through the concurrence of man's own volition, is transformed into saving 'efficacious grace'. In this way, and in accordance with his title, Molina reconciled the gifts of grace with human free will. Inevitably there was Protestant opposition to this relatively humanistic and optimistic theology, and opposition also to some of the moral consequences drawn from it. But there were also those within the Catholic Church itself—among them Cornelius Jansen, Bishop of Ypres, and his close friend Saint-Cyran—who sought to recall the Church to a more demanding conception of man's relation to God which would both purify the Church and place it beyond the

moral attacks of Protestantism. Jansen and Saint-Cyran went back
to Saint Augustine for this purer teaching and the eventual result of
their years of study was the *Augustinus* of Jansen published in 1640
two years after his death. The book was condemned by the Inquisi-
tion in the following year and by the bull, *In eminenti*, of Pope Urban
VIII in 1643. Ten years later Pope Innocent X, in the bull *Cum
occasione*, condemned as heretical five propositions said to be
contained in the *Augustinus*. The fight in defence of Jansen's
Augustinian ideas, which soon came to be called Jansenism, was
first carried on by Saint-Cyran and, since he was a spiritual director
of the nuns of Port-Royal in Paris between 1634 and 1643, Jansenism
and the abbey of Port-Royal became virtually synonymous. In the
meantime, in 1637, the earlier abbey from which the nuns had
moved in 1625—Port-Royal-des-Champs in the valley of the
Chevreuse outside Paris—had been reoccupied by a small group of
men (including Antoine Le Maître), the so-called 'solitaires' of
'messieurs de Port-Royal'. After the death of Saint-Cyran in 1643
one of their number, Antoine Arnauld, became leader of the
Jansenist cause and published such works as *La Frèquente Communion*
(1643) and *Apologie de M. Jansénius* (1644). Following the bull of
Innocent X Arnauld could not easily defend the five 'Jansenist'
propositions as such, but he claimed that they were not to be found
in the *Augustinus* (only one of them, in fact, occurs textually in the
book). This is the famous distinction between *droit* and *fait* which
became an important element in the rearguard action which the
Jansenists were now fighting. However, Arnauld himself did not let
the matter rest here, and the second of his two *Lettres à un duc et
pair* (1655), with its bold reiteration of the main Jansenist positions,
led to his arraignment before the Faculty of Theology (the Sorbonne)
in Paris. It was at this point, during one of Pascal's visits to Port-
Royal, that he and Arnauld met. Pascal's sister, Mme Périer,
describes how the *Lettres provinciales* were born from the
encounter:

[Pascal] était allé à Port-Royal-des-Champs pour y passer quelque
temps en retraite, comme il faisait de temps en temps. C'était alors qu'on
travaillait en Sorbonne à la condamnation de M. Arnauld, qui était aussi
à Port-Royal. Tous ces Messieurs le pressaient d'écrire pour se défendre,

et lui disaient: 'Est-ce que vous vous laisserez condamner comme un enfant, sans rien dire?' Il fit donc un écrit, lequel il lut en présence de tous ces Messieurs, qui n'y donnèrent aucun applaudissement. M. Arnauld, qui n'était point jaloux de louanges, leur dit: 'Je vois bien que vous trouvez cet écrit mauvais, et je crois que vous avez raison.' Puis il dit à M. Pascal: 'Mais vous, qui êtes jeune, vous devriez faire quelque chose.' M. Pascal fit la première Lettre, la leur lut; M. Arnauld s'écria: 'Cela est excellent; cela sera goûté; il faut le faire imprimer.' On le fit, et cela eut le succès qu'on a vu.

No doubt Pascal began writing the *Lettres provinciales* because of a genuine commitment to the cause of his friends at Port-Royal. No doubt, also, they encouraged him because of his sharp intelligence and the polemical gifts which he had already displayed, on a rather different subject, in his correspondence with Père Noël. At the same time, although he took a keen interest in theology, Pascal was not a professionally trained theologian, and there is evidence that he was provided with some of his material by both Arnauld and Nicole from whose own earlier writings he also drew. As regards the polemical method which he used, this is so varied and vigorous that even Voltaire, who certainly possessed no initial prejudice in Pascal's favour, greatly admired the letters as an outstanding example of the controversialist's art.

In the first three letters Pascal adopts a deliberately straightforward and practical approach calculated to lower the temperature of this theological quarrel. He demonstrates the argument to be chiefly about terminology—and highly technical terminology at that —rather than about real or fundamental differences. This attitude of relatively uninstructed common sense combined with penetrating intelligence enables him to mock the experts caught in an intricate verbal web of their own devising. The same attitude makes it natural that he should appeal to the fair-mindedness of men of goodwill rather than to theologians holding entrenched positions. He effectively broadens the debate, takes it outside the Parisian Faculty of Theology, and significantly addresses his letters to a 'provincial' rather than to the Sorbonne doctors. In doing this, Pascal not only exposes and exploits the inconsistencies and divisions of the opposition; he enlivens the satirical element further by means of imaginary

que vous cherchez dans vous-mêmes les remèdes à vos misères. Toutes vos lumières ne peuvent arriver qu'à connaître que ce n'est point dans vous-mêmes que vous trouverez ni la vérité ni le bien' (L. 149, B. 430).

On the metaphysical level, Pascal sees man as solitary, alienated, contingent. In a famous fragment entitled 'Disproportion de l'homme' (L. 199, B. 72) he measures man against the infinite vastness of space, then against the infinite smallness of the elements which compose the most minute living organisms, and describes him as 'un néant à l'égard de l'infini, un tout à l'égard du néant, un milieu entre rien et tout, infiniment éloigné de comprendre les extrêmes . . .'. Again, this unique and solitary creature that is man owes his very existence to chance: '. . . moi qui pense n'aurais point été, si ma mère eut été tuée avant que j'eusse été animé, donc je ne suis pas un être nécessaire' (L. 135, B. 469). But man is not merely solitary and contingent. His condition is one of suffering, condemnation, and imprisonment. We are all condemned to death—'le dernier acte est sanglant quelque belle que soit la comédie en tout le reste'—and we await our sentence:

Qu'on s'imagine un nombre d'hommes dans les chaînes, et tous condamnés à la mort, dont les uns étant chaque jour égorgés à la vue des autres, ceux qui restent voient leur propre condition dans celle de leurs semblables, et, se regardant les uns et les autres avec douleur et sans espérance, attendent à leur tour. C'est l'image de la condition des hommes. (L. 434, B. 199)

This last fragment is both sombre and dramatic enough for any philosophical nihilist or devotee of 'the absurd'. Pascal uses it not only to convey a picture of 'unaccommodated man' but also to point up the unbearable truth which obliges men to banish it from their minds through those various forms of action and distraction which he calls *divertissement*. The almost frenetic human need to be diverted from reality is, for Pascal, a psychological symptom of a metaphysical and spiritual *malaise*. Normally, *divertissement*—which may take the form of work or play, self-discipline or self-abandonment—is not a conscious response to the 'human condition'. Indeed, most men are unaware of that condition. Nevertheless, *divertissement*

dialogues between the writer and various theologians. A typical passage from the first letter, on the term *pouvoir prochain*, conveys something of the general flavour:

Car enfin, mes Pères, dites-moi, je vous prie, pour la dernière fois, ce qu'il faut que je croie pour être catholique.

— Il faut, me dirent-ils tous ensemble, dire que tous les justes ont le *pouvoir prochain*, en faisant abstraction de tout sens: *abstrahendo a sensu Thomistarum, et a sensu aliorum theologorum*.[1]

— C'est-à-dire, leur dis-je en les quittant, qu'il faut prononcer ce mot des lèvres, de peur d'être hérétique de nom. Car enfin est-ce que ce mot est de l'Écriture?

— Non, me dirent-ils.

— Est-il donc des Pères, ou des Conciles, ou des papes?

— Non.

— Est-il donc de saint Thomas?

— Non.

— Quelle nécessité y a-t-il donc de le dire, puisqu'il n'a ni autorité, ni aucun sens de lui-même?

— Vous êtes opiniâtre, me dirent-ils. Vous le direz, ou vous serez hérétique, et M. Arnauld aussi . . .

Heureux les peuples qui l'ignorent! heureux ceux qui ont précédé sa naissance! Car je n'y vois plus de remèdes si MM. de l'Académie ne banissent par un coup d'autorité ce mot barbare de Sorbonne qui cause tant de divisions . . . Je vous laisse cependant dans la liberté de tenir pour le mot de *prochain* ou non; car j'aime trop mon prochain pour le persécuter sous ce prétexte. (374-5)

The pun in this last sentence should not prevent us from seeing the essentially practical and human emphasis of Pascal's attitude.

Between the publication of the third and fourth letters Arnauld was condemned and deprived of his status as a doctor of the Sorbonne. This fact may explain in some measure the change of tone and tactics which come with the fourth letter itself. From what was primarily a rearguard action concerned to expose theological mumbo-jumbo, Pascal turns (letters 4–10) to a direct attack on what he claims to be the Jesuit moral teaching that largely follows from Jesuit theology. As the object of attack changes, so the tone alters from mockery to moral indignation. The following passage from

---

[1] Leaving aside the meaning of the Thomists and the meaning of other theologians.

the sixth letter is typical of the manner in which Pascal exposes some of the worst aspects of casuistry:

Ce bon Père me parla donc de cette sorte:
— Une des manières dont nous accordons ces contradictions apparentes, est par l'interprétation de quelque terme. Par exemple, le pape Grégoire XIV a déclaré que les assassins sont indignes de jouir de l'asile des églises, et qu'on les en doit arracher. Cependant nos 24 Vieillards disent en la page 660: *Que ceux qui tuent en trahison ne doivent pas encourir la peine de cette bulle.* Cela vous paraît être contraire, mais on l'accorde, en interprétant le mot d'*assassin* comme ils font par ces paroles: *Les assassins ne sont-ils pas indignes de jouir du privilège des églises? Oui, par la bulle de Grégoire XIV. Mais nous entendons par le mot d'assassins ceux qui ont reçu de l'argent pour tuer quelqu'un en trahison. D'où il arrive que ceux qui tuent sans en recevoir aucun prix, mais seulement pour obliger leurs amis, ne sont pas appelés assassins.* De même, il est dit dans l'Évangile: *Donnez l'aumône de votre superflu.* Cependant plusieurs casuistes ont trouvé moyen de décharger les personnes les plus riches de l'obligation de donner l'aumône. Cela vous paraît encore contraire; mais on en fait voir facilement l'accord, en interprétant le mot de *superflu*, en sorte qu'il n'arrive presque jamais que personne en ait. Et c'est ce qu'a fait le docte Vasquez en cette sorte, dans son Traité de l'Aumône, c. 4: *Ce que les personnes du monde gardent pour relever leur condition et celle de leurs parents n'est pas appelé superflu. Et c'est pourquoi à peine trouvera-t-on qu'il y ait jamais de superflu dans les gens du monde, et non pas même dans les rois.* (392)

This type of exposure continues up to the end of the tenth letter as Pascal scrutinizes in turn such concepts as 'probabilism', 'the interpretation of terms', and 'direction of intention'. Also, particularly in letters 9 and 10, the effect of casuistry on piety, as well as on morality, is examined. The remaining eight letters are chiefly concerned with answering attacks already provoked by the first ten and with defending Jansenism against the accusation that it is thinly disguised Calvinism. The *Lettres provinciales* caused a great stir and passions ran high on both sides. The Parlement of Aix had the letters publicly burnt, whereas the Parlement of Bordeaux refused to make this gesture. Pascal's display of passion and skill was admired and applauded by many who were not themselves Jansenists, although the book was placed on the Index by Pope Alexander VII. Bayet, in his book on the *Lettres*, sums up the situation when he

writes: 'Devant l'opinion, Pascal est vainqueur. Offi[...] est vaincu.' This double experience of practical victory [...] defeat is perhaps the surest sign of polemical triumph. [...]

In the nature of things, the polemicist can have a shr[...] the effect he has achieved. The less overtly militant [...] influence is less easily calculated, though its effect ma[...] lasting. Pascal clearly enjoyed a wide and immediate su[...] the *Lettres provinciales*, but it is as an apologist for Christi[...] he has continued to be best known since his death. The no[...] he made while preparing a systematic disclosure and defen[...] truths of Christianity—the *Pensées*—remain his major cont[...] to literature and thought.

Running through the whole of Pascal's advocacy of the C[...] position we find a continuing emphasis, in keeping with his p[...] attitudes elsewhere, on man—his nature, his needs, and the p[...] of his existence. Pascal argues that human nature and the 'h[...] condition' can only be adequately accounted for in terms of Chr[...] teaching. Furthermore, it is only by accepting the full consequ[...] of this teaching that we can live in accordance with our full hu[...] potential and face the otherwise terrifying nature of our m[...] physical situation.

At the psychological level, discussing man's nature, [...] emphasizes the thoroughly contradictory qualities of human [...] both individually and collectively. In a passage of typical rh[...] bravura he writes: 'Quelle chimère est-ce donc que l'homme [...] nouveauté, quel monstre, quel chaos, quel sujet de contra[...] quel prodige? Juge de toutes choses, imbécile ver de terre [...] taire du vrai, cloaque d'incertitude et d'erreur, gloire et [...] l'univers' (L. 131, B. 434). The same contradictory [...] conveyed in rather different terms in another fragme[...] sommes incapables de ne pas souhaiter la vérité et le [...] sommes incapables ni de certitude ni de bonheur' (L. 4[...] Having made this point in a variety of ways, Pascal insi[...] impossible to find within man himself a means either [...] this double nature or of bridging the gap between as[...] realization, between the pursuit of truth and happi[...] continuing elusiveness of both these goals: 'C'est en va[...]

is no less significant on that account. Indeed, it has the value that it may be used as a distinctively 'human' way of ultimately bringing individuals to a consciousness of their condition and hence to a consciousness of their need, as Pascal sees it, of God.

It is clear, then, that Pascal first shows the possible relevance of Christian teaching not by propounding religious dogmas but by focusing attention exclusively on the nature of men as revealed by close psychological scrutiny. This means that he relates religion first and foremost to human concreteness, not to metaphysical abstraction. He goes on to claim that the doctrine of the Fall explains man's double nature (his fallen nature contains elements of an antecedent perfection), while the redemptive role of Christ offers escape from an otherwise imprisoning human condition. At the same time, Pascal does not simply try to drive human beings, in desperation, to Christian remedies. Nor does he hold that Christianity can work effectively simply by dint of our giving intellectual assent to it. On the contrary, he repeatedly asserts that a purely rational approach to religion neither constitutes belief nor does it bring us knowledge of God. Religion requires a response from the whole of our being, and when Pascal defines faith as 'Dieu sensible au cœur, non à la raison' (L. 424, B. 278) he is not putting a premium on irrationality but claiming that our response must be more than solely intellectual. In fact, the term cœur is used in at least three different senses in the Pensées. Firstly, and in secular contexts only, it is used in the familiar meaning of the emotional or sentimental part of our nature. Secondly, it is used in a way that recalls the Kantian categories and means the innate apprehension of certain general principles. For example: 'Le cœur sent qu'il y a trois dimen-sions dans l'espace et que les nombres sont infinis et la raison démontre ensuite qu'il n'y a point deux nombres carrés dont l'un soit double de l'autre. Les principes se sentent, les propositions se concluent et le tout avec certitude quoique par différentes voies . . . (L. 110, B. 282). Thirdly, Pascal uses the term cœur to mean some-thing like that focal point in the personality at which thought, feeling, and will come together in such a way that they provide know-ledge which is direct, concrete, and, to that extent, intuitive. This is no doubt the sense of such phrases in Psalm 119 (a psalm much admired by Pascal) as 'With my whole heart have I sought thee . . .'. It is the sense in which Pascal uses the term *cœur* in another fragment: 'Le cœur a son ordre, l'esprit a le sien qui est par principe et démonstration. Le cœur en a un autre. On ne prouve pas qu'on doit être aimé en exposant d'ordre les causes de l'amour; cela serait ridicule' (L. 298, B. 283). Sir Arthur Eddington made a closely related point when he wrote:

> In the case of our human friends we take their existence for granted, not caring whether it is proven or not. Our relationship is such that we could read philosophical arguments designed to prove the non-existence of each other, and perhaps even be convinced by them—and then laugh together over so odd a conclusion. I think it is something of the same kind of security we should seek in our relationship with God. The most flawless proof of the existence of God is no substitute for it; and if we have that relationship the most convincing disproof is turned harmlessly aside.

It is such a relationship, using the word *cœur* in the third sense above, that Pascal tries to make accessible to us, and this aim goes far towards explaining his rejection of Descartes's 'ontological proof' of God's existence. At best, the relevant passage in the *Discours de la méthode* offers a 'rational' proposition about some kind of First Cause or Prime Mover. Even if such a proposition convinced us, it would convince the intellect only. By failing to engage feeling and will, as well as thought, it would have no power of permanent and full conviction.

The claim put forward by Pascal when he uses the term *cœur* in the second sense above—'Les principes se sentent, les propositions se concluent et le tout avec certitude quoique par différentes voies'— goes some way towards explaining the over-all intellectual shape of his apologia. Where Descartes, for example, moves from argument to belief in his discussion of God's existence, Pascal moves in something like the opposite direction—from belief to argument. This distinction is related to one made by Pascal himself between what he calls the *esprit de géométrie* and the *esprit de finesse*. It may also remind us that his method, which seeks to bring antecedent belief to consciousness of itself, resembles that of Saint Anselm in his *Proslogion*: 'For I do not seek to understand in order that I may believe, but I believe in order that I may understand.' Nevertheless, Pascal does not claim that man can have any adequate understanding, of a direct kind, of God. He is at pains to insist that we can only know God indirectly, through the intermediacy of Christ—and we can do so because Jesus Christ was both man and God, a means of access for man to God. The importance which he attaches to this mediating role of Christ is clear:

Non seulement nous ne connaissons Dieu que par Jésus-Christ, mais nous ne nous connaissons nous-mêmes que par Jésus-Christ. Hors de Jésus-Christ, nous ne savons ce que c'est ni que notre vie, ni que notre mort, ni que Dieu, ni que nous-mêmes. (L. 417, B. 548)

This emphasis on the person and role of Christ represents a culminating point in Pascal's apologia. It receives most moving expression in the long fragment entitled 'Le Mystère de Jésus' (L. 919, B. 553 and 791). Nevertheless, to insist on the centrality of Christ's teaching and of his mediating function is clearly not to 'prove' that Christianity is 'true'. Indeed, given the particular form of Pascal's discussion and the anti-cartesian theory of knowledge which he advances, intellectual conviction cannot precede acceptance of Christ's teaching. This remains true however closely religious claims may be shown to have relevance to man's psychological make-up and his metaphysical plight. What Pascal has done is to show that Christianity looks relevant and may therefore merit serious consideration. (He even suggests, by means of his famous 'wager' (for example L. 418, B. 233), that the sceptic has nothing to lose if he assumes the truth of Christianity and acts accordingly, whereas he stands to lose a great deal if he chooses to wager against it and it turns out to be true.) In the end, Christianity must first be accepted by an act of faith—we must believe in order that we may understand. Understanding will follow faith if that faith is a genuine act of mind and will, if it involves the whole personality as all positive knowledge must do. To adopt a distinction made by Kant, Pascal is concerned to expound not *passive* knowledge (for example of the theorems of geometry) but *active* knowledge (in this case, knowledge of Christ as Redeemer through worship and prayer). This is the main purpose and central theme of the *Pensées*.

NOTE

BLAISE PASCAL, 1623–62, was born at Clermont-Ferrand. His father, Étienne Pascal, a magistrate, took charge of his own children's education under the influence of Montaigne's pedagogical ideas. The family moved to Paris in 1631 and Étienne Pascal mixed with some of the leading scientific men of his day— Mersenne, Desargues, Roberval, etc. In 1639 Étienne's post as *commissaire pour l'impôt* in upper Normandy took the family to Rouen where Blaise soon gave evidence of his outstanding mathematical and scientific gifts. His essay on conic sections was written at the age of sixteen, he invented a calculating machine three years later, he did further mathematical work, and wrote several treatises in connection with his experiments on atmospheric pressure. In 1646, while still in Rouen, the Pascal family became deeply influenced by Jansenist ideas but Blaise continued his scientific work and eventually also mixed with such *mondains* as Méré, the duc de Roannez, and Damien Mitton. His conversion and complete commitment to Christianity occurred in the course of a mystical experience during the night of 23 November 1654. From this point onwards he devoted himself mainly to religious activities, published his *Lettres provinciales* (1656–7), and conceived an *Apologie de la religion chrétienne* which was still in note form when he died, at the age of 39, in 1662. These notes were first published, as the *Pensées*, in 1670.

Editions. The *Œuvres complètes* edited by L. Brunschvicg and P. Boutroux (14 vols. 1903–14), though dated in some respects, is still essential. There are practical one-volume editions by J. Chevalier (1954) in the Pléiade series and by L. Lafuma (1963) in the Intégrale collection. The *Œuvres complètes* edited by J. Mesnard, of which one volume only has so far appeared (1964), brings together a great deal of illuminating material from other seventeenth-century writers and promises to be quite indispensable for a thorough study of Pascal's thought.

   The *Lettres provinciales* exist in several separate editions of which the best are: H. F. Stewart (ed.), *Les Lettres provinciales de Pascal* (1919, repr. 1951), and L. Cognet (ed.), *Pascal: Les Provinciales* (1965). The *Pensées* can be read in a variety of arrangements by different editors. The three most valuable arrangements, in my view, are by L. Brunschvicg (1897, frequent reprints), J. Chevalier (1924, and reprinted in 'Livre de poche' series, 1962), and L. Lafuma (3 vols., 1951). Incidentally, the whole story of the different editions, arrangements, and corrections which the *Pensées* have undergone can be read in L. Lafuma, *Histoire des « Pensées » de Pascal* (1954).

Criticism. Pascal's ideas are excellently placed within a wider intellectual context by F. Strowski, *Pascal et son temps* (3 vols., 1907), H. Busson, *La Pensée religieuse française de Charron à Pascal* (1933), and J.-E. d'Angers, *Pascal et ses précurseurs* (1954). Pascal's religious ideas are examined by H. Bremond, *Histoire littéraire du sentiment religieux en France* (12 vols., vol. iv, 1920), J. Laporte, *La Doctrine de Port-Royal* (2 vols., 1923 and 2 posth. vols., 1951–2), J. Russier, *La Foi selon Pascal* (2 vols., 1949), F. T. H. Fletcher, *Pascal and the mystical tradition* (1954), and R.-E. Lacombe, *L'Apologétique de Pascal, étude critique* (1958). A more thoroughly philosophical approach is adopted by E. Baudin, *La Philosophie de Pascal* (4 vols., 1946–7) and C. Baudouin, *Pascal ou l'ordre du cœur* (1962). A challenging neo-marxist account of Pascal's pessimism is included in L. Goldmann, *Le Dieu caché* (1955). There is a discussion of Pascal's social and political ideas in G. Chinard, *En lisant Pascal* (1948), while E. Auerbach's *Scenes from the drama of European literature* (1959) has an excellent chapter entitled 'On the Political Theory of Pascal'. The volume *Blaise Pascal, l'homme et l'œuvre*, in the Cahiers de Royaumont series (1956), contains some fundamental articles including A. Koyré, 'Pascal savant'. On this subject see also P. Humbert, *L'Œuvre scientifique de Blaise Pascal* (1947). An aspect of Pascal's apologetics, scarcely touched on in the above chapter, is dealt with at some length by G. Brunet, *Le Pari de Pascal* (1956). As regards his qualities as a stylist, these are examined by J.-J. Demorest, *Pascal écrivain* (1957) and Patricia Topliss, *The Rhetoric of Pascal* (1966). Finally, among the many general studies, special mention should be made of J. Chevalier, *Pascal* (1922), J. Mesnard, *Pascal, l'homme et l'œuvre* (1951, repr. 1964), J. Steinmann, *Pascal* (1962), J. H. Broome, *Pascal* (1965), and J. Mesnard, *Pascal* (1965) in the series 'Les Écrivains devant Dieu'.

5. Social Structure and Social Change

THE France of Richelieu and Mazarin, of Colbert and Louvois, of Louis XIII and Louis XIV was a unique society. Its assumptions rested upon a view of history stretching back for many centuries, in which the emphasis was upon the individual role of the nation in western Europe. 'Gesta Dei per Francos' was a tag which implied that the French were a chosen people, with a distinct place in the divine plan.

However, if we step back and look at this society from a more general point of view, we may conclude that seventeenth-century France was not unique. In its organization into peasantry, middle class, and nobility, with the peasantry an overwhelming majority, it resembles other traditional societies, some of which survive in the twentieth century. If we seek an appropriate analogy for the society of Louis XIV, we might do worse than turn to the India of the British Raj with its wealthy princes, some of whose palaces put Versailles to shame by their ostentation and splendour. France, like other traditional societies, was rigidly stratified socially (here again the Indian caste system comes to mind). It was an overwhelmingly religious society, with religious observance and custom bound into daily routine and seasonal change. It was a society in which the few enjoyed luxury, while the majority lived near subsistence level, a condition difficult to change owing to a high degree of under-employment. In all these features, and many more, France was not unique, but a typical traditional society. (So also, for that matter, was English society, much as English historians may like to stress the individuality of England.)

One aspect in particular of seventeenth-century France recalls parallels in other traditional societies, namely the persistent economic stagnation of the period. Political and literary historians alike tend to look upon the seventeenth century as 'Le Grand Siècle'. Yet for the economic historian this is no longer possible, particularly in the light of the pioneer work of Goubert.[1] The evidence of population statistics provides a picture of almost unrelieved gloom, in which semi-starvation was the normal lot of the peasantry, made intolerable by famine at regular intervals, 1625–7, 1649–52, 1661–2, and 1693–4. Economically the seventeenth century stretches from the 1620s to the 1730s, when at long last France began to emerge from the doldrums into the relative prosperity of the eighteenth century.

This newly discovered economic dimension means that we must look again at almost every aspect of French life during this period. The war policy of Richelieu, with its inevitable increased burden of taxes, was imposed upon a society already badly hit by depression, and hence all the more sensitive to new demands. On top of this the rebellion of the 1640s and the 1650s, the Fronde, was a crisis of the first order, the extent of which is only now coming to be realized. Indeed, the very title 'Fronde', meaning a sling or child's catapult, may mislead us if it implies that this was a short-lived episode, confined to a few irresponsible aristocrats. Perhaps we should think of it more in terms of the Puritan Revolution in England—as a crisis which marked a crucial change in French society, and as a result of which both aristocracy and peasantry collapsed, to the advantage of a new middle class.

Taking the above as a general introduction, we may now turn and look in more detail at the fortunes of the three main social groups: nobility, middle class, and peasantry.

In 1600 the ruling élite of France was a military aristocracy—the French equivalent of the Japanese *samurai*. This nobility was a caste, entered in theory only by birth, and it lived by a code of honour in which the duel possessed a symbolic value. La Rochefoucauld, a member of the *noblesse d'épée*, describes a duel in his *Mémoires*:

Cependant, le duc d'Enghien trouvant à son retour tout le changement que je viens de dire et ne pouvant témoigner au duc de Beaufort, qui était en prison, le ressentiment qu'il avait de ce qui s'était passé entre Mme de Longueville et Mme de Montbazon, il laissa à Coligny la liberté de se battre contre le duc de Guise, qui avait été mêlé dans cette

[1] For Goubert's work, see Note at the end of this chapter.

affaire. Coligny était faible, peu adroit, et il relevait d'une longue maladie; il choisit d'Estrades, qui depuis a été maréchal de France, pour appeler le duc de Guise, qui se servit de Bridieu, et ils prirent leur rendez-vous à la place Royale. Le duc de Guise, en mettant l'épée à la main, dit à Coligny: 'Nous allons décider les anciennes querelles de nos deux maisons, et on verra quelle différence on doit mettre entre le sang de Guise et celui de Coligny.' Le combat fut bientôt fini: Coligny tomba, et le duc de Guise, pour l'outrager, lui ôtant son épée, le frappa du plat de la sienne. D'Estrades et Bridieu se blessèrent dangereusement l'un et l'autre, et furent séparés par le duc de Guise. Coligny, accablé de douleur d'avoir si mal soutenu une si belle cause, mourut quatre ou cinq mois après d'une maladie de langueur.

As the remark by the duc de Guise in this passage suggests, the quality most prized by the nobility was pride, pride in ancestry above all. All that a nobleman needed was a rudimentary knowledge of letters, acquired at the hands of a tutor, before he was apprenticed to arms or went off to the wars. The cultivation of military virtues was accompanied by scorn for those who followed the occupations of trade or administrative office. The aristocrat was destined for a higher life, marked by 'conspicuous consumption' and lavish expenditure. There was some parallel here with the Elizabethan aristocracy, though in England at least some members of the aristocracy had an eye to business.

François de La Rochefoucauld himself can be regarded as a typical member of the *noblesse d'épée*. Born in 1613, La Rochefoucauld received only a rudimentary education from his tutor before entering upon the inevitable military career. He served in the Italian campaign of 1629, and from then on much of his life was spent in war. He served in the Spanish Netherlands in 1635/6, he was present at the battle of Rocroi in 1643 and at the siege of Gravelines in 1644. During the last years of his life he took part in the siege of Lille. He died in 1680. His intervention in the Fronde as a member of the *noblesse d'épée* falls into place as entirely characteristic, and it is understandable that the Angoumois area, where his château was situated, was a centre for aristocratic criticism of Mazarin (see pp. 74–5). Where he differed from other members of his social group was in possessing literary talents which he put to considerable use.

The French nobility were a privileged class and their most significant privilege was exemption from royal taxation. In particular, they were largely exempt from the heaviest of all taxes, the *taille*, which, because it fell on the peasantry, carried with it social degradation as well as a harsh financial burden. However, the exemption was not absolute. In certain areas of France the *taille* was a land tax; in other areas it was a personal tax. This meant that sometimes a noble holding *taillable* land was directly liable to tax; in other cases he paid indirectly by having *taillable* persons as his tenants. It was in this twilight area of ambiguity that the nobility tried to extend their personal exemption as far as possible, and clashed with the expanding state of Richelieu.

The second social group in France was the bourgeoisie, the 'third estate', consisting of royal administrators (*officiers*) and merchants. Socially, there was no clear dividing line between these. Intermarriage between an *officier* family and a merchant family was common, and perhaps the only difference between the two was that merchant wealth was newer. The *officiers* represented the major profession in France, the lay equivalent of the Church, with as many internal distinctions and ramifications. At the heart of the administration was the system of law courts or *parlements*, with the Parlement of Paris at its head. (The English 'High Court of Parliament' was not so very different at this date.) There were local *parlements* in various provinces—at Dijon, Aix-en-Provence, Rouen, and Bordeaux, for example. As in other countries of western Europe, including England, these offices were for sale and, in the depressed economic circumstances of seventeenth-century France, an office offered a sound investment for a family. There was a whole range of prices for offices with greater or less prestige and greater or less possibility of profit. All in all, office-holding was the only expanding 'industry'.

In many ways, the Church was part of this office-holding empire. A family might well send sons into the Church as well as the royal administration, since an ecclesiastical office was often as profitable as a lay one. It might also regard a socially distinguished convent as a haven for unmarriageable daughters—they would still need a dowry, but the cost would be much less than its secular equivalent.

Trade was also an acceptable avenue for the middle class, though for the better-established families money-lending to the nobility or advances to the peasantry became more agreeable alternatives than the hurly-burly of actual buying and selling.

If we seek an example of an office-holding family at a very high social level we may turn to the Dijon family network which produced Jacques-Bénigne Bossuet, Bishop of Meaux. Bossuet was born into a group of families—Bossuet, Bretagne, Mochet, and Humbert—which held high office in the Parlement of Burgundy. It was not surprising that one of their number should reach high office in the Church under Louis XIV. This group of families had shown its loyalty to the Crown during the troubled reign of Henri III in face of the hostility of the *noblesse d'épée*, and perhaps we should look upon Bossuet's exposition of the Divine Right of the monarchy as putting into words that attitude which his kinsmen had adopted, not without profit, since the Wars of Religion.

These two social groups—robe and sword—remained on terms of general hostility. Only on one occasion, during the early days of the Fronde in 1648, did anything like a political alliance develop between the two, resting on their common hostility towards Mazarin. But this proved no more than a temporary basis of unity. The 'Fronde of the Parlements' ended when the ambitions of the aristocracy became clear. In fact, some of the *parlements* did not join in the Fronde. At Dijon, for example, the memory of the Wars of Religion was more than enough to secure loyalty to the Crown. The days when robe and sword would be permanent allies were still to come.

It was the clerical and administrative bourgeoisie which provided the bulk of the students at the universities of France. The *noblesse d'épée* did not regard higher education as necessary for the cultivation of the military virtues. The merchants, for their part, did not need university education, since their educational requirements were met by apprenticeship with a fellow merchant. The typical merchant's library consisted of a copy of Savary's *Le Parfait Négociant* and a few works of piety.

The third social group—the peasantry—included the great majority of the French people, but it remains something of an enigma and its history has only just begun to be written. Historians have been only too quick to take their cue from the famous description of La Bruyère, which suggested that the condition of the peasantry was very near that of the beasts of the field (see ch. 9, pp. 148–9).

In fact, we know that among the peasantry there was a hierarchy as marked as that within the bourgeoisie. At the top of the social ladder was the *laboureur*, the French equivalent of the English yeoman. A *laboureur* typically had a farm of under twenty hectares, which he ploughed with his own pair of horses. (A hectare is roughly 2·5 acres, which makes this under 50 acres.) But the *laboureurs* were the élite of the peasantry and represented only about 10 per cent of the total number. More typical of the French peasantry as a whole were the *haricotiers* and the *manouvriers*. An *haricotier* normally rented a holding of under ten hectares (i.e. 25 acres) and had a net annual income of 50 *livres* after paying *taille* and tithe at the rate of 20 *livres* and 18 *livres* respectively. Below him was the *manouvrier* with only a garden holding and maybe a pig and a few poultry; and below all these there was a submerged rural proletariat about which we know nothing.

Upon all these peasant groups, threatened as they were by starvation and famine, the weight of royal and clerical taxation pressed very hard indeed. Goubert has estimated that the *taille* and the tithe took a third of a peasant's income, which at the outset was scarcely enough for subsistence. But this was not the whole story. The peasantry was in a state of chronic indebtedness to the urban bourgeoisie. Of sixty peasants at Beauvais, not one was out of debt. In time of famine the situation became much worse, and it was then that the local usurers laid the foundations of their substantial fortunes. In this respect, as in others, French peasant society was not unique. The usurer of India and the 'gombeen man' of Ireland belong to the same recognizable category as the French *receveur*.

For an example of a *receveur* we may turn to a certain Claude Dusmesil of Goincourt, the local agent for the estates of an order of nuns and of several bourgeois. He was responsible for levying the tithe and seigneurial rights to a total figure of 1,200 *livres* and 40 *hectolitres* of corn. In the local village, 36 of the 80 families owed him a total of 1,691 *livres*, and in the surrounding villages there were other debts as well. Dusmesil left 16,000 *livres* when he died, the nuns' good servant. Almost inevitably, the Church, as an absentee landlord, created pockets of anti-clericalism in the countryside.

Against this background, it is no surprise to find that revolt among the peasantry was endemic during the seventeenth century. In almost every decade and in almost every province, peasant unrest made itself felt. The most widespread, and the one which Richelieu repressed most savagely, was the revolt of the *nu-pieds* in Normandy. The date was 1639, after four years of war, which almost certainly indicates that one of the grievances of the rebels was the heavy weight of war taxation. Richelieu himself was the target of many of the rebel poems:

> Quoy, nous deffendre est-il trop tard?
> Nous sommes trop dans la détresse;
> Les armées et le cardinal
> Ont tous noz biens et noz richesses
> Après n'avoir plus rien du tout,
> Pourrions-nous bien venir à bout
> D'un sy grand nombre de merveilles?
> Ouy, le proverbe de nos vieilles,
> Dict qu'il vault mieux tard que jamais.
>
> Jean Nudz-piedz est vostre suppost,
> Il vengera vostre querelle,
> Vous affranchissant des impostz.
> Il fera lever la gabelle,
> Et nous ostera tous ces jeunes
> Qui s'enrichissent aux despens
> De vos biens et de la patrie.
> C'est luy que Dieu a envoyé
> Pour mettre en la Normandie
> Une parfaicte liberté.

But something more was involved than taxation, as the following poem shows:

> César, dans le sénat, fut occis par Brutus,
> Pour avoir conjuré contre tous les Romains.
> Catilina fut tué après un tas d'abus,
> Qu'il avoit entrepris aux despens des humains;

Et moy je souffriray ung peuple languissant
Dessoubz la tyrannie, et qu'un tas de horzains
L'oppressent tous les jours avecques leurs partys!
Je jure l'empescher, tout Nuds-piedz que je suis.

Je ne redoubte point leurs menaces hachées;
Mes gens sont bons soldatz, et qui, en m'appuyant,
Me fourniront assez de compagnies rangées
Pour soustenir hardis, assistéz de paisans,
Contre ces gabeleurs, vrays tyrans d'Hircanie,
Qui veulent oppresser peuples et nations
Par des sollicieteurs de tant de tyrannies,
Où s'opposent Normandz, Poittevins et Bretons.

But the revolt failed. Richelieu sent a strong army under Gasson which easily overcame peasant resistance. The aftermath saw the immediate execution of surviving rebels, though the leaders were paid the compliment of torture and a more formal execution in the square at Rouen.

We tend to assume that these peasant revolts were the simple response of simple people to intolerable material conditions. But this is perhaps too narrow a view. Examination of other peasant societies reveals that complex systems of values and beliefs may go hand in hand with a primitive economy, and there is no reason to believe that French peasant society was in any way different. Something of the general kind of complexity which we may assume existed lies behind what is admittedly a special case—the revolt (1702–3) of the Protestant *camisards* in the Cevennes following upon the Revocation of the Edict of Nantes (1685). This peasantry was unique in France in being Protestant. Here, Calvinist missionaries of the sixteenth century had enjoyed a success which was denied to them elsewhere. As a result Calvinist hymns replaced traditional peasant songs, puritan attitudes introduced a more rigid sexual code, new taboos took the place of the old. The picture need not be overdrawn, since it can be maintained that this was happening to the Catholic peasantry also, exposed to the puritanism of the counter-Reformation.

After 1685 the peasantry of the Cevennes seemed to be confronted with a loss of social identity. Their ministers were taken away from them and their spiritual tradition faced extinction. The response was characteristic of other peasant societies in comparable situations. A wave of millenarianism swept over the region, similar to those which captured the imagination of fifteenth-century Bohemia, or sixteenth-century Münster, or the 'Old Believers' in mid seventeenth-century Russia. The new messiah, destined to save the people of France for the true faith, was William of Orange, King of England since 1688. His local prophets were the schoolmaster François Vivent and the lawyer Claude Brousson, both of them disciples of the Huguenot exile, Jurieu, who was prophesying the end of the Scarlet Woman. The results were seen a few years later, in 1702, when the Cevennes erupted in a wave of apocalyptic enthusiasm. This time the leader was a peasant, Abraham Mazel. The local Catholic curé was killed, the images in his church destroyed, and an extraordinary wave of fervour swept the countryside, nourished by resentment against the *taille* and the tithe as well as by religious grievances. But Babylon did not fall. Instead the royal troops destroyed 53 villages and as many hamlets. This was the last peasant revolt of the *ancien régime*.

Nobility, bourgeoisie, peasantry, such was the basis of the social structure of France in 1600. We may now turn to discuss the most significant social change of the seventeenth century, namely the decline of the *noblesse d'épée*. The decline had begun during the Wars of Religion when the League of nobility failed in its bid for power. Under Henri IV the nobility declined still further, though later in the century they looked back to his reign as a golden age. Finally, under Richelieu, government policy was aimed directly at curtailing the local power and privileges of the aristocracy.

The nobles from the Angoumois area complained that they and their peasantry were being squeezed dry, while the tax-farmers and lawyers prospered at their expense. They blamed the royal ministers as the root cause of the undesirable changes which were taking place. They blamed the government (though not the King) for using the system of selling offices as a means of revenue, which meant that men of wealth were replacing men of birth and quality in the administration. The nobles also blamed the government for introducing tax-farming as its chief method of collecting revenue. The effect of this was to transfer a good deal of local power from the gentry into the hands of the financiers, or their agents, who were willing to 'farm' the revenue (i.e. pay a fixed sum to the government) and take as their profit the difference. Finally, the nobles saw the government as responsible for introducing the *intendants* into the provinces as a powerful new instrument of policy. In some ways this had been the most decisive change of all. Richelieu's *intendants* were not office-holders but selected men from the central administration. The result again was to cut down the informal influence which the local nobility could exercise. The governorship of the various provinces of France, which had once been the most important post open to the nobility, was dwindling into relative insignificance in the face of the 'new men' from the bourgeoisie.

Behind the grievances of the nobility lay the assumption that they were the 'natural leaders' of the country, to whom its defence was entrusted in time of war and its administration in time of peace. It seemed intolerable that the ability to pay for an office should be more important in the eyes of the Crown than natural position. This and other grievances are illustrated in the following extracts, taken from a *cahier de doléances* of the Fronde period recently published under the auspices of Professor Mousnier:

Sera aussy represante ausdicts estats ce quy a esté en pluzieurs aultres, le notable preuidice que la noblesse resoit par la *venellité des charges* tant de la maison du roy, de la guerre que de la justice dans lesquelles l'antrée luy est presque impossible par leur prix excessif, ce quy luy est bien sensible de ce voir privée des charges qu'elle a autrefois poceddé à les voir à présent entre les mains de personne la plus par sans naissance, sans meritte ou sans capacitté, c'est pourquoy Sa Majesté est trés humblement supliée de voulloir apporter a son estat cette refformation comme la plus utille et la plus souhaittée de touttes en hostant cette vennalitté des charges du royaume, ce que s'il luy plaist, pour celles de la guerre et de sa maison, leur véritable prix sera le sang de sa noblesse qu'elles respandra genereuzement pour son service et pour celles de justice la juste récompanse sera la fidellité, intégrité et suffizance de ses subjects et par preferance celle des gentilshommes mais sy la nécessité de l'estat empeschoit que les peuples ne pussent jouir sy prontement dudict bien quy a toujours esté jugé sy necessaire, le roy sera tres humblement supplié s'abollir cependant le droict annuel par le moyen duquel les charges de justice se randent hereditaires et quasy toutes affectées aux familles ou elles se trouvent et hostant a la noblesse toute espérance dy pouvoir jamais entrer et au roy les moiens de choizir des magistrats bons et inteligens.

The nobility also protested against the weight of taxation upon the peasantry for the interested reason that the peasantry was the direct source of their own income:

Et d'aultant que la misere et pauvreté du peuple quy rejaillist et passe de nescessitté jusqu'à la noblesse quy en tire ses revenus et les moyens de sa subcistance ne justifie que trop combien il a esté ruyneux a tout le royaume et principallement a cette province que les tailles ayent ete mises en party, sa Majesté sera très humblement supliée que suivant ses royalles promesses, les tailles soient diminuées autant que les necessites de l'estat le pourront permettre et ne soient plus à l'advenir données en party mais levées par les voyes accoutumées devant que les intendants et partizans s'en meslassent, estant asses congneu que lesdits partizans, pour satisffaire à leur avarice et rapacitté, ont emploié des fuziliers, sergents et autres officiers qu'ils ont introduict dans les eslections dont ils avoient les partis, avec lesquels ils partageoient les frais que les sergens faisoient et quy estoient ensuite taxées par les officiers, surchargeant tellement le pauvre peuple qu'outre le principal de la taille et autres commissions ordonnées estre levée par sa Majesté quy sont montées à des sommes immanses et comme incroiable, les fraits que les recepveurs et partizans ont faict pour la collecte des deniers se sont trouvés monter souvent au tiers ou cart du principal de la taille dont le peuple est tellement ruyné et la noblesse incommodée, pour ne pouvoir estre payée de ses ranthes que le service de sa Majesté en est empesché, les gentilshommes n'ayant que de quoy se mettre en equypage pour le servir, a raison de quoy sa Majesté est très humblement supliée de commettre au plus tost un gentil-homme de chaque province avecq un officier de justice, gens de probité et capacitté recognue pour informer des levées de deniers qui ont esté faites tant par les intendants que partizans, outre ceux quy leur estoient ordonnées et des concussions et malversations commises tant par eux que leurs fusilliers, commis, sergens at autres officiers quy ont travaillé par leur ordre dont il se tirera non seullement de quoy paier les frais de ses commissaires, mais encore des sommes considérables pour estre emploiées aux affaires de sa Majesté ou nécessités de la province.

Hence in some parts of France there seems to have been an

alliance at this time between two groups who should have been economic enemies, the nobility and the peasantry, united in their common enmity towards the tax-farmer. The countryside, indeed, was turning against the town:

Cependant comme il n'y a rien quy provoque et multiplie tant les crimes que l'impunité et qu'il n'est que trop congnu, voire resanty par tous les ordres du royaume combien il c'est commis d'abus, de larsins et volleries au maniement et dispansation des finances, de quoy quant nous nous tairions, les despances prodigieuzes soit en festins meubles et bastimens et en un mot les richesses immenses d'une infinie de partizans quy surpasse en revenu celle des plus grandes et illustres maisons du royaume et esgalle celle de quelque prince n'en parlent que trop et quy faict que le roy es très humblement suplié, non seullement de trouver bon qu'il y soit estably un meilleur ordre a l'advenir par les estazts qu'il appleu a sa majesté de faire assembler mais que de plus lesdictz estats nomment et choizissent nonbre suffizans de gens de probité et capacité recognue et quy soient hors de soubcon d'estre interessés avecq les partizans et financiers pour en compozer une chambre de justice, à laquelle sa majesté est supliée de donner tous les pouvoirs et lettres nécessaires pour informer des abus et malversations de tous traitans, soubstraitans, partizans, financiers et autres quy ont heu part en quelque sorte que ce soit au maniement et droiction des finances despuis les recherches faites par la dernière chambre establie pour mesme effect, faire et parfaire le procés a ceux quy ce trouveront coulpables desdits abus et maleversations, soit par punition corporele, amende pécuniere, confiscations de biens et aultres telles punitions qu'il se trouveront avoir mérittés selon la quallité et condition de leurs crimes.

There seems to have been a good deal of justification for these complaints. The desperate financial straits of the Crown had led to desperate remedies, and Mazarin, himself far from a model of probity, had turned to men whose objective was to make money quickly and easily. The revenue at this date was being collected by men who earned over 30 per cent interest on their loans to the Crown, six times more than the legal limit of 5 per cent.

The grievances of the nobility were also based upon a keen hostility towards the *robins*, as they termed the lawyers. There was no hint of the *noblesse d'épée* recognizing the robe as a kind of nobility. They saw the lawyers as bourgeois buying their way into offices which belonged by right to gentlemen. Hence the nobility pressed the Crown to do away with the sale of offices, and if this proved to be impossible, at least to abolish the *paulette*, the financial device which enabled office-holders to keep an office within the same family by paying an annual tax. There was little hint in the behaviour of the mid-century nobility that their attitude towards the robe would ever change.

The protests of the Angoumois nobility and the 'Fronde of the Princes' which followed were the death-throes of a declining social group. By the end of the century power had passed to the upper bourgeoisie, notably the major office-holders of the Crown and the financiers. In the eyes of the older élite the newcomers were upstarts and swindlers, but we should not take the literary evidence too literally. The kind of complaints made during the century in France are to be found equally in seventeenth-century Japan and seventeenth-century England. Looked at from another point of view, the tax-farmers and the *officiers* represented an element of modernization and social mobility in the rigid French social structure.

Yet in a sense the ideal of nobility remained and was incorporated within the social changes. The upper bourgeoisie was transformed into a *noblesse de robe*. Even the financiers acquired titles or married their daughters into the nobility. This process was due in part to the imitation of the aristocratic way of life, but it also owed a good deal to the direct policy of the Crown. Louis XIV enforced purchase of noble titles upon his *officiers*, partly as a means of drawing them closer into the system of social hierarchy, but also as a means of revenue. The new peers were repeatedly forced to have their titles confirmed by a formal *réhabilitation*, which was in effect a form of tax. There were eight *réhabilitations* between 1664 and 1715, five of them in the 1660s. What appears at first sight to be a piece of pure snobbery on the part of the Crown falls into place as a means of selling titles much as Charles I had done in England. By 1789 the nobility had changed completely in character from what it had been in 1600. Of nearly sixty Beauvais noblemen in 1789, only ten came from families that had been noble in the time of Henri IV, and most of them had been ennobled before 1740.

The result of these changes was a working alliance between robe and sword during the eighteenth century. An equally significant result, and perhaps a more lasting one, was the extension of social prejudice against trade. In becoming a *noblesse*, the *robins* took over the snobberies of their social superiors and transmitted them to a larger proportion of the population. This attitude remained common in the nineteenth century and lasted even into the twentieth.

Commerce went on, in spite of the contempt of the *noblesse*, but it cannot be said to have flourished. The commercial conditions of the century were those of a protracted recession, and this remained the case even in 1700. This endemic depression has led historians to overestimate the effects of the Revocation of the Edict of Nantes in 1685. Pamphleteers found an obvious reason for commercial stagnation and decline in the emigration of so many of Louis XIV's industrious Huguenot subjects. Recent research has shown that the Revocation seems to have made very little difference. There was recession, but at no worse a rate than before.

Louis XIV's wars, which have so often been described as economically disastrous, may well have acted as a social and economic catalyst. The battles of these wars and the diplomatic background have been described on many occasions, but the most interesting aspect of this prolonged period of war (1667–79, 1688–1713), namely its social impact, has scarcely been touched upon. Yet there are good grounds for regarding the wars as providing an economic stimulus in a society where this was sadly lacking. The war encouraged the development of particular industries, especially shipbuilding and metal foundries. The provision of uniforms for half a million men was in itself a major industry, while the new training and drill under Louvois forced acceptance of a changed and possibly more 'rational' routine upon a traditionally-minded peasantry. The war also created financial opportunities on a scale unknown before. Samuel Bernard (1651–1739) was one of those who took advantage of them and left thirty-three million *livres*. Antoine Crouzat was another, and the Pâris brothers made up a triumvirate of their own in the world of finance. All these social changes pointed towards the eighteenth century, which was to see the development of French trade and the rise of a commercial bourgeoisie on the grand scale.

In conclusion, we may say that the seventeenth century in France was an age which saw the disappearance of the *noblesse d'épée*, a change which in a real sense marked the end of the Middle Ages. By 1700, a new nobility, the *noblesse de robe*, had come into being. The social ideal of the *honnête homme* marks the shift. There were also signs of a rising commercial class even though, it cannot be too often repeated, the age of *gloire* was an age of economic decline for France. As for the peasantry, they, like their masters the *noblesse d'épée*, seem to have met with almost unmitigated disaster throughout the century, though during the following century their position was to improve.

NOTE

J. Lough, *An Introduction to Seventeenth-Century France* (1954), is still in many ways the most convenient introduction to the subject-matter of the above chapter. Since this book was published, however, historical studies of France at this period have undergone something of a renaissance under the inspiration of Marc Bloch and Lucien Febvre. Among recent writers in the field, R. Mandrou has attracted a good deal of attention for his imaginative insight and all-embracing approach, particularly in his *Introduction à la France moderne, 1500–1640* (1961) and his *La France au XVIIᵉ et XVIIIᵉ siècles* (1967), which also contains an excellent bibliography. The most influential single work on seventeenth-century France has been P. Goubert, *Beauvais et le Beauvaisis de 1600 à 1730* (2 vols., 1960), in which a limited area is subjected to detailed analysis over a long period. The same author's *Louis XIV et vingt millions de Français* (1966) is a valuable *œuvre de vulgarisation*. Two books, both of immense interest, on very specific topics are P. Ariès, *L'Enfant et la vie familiale sous l'Ancien Régime* (1960; Eng. trans. *Centuries of Childhood*, 1962), and M. Foucault, *Histoire de la folie à l'âge classique: folie et déraison* (1961).

On the peasantry, the work of the Russian historian B. Porchnev, *Les Soulèvements populaires en France de 1613 à 1648* (1963), has stimulated a great deal of discussion. An excellent recent work on the peasantry is E. Le Roy-Ladurie, *Les Paysans de Languedoc* (2 vols., 1966). On the nobility the most convenient recent work is the introduction by R. Mousnier to *Deux Cahiers de la noblesse pour les États-Généraux de 1649–1651* (1965). F. L. Ford, *Robe and Sword: the Regrouping of the French Aristocracy after Louis XIV* (1953) and the relevant chapter in B. Moore, *Social Origins of Dictatorship and Democracy: Lord and Peasant in the Making of the Modern World* (1966) are both important. A useful selection of documents is to be found in H. G. Judge (ed.), *Louis XIV* (1965).

Some books in English on social history are relevant, notably T. Aston (ed.), *Crisis in Europe, 1560–1660* (1965), L. Stone, *The Crisis of the Aristocracy,*

1558–1641 (1965), and H. Trevor-Roper, *Religion, Reformation and Social Change* (1967). There is also an informative chapter by M. Prestwich in J. M. Wallace-Hadrill and J. McManners (eds.), *France: Government and Society* (1957).

Articles in French periodicals include R. Mousnier, 'Quelques raisons de la Fronde' in *XVIIe Siècle* (1949) and P. Deyon, 'La noblesse française et la monarchie absolue' in *Revue historique* (1964). The periodical *Annales: Économies -Sociétés-Civilisations* is standard reading for social historians.

6. Louis XIV and the Arts

C'ÉTAIT un temps digne de l'attention des temps a venir que celui où les héros de Corneille et de Racine, les personnages de Molière, les symphonies de Lulli, toutes nouvelles pour la nation, et (puisqu'il ne s'agit ici que des arts) les voix des Bossuet et des Bourdaloue, se faisaient entendre à Louis XIV, à Madame, si célèbre par son goût, à un Condé, à un Turenne, à un Colbert, et à cette foule d'hommes supérieurs qui parurent en tout genre. Ce temps ne se retrouvera plus où un duc de La Rochefoucauld, l'auteur des *Maximes*, au sortir de la conversation d'un Pascal et d'un Arnauld allait au théâtre de Corneille.

(Voltaire, *Le Siècle de Louis XIV*)

On 4 July 1674, in the palace and gardens of Versailles, began the first of a series of festivities which was destined to last some eight weeks. Having just triumphantly wrested the Franche Comté from the Spanish, Louis XIV, together with Madame de Montespan, had come with his Court on his annual visit to Versailles (the Court officially settled there in 1682) determined to celebrate his latest victory and to surprise Europe yet again with a magnificent display of power, resources, and artistic achievement. Plays by Molière and Racine, operas by Quinault and Lully, monstrous collations and ballets, concerts on the water, and miracles of pyrotechnics were arranged to delight the members of a Court whose only release from boredom was a steady round of intrigue, back-biting, and gambling. About four o'clock the King and his Court took their afternoon walk in the direction of the Marais. There, artificial trees had been loaded with exotic fruit, shrubs and hedges had been transformed into vases, baskets, and large dishes of flowers and sweetmeats. Amid the sound of the waterfalls the Court ate for several hours until it was time to go back to the palace where, in the courtyard, a theatre had been erected and members of the Académie Royale de Musique were ready to perform Quinault's opera *Alceste*, set to music by the inimitable Lully. The opera had not enjoyed much success at its first Paris performances in January—spectators had called it a travesty of Euripides—yet Louis XIV liked it; he enjoyed the music and no doubt appreciated compliments such as:

Après avoir couru de victoire en victoire
Prenez un doux relâche au comble de la Gloire.

Increasingly jealous of his reputation in the world, he must have approved the sentiments expressed by *la Gloire*: 'Il laisse respirer tout le monde qui tremble.'

In spite of the splendour of such *divertissements* it is probable that Louis's own thoughts were more concerned with military matters. Corneille suggests as much in his *Vers présentés au Roi sur ses campagnes* when he writes:

Au milieu de sa Cour au spectacle empressée,
La guerre s'emparait de toute sa pensée.

The King felt the need to amuse his Court while he solved weightier problems of state. So a week went by before the next day of festivity. Near the newly built Petit Trianon an octagonal salon of greenery had been made in which was sung Quinault's *Églogue de Versailles*, then the day's delights ended in a superb collation with musical accompaniments. The 19th of July began with a visit to the Ménagerie where strange and fierce animals were on show; then the Court set out in gondolas to float down the Grand Canal and listen to the music of violins; they finally returned to the Grotto where a theatre had been erected by the Florentine Vigarani for a performance of Molière's *Malade imaginaire*. According to the official account the marvellous lighting effects drew most admiration from the spectators. A collation began the festivities of 28 July; then all made their way to the Water Tower to hear the King's favourite work *Les Fêtes de l'Amour et de Bacchus*, written by Quinault two years before and set to music by Lully; it was a work which combined music, dancing, and astonishing theatrical machines where magicians, sorcerers, and demons came up out of the earth and disappeared into the clouds. Fireworks were then let off, and a midnight supper was taken in full view of the Grand Canal illuminated with 600 candles. On 18 August there were particular reasons for celebration, since seventeen standards had been captured from the Spanish. As usual, the proceedings began with food; there followed a visit to the Orangerie where, in a theatre filled with machines borrowed from the Tuileries, all had been prepared for a performance of Racine's *Iphigénie*. This play was so successful that the gazetteer Robinet reported:

> L'auteur fut beaucoup applaudi . . .
> Et même notre auguste Sire
> L'en louangea. fort: c'est tout dire.

Félibien, writing the official account of the *fêtes*, is more laconic: according to him, Racine 'reçut de toute la Cour l'estime qu'ont toujours eue les pièces de cet auteur'. Praise and adulation, more than twenty pages of them, were kept for the most spectacular side of the festivities—the illuminations. These were devised by Le Brun; they showed Hercules, Pallas, and Les Amours, and all contained a certain 'sens mystérieux', a meaning which held no secrets for Louis XIV and his Court, since this sun-king had for years been accustomed to seeing himself portrayed in the guise of the gods. The royal device—the sun—stood high on an obelisk by which 'on prétendait marquer la Gloire du Roi toute éclatante de lumiere et solidement affermie au-dessus de ses ennemis'. Of all the entertainments provided in these weeks, illuminations and fireworks seem to have been those which aroused the most enthusiasm and were repeated most often; they were also the most expensive. On 31 August Vigarani produced the most astounding of all the pyro-technic creations. The entire park of Versailles seemed alight, and as the King's gondola made its way down the Grand Canal, observers could hardly distinguish air from fire and water.

This fusion of the elements brought to an end the most extrava-gant and the last of all the important *fêtes* ordered by Louis XIV. Within a few years his active patronage of the arts was much diminished. From the young King who first donned the role of 'le Roi Soleil' in Benserade's *Ballet de la Nuit* of 1653, who danced as well as any professional, who had ridden as Roger in the Versailles *fêtes* of 1664, he had become a spectator more preoccupied with responsibilities of State. It is indeed difficult to trace exactly the extent of his personal influence on the arts which helped to make him great. The traditional view of 'le siècle de Louis XIV' probably attributed too much influence to him.

His tastes are fairly well defined. The Prussian ambassador Spanheim wrote of him: 'Sans être savant, Louis XIV écrit bien. Il aime les beaux-arts et les protège; il se connaît particulièrement en musique, en peinture et en bâtiments.' The King's passion for music and dance found expression in the favours he lavished on Lully—'il ne pouvait se passer de cet homme-là'—and in the marked preference he always showed for opera. In the *fêtes* we have just described, opera takes pride of place among the dramatic productions, even influencing other forms: Molière's *Malade imaginaire* is designed to include music and dance interludes, Racine's *Iphigénie* reproduces the atmosphere of opera with its theme and crowd scenes. In architecture, painting, sculpture, and landscape-gardening Louis liked the noble and the symmetrical. In these domains he was so well informed that he could discuss for hours themes for painting, and the detail of building projects. Above all, he loved everything that was grandiose, in literature as in the fine arts; Saint-Simon, who did not think much of the King's taste, wrote in his memoirs: 'il aima en tout la splendeur, la magnificence, la profusion.' There are, however, indications that this tendency towards the grandiose stopped short of the extravagant; Louis commented on the panegyric of himself delivered by Racine to the Académie: 'Je vous louerais davantage, si vous ne me louiez pas tant.' There are also signs that Louis actually tired of the constant flood of works specifically designed to glorify his name; a contemporary wrote: 'à force d'entendre des sermons, des poésies, des harangues et la lecture des livres qu'on lui dédie, il en est fatigué.' However this may be, Louis's personal share in the forming of the official taste of his reign is hard to distinguish from that of such influential members of his entourage as Colbert or Madame de Montespan. In the second half of his reign the King certainly counted for less and less in the development of the arts.

The reasons for the flourishing of official art and royal *divertissement* are to be sought more in politics than in the King's personal taste. Louis XIV, his Court, and his ministers had been nurtured in the belief that to appear great was indeed to be great. Reputation in the world was what counted, and at least from the time of François Ier, writers and artists had been specifically employed to project an image of the prince which the world could admire and even fear. In the 1660s works publishing the greatness of Louis proliferated. As Sorel wrote in 1667: 'Il faut que la grandeur et la dignité de notre Roi soient connues de tout le monde.' Princely magnificence and display, nonchalant extravagance in buildings, festivities, and dress were thought to be excellent prestige propaganda for a monarch whose armies encroached increasingly on the rest of Europe. The festivities of 1674 had the achievements of Louis XIV as their focal point; Félibien was ordered to write a detailed account of the proceedings so that the brilliance of the occasion might be known abroad. Israël Sylvestre and others were commanded to record the events in a series of engravings which also advertised the size and beauty of Versailles. Félibien stressed the importance of the most spectacular elements of the *fêtes*, Sylvestre showed the splendour of the settings, both were inclined to dismiss the work of Molière and Racine as incidental—entertainments which were a necessary part of such occasions and which happened to please.

It was Colbert who had had the idea of leaving a visual record of Louis XIV's deeds and *divertissements*; he also worked to strengthen royal authority by gradually bringing various academies under the direct protection of the King. Richelieu had seen the advantages of establishing close links between writers and political authority when he associated himself with the Académie Française in 1635; following his example Louis became its official protector in 1672. The Académie Royale de Peinture et de Sculpture, from its inception in 1648, and through the activities of its founder Le Brun, always enjoyed royal favour. Further institutions were formed on the model of these two academies. The Académie des Inscriptions came into being in 1663, the Académie des Sciences in 1666; by 1671 the Académie de l'Architecture was flourishing, and the following year Lully formed the Académie Royale de Musique. Such centralization ensured the possibility of royal interference at any time in every sphere of artistic and scientific endeavour. Louis supported Boileau for election in 1683 against the claims of La Fontaine and the wishes of the majority of academicians; Boileau was elected and La Fontaine had to wait another six months. Although we know that the King had the power to approve candidates for these various institutions and that he could propose themes for discussion and lectures, and works for analysis, that he visited the academies and so on, it is not clear (except for the incident quoted above) how far he meddled in the detail of their activities. The members of the academy, however, understood that part of their function was to praise the virtues of the King and glorify his acts. This understanding is clearly expressed by Racine in the public *Discours* he pronounced in 1685, on the reception of Thomas Corneille to the Académie, when he said:

Dans l'histoire du Roi, tout vit, tout marche, tout est en action. Il ne faut que le suivre, si l'on peut, et le bien étudier lui seul. C'est un enchaîne-ment continuel de faits merveilleux, que lui-même commence, que lui-même achève, aussi clairs, aussi intelligibles quand ils ont exécutés, qu'impénétrables avant l'exécution. En un mot, le miracle suit de près un autre miracle.

Even more than the academies the system of pensions shows authority's attempt to enlist literary and artistic talent in the cause of propaganda. At the beginning of Louis's personal reign there was a particularly determined attempt to bring under the royal patronage men of letters who had previously depended on private patrons as well as the King. Colbert instructed the poet Chapelain to draw up a list of writers who might be induced to produce panegyrics of the King in prose and verse in exchange for 'gratifications'. Chapelain's letters to Colbert give a good idea of the way he saw the relation between patron and poet; thus he writes of Cotin:

C'est un de nos plus fameux académiciens et que j'ai engagé par votre ordre à cet éloge royal que nous épluchons et qui nous semble répondre à notre attente. Je laisse à votre prudence de considérer si un homme aussi approuvé qu'il est ne mériterait pas d'être du nombre des gratifiés, et pour ce qu'il a fait, et pour ce qu'il est capable de faire en prose et en vers.

In this way Colbert and Chapelain were able to inspire the flood of sonnets and odes which greeted such occasions as the convalescence of the King in 1663.

The encouragements given to artists took various forms: single payments, pensions, houses, food, sinecures, ecclesiastical preferment. In some cases they provided most of an artist's income. Actors for instance depended largely on the royal bounty: 'Le soin principal des comédiens est de faire leur cour chez le roi, de qui ils dépendent' (Chappuzeau, *Le Théâtre français*, 1674). In other cases royal remuneration was less important. Though few gained much from publishers or theatrical companies, many writers had private means or a regular income from some other employment (this did not, however, apply equally to other artists). And although there were no great private patrons to equal the tax-farmer Fouquet, who had fallen from power in 1661, patrons other than the King were of course an important source of income for many artists and writers. Moreover, after a boom period around 1664, the amount paid out in pensions and gratifications declined and the pension years grew to be sixteen months in length—as Corneille and others complained.

Nevertheless, pensions gave the authorities a hold over artists, channelling their talent into the officially desirable direction and suspending over their heads the threat of a sudden reduction in income. We see a hint of the positive side of this in Chapelain's appraisal of the satirist Furetière: 'S'il se pouvait laisser conduire, il serait capable de grandes choses', and an indication of the negative side in the reduction and suppression of the pension paid to the historian Mézeray after he had dared to criticize the economic policies of the regime.

As well as encouraging conformism financially, Louis's government, like its predecessors, actively discouraged literary subversion. The century saw a gradual increase in the control exercised by the central power over the book trade. It is true that throughout the *Ancien Régime* the control of opinion, though sometimes fierce, was at best spasmodic. At the end of the seventeenth century it was not difficult to have forbidden works printed clandestinely in Paris or openly in Holland, whence a well-established distributive chain led back through Rouen to Paris. All the same, beyond the loss of a pension, the sanctions against undesirable books went as far as exile or even death. In 1662 a Paris lawyer was burnt for writing verse which did not show sufficient respect for the political and religious authorities. In general, one can accept La Bruyère's view that 'un homme né chrétien et Français se trouve contraint dans la satire; les grands sujets lui sont défendus' (*Les Caractères*, ch. i).

In painting and sculpture in particular a certain conformism seems to have established itself fairly quickly. Charles Le Brun with his multifarious activities, designing tapestries, planning buildings, painting royal portraits and the ceilings of Versailles, planning illuminations and fireworks for court entertainments, inventing devices for carousels and costumes for ballets and masquerades, was probably largely responsible for the grandiose style which dominated the first forty years of Louis XIV's reign. Richness and magnificence are basic elements in his style; they match the grandeur of the conception of Versailles. His themes are pompous and solemn, they show Louis as a god, Jupiter, Mars, or Hercules, his deeds as surpassing those of the heroes from antiquity and romance literature, and in the *fêtes* where variety and ingenuity were so important these themes ultimately acquired a disturbing sameness.

Even the skill with which, in the space of seconds, theatrical machines could break down notions of reality and illusion, showing the startled spectator at one moment the splendours of a super-natural scene, at the next changing to the horrid landscape of hell, and a moment later transforming the whole into an enchanted forest, even this skill could not hide the fact that the themes of the opera were basically the same as those Le Brun used elsewhere to extol Louis XIV's virtues. These heroic themes we know were specifically chosen by Louis himself. Quinault and Lully always submitted two or three ideas for an opera to the King, and only when he had made his choice of Alceste or Armide did they begin serious work. It seems that at every stage of its progress towards a finished work of art Louis was consulted, and it may well be that the considerable favour Lully enjoyed stemmed precisely from this close collaboration of monarch and musician. But if the themes and their development were closely watched by the King, their musical elaboration was left entirely to the genius of Lully. Here, at least, was an art form which could develop fairly freely, at times almost independently of the themes around which the notes were embroidered. Lully wrote his overtures, the music to *ballets-intermèdes*, untrammelled by the exigences of poet or choreographer. Records show that he was the dominant personality, that he was the genius who required of Quinault that he sacrifice one third of his opera as being too wordy, that he rewrite up to six times a scene for *Alceste*; he was the musician who could tell La Fontaine that his verse was not worthy of being set to his music. Lully not only showed he could express the grandiose powerfully in the Prologues to his operas; he also revealed an ability to give depth to the sentiments of the gods and heroes whose amorous exploits he sang. Their lyrical expressions of love seemed so poignantly real that, paradoxically, gods became men of flesh and blood. Lully's success came from a satisfactory blending of the pompous scope of heroic themes with a more intimate expression of the feeling of love—his talent coincided with the tastes of his monarch.

In the case of other artists such coincidence was undoubtedly much more rare. The users of words in particular can tell us a lot about the discomfort of conformism. Most of the important literature of the age not only shows the direct influence of the state machine, but also reveals the problems and tensions which the system created for the artist.

The case of Mézeray's history indicates one way in which this system operated. Here financial pressure was exerted in an attempt to discourage political non-conformism. The least that was expected of writers was that they should refrain from criticism of the established authorities—further, they were encouraged to play a positive and enthusiastic part in the glorification of the Sun-King and in the worldly ceremony which surrounded him. Not that a great deal of encouragement was always needed: particularly in the early years of Louis's personal reign, when the Court was young, vigorous, and as yet unrepentant, the monarch himself, his courtiers, and their splendid setting might well dazzle and subdue the minds of writers. Even in 1689, when Racine's *Esther* was being performed in what developed into a sort of court ritual, Madame de Sévigné, for all her pretentions to level-headedness, reveals in a letter to her daughter (21 February 1689) a hero-worship which we can find similarly in the works of most contemporary writers.

The influence naturally worked most strongly on those who lived at the Court or depended on it for money and fame; thus the King and his Court are of crucial importance for Molière or for Racine and Boileau after 1677. But even those who were relatively independent or remote from the central power felt the pull of the Court and all it stood for. To a greater or lesser extent almost all the writing of the period shows a tension between attachment to the King, the Court, or worldly values in general and the rejection of these in the name of such ideals as honesty, independence, artistic integrity, or religious belief.

As far as we know, Bishop Bossuet experienced little of this inner tension, devoted as he was to the service of his religion. As tutor to the Dauphin, Bossuet combined his belief in the absolute monarchy with a constant insistence on the duties of the Christian king. As director of the royal conscience he could be more frank in his advice than poets and historians; he wrote outspoken letters to Louis about his scandalous private life and about the misery of his overtaxed people. Preaching before the King at the Louvre in Lent 1662, he spoke to his audience in vigorous, threatening terms of the poor at their gate, accusing them of 'cette dureté qui fait des voleurs sans dérober, et des meurtriers sans verser le sang'. And yet Bossuet was conscious of the need for royal magnificence and as court preacher he took part in ceremonies whose worldly nature is suggested by La Bruyere's subsequent description of the chapel of Versailles:

Les grands forment un vaste cercle au pied de cet autel, et paraissent debout, le dos tourné directement au prêtre et aux saints mystères, et les faces élevées vers leur roi, que l'on voit à genoux sur une tribune, et à qui ils semblent avoir tout l'esprit et tout le cœur appliqués. (*Les Caractères*, ch. viii)

Frequently in his sermons Bossuet is obliged to remind his fashionable audience that they should come to sermons for edification and not theatrical pleasure. The funeral oration in particular was a splendid dramatic occasion where elaborate settings with drapery, cannons, pyramids, and death's-heads evoked the splendour and vanity of the life of the great. All this was reflected in the words of the preacher, who had to combine eulogy with his *memento mori* and seemed to participate in the very pomp (the word recurs constantly) which his words undermined. In the first sentence of his first funeral oration Bossuet insists on the edifying side of his work: 'Quand l'Église ouvre la bouche des prédicateurs dans les funérailles de ses enfants, ce n'est pas pour accroître la pompe du deuil par des plaintes étudiées, ni pour satisfaire l'ambition des vivants par de vains éloges des morts.' And yet in the nature of things, as he later comes to preach on the death of Henriette-Marie de France, reine d'Angleterre, of Queen Marie-Thérèse, or of the great Condé, Bossuet finds himself praising the great and flattering his King even while he is humbling man in general. He may warn against the dangers of court life (*Oraison funèbre d'Anne de Gonzague de Clèves*) or even discreetly reprimand the King for his past love affairs (*Oraison funèbre de Marie-Thérèse*), but these moral lessons are encompassed in a whole whose grandiose form and often flattering content may be seen as contributions to the glorification of King and Court.

Nevertheless, in Bossuet's orations, edification does always have the last word. This is notably so in the oration for Condé, where, after evoking the many-sided greatness of the dead man, Bossuet enfolds the whole splendid setting in his peroration:

Jetez les yeux de toutes parts: voilà tout ce qu'a pu faire la magnificence et la piété pour honorer un héros: des titres, des inscriptions, vaines marques de ce qui n'est plus; des figures qui semblent pleurer autour d'un tombeau, et des fragiles images d'une douleur que le temps emporte avec tout le reste; des colonnes qui semblent vouloir porter jusqu'au ciel le magnifique témoignage de notre néant.

And finally, perhaps conscious of the sacrifices demanded of him by the role he must play in such ceremonies, Bossuet says farewell to the funeral oration: 'Au lieu de déplorer la mort des autres, grand prince, dorénavant je veux apprendre de vous à rendre la mienne sainte.'

Even more closely bound to Louis were the two royal historians, Racine and Boileau, who owed their fortune largely to the King's favour (particularly in the case of Racine) and who in the later part of their careers devoted themselves wholeheartedly to his praise and service. Racine had launched his career with two or three official odes, but he owed his worldly success rather to his tragedies—for tragedy too took its place in the ceremonies of the Court. In his early play *Alexandre*, where he is at his most conventional, Racine includes an official portrait of his young king which begins:

> D'abord ce jeune éclat qu'on remarque en ses traits
> M'a semblé démentir le nombre de ses faits.
> Mon cœur, plein de son nom, n'osait, je le confesse,
> Accorder tant de gloire avec tant de jeunesse;
> Mais de ce même front l'héroïque fierté,
> Le feu de ses regards, sa haute majesté,
> Font connaître Alexandre. (III, iii)

Alexandre, hero in love as in war, must be taken as Louis. This heroic image is perpetuated in the heroes of the opera, with the support of machines and pageantry, but in Racine's next play, *Andromaque*, the image of the heroic ruler is already tarnished. Then, four years after *Alexandre*, Racine gave his audiences, in *Britannicus*, the emperor Néron, a weak-willed, cruel, vain, play-acting ruler who is the very opposite of all the conventional patterns of eulogy. Although the anecdote may be spurious which tells us that Louis stopped dancing at Court festivities after hearing this play's denunciation of such activities on the part of Néron, although Racine could not openly allegorize the King as Néron, there can be little doubt that this tragedy, with its fierce picture of Court life, had some bearing on contemporary reality. Thereafter in Racine's plays, as in *La Princesse de Clèves*, kings are rarely happy and courts are rarely virtuous, but this will not prevent Racine personally from becoming one of the King's most valued servants and an expert in Court life. The problem of divided allegiance, if problem there was, was made easier when Louis, like Racine, was won over to the devout life.

Although Racine's tragedies may have implications which are hard to reconcile with his enthusiastic participation in the life of the Court, after 1677 it is rather in Boileau's letters and poems that we get some hint that the role of servant and official flatterer may not always have been congenial to the artist. Boileau began his career as a fairly disreputable satirist. He was passed over in the 1663 distribution of 'gratifications'; after this setback it took him many years to win the royal favour and the money which went with it—he speaks quite plainly of the financial advantages of conformism in *Satire IX*, addressed to himself:

> Osez chanter du roi les augustes merveilles:
> Là, mettant à profit vos caprices diverses,
> Vous verriez tous les ans fructifier vos vers.

Eventually, after several overtures in verse, Boileau gained the ear of Louis and thereafter his future was assured; he could become royal historian and 'législateur du Parnasse'.

But even after his success Boileau retained the taste for independence—or at any rate the posture of independence—which he had cultivated in his earlier writing. To reconcile this with his role as official poet he was forced back on to the constant use of self-deprecating irony when he wrote panegyric. His is the flattery which rejects flattery and gains greater weight by its appearance of plain speaking—sometimes more than appearance, for on occasion Boileau does in fact presume to advise the King. He is not so bold as this in his *Épître IV*, where he complains instead about the impossibility of eulogizing Louis's Dutch campaigns, which involve such unversifiable proper names as:

> Zutphen, Wageninghen, Harderwic, Knotzembourg.

and makes fun of the official ode:

> Vous savez des grands vers les disgraces tragiques,
> Et souvent on ennuie en termes magnifiques.

Acutely conscious of the banal pomposity of most verse of the sort he is composing, and embarrassed by his mercenary status, he says in his *Épître VIII*:

> J'ai peur que l'univers, qui sait ma récompense,
> N'impute mes transports à ma reconnaissance.

Boileau steps back from his subject and, instead of praising directly, talks with mock modesty of the problems of praising.

There are similar tensions in La Fontaine's attitude to his protector Fouquet. La Fontaine too attempts to make flattery and mercenary verse more palatable—both for author and recipient—by wit. After Fouquet's disgrace in 1661 La Fontaine combines a theoretical attitude of independence and even of occasional hostility to the court ceremonies with the production of official verse of the most banal kind and a series of embarrassed, half-ironical epistles attempting to win Louis's favour.

The same sort of ambiguity can be found in the *Fables*. On the whole, these are much concerned with the relations between 'les grands' and 'les petits' and show a wry awareness of the injustices of the social order. It is true that some of the fables, particularly those written when La Fontaine had attained some familiarity with Court circles, are contributions to the work of official propaganda (for example 'Le Soleil et les Grenouilles'), but often La Fontaine criticizes the ways of kings—perhaps by implication the ways of Louis XIV. Thus in 'Le Lion, le Loup et le Renard' the Lion—who is clearly intended to be a king—is shown as cruel and unreasonable, while in 'Les Animaux malades de la peste' and 'Le Lion, le Singe et les deux Ânes' he appears totally impervious to criticism. But more than kings, it is the Court which is spoken of with disdain:

> Je définis la cour un pays où les gens,
> Tristes, gais, prêts à tout, à tout indifférents,
> Sont ce qu'il plaît au prince, ou, s'ils ne peuvent l'être,
>   Tâchent au moins de le paraître:
> Peuple caméléon, peuple singe d'un maître.
>   ('Les Obsèques de la Lionne')

The fox is the master of the courtier's art. He not only adapts himself to changing circumstances, but is quick to see his way out of difficulties and turn every situation to his advantage, gaily profiting from the stupidity and innocence of his fellow-animals (for example in 'Le Renard et le Bouc'). A natural Machiavellian, he never allows considerations of conventional morality to stand in his way. But note that La Fontaine's harshest words against crafty villains are reserved for the cat, who is not a courtier:

> Celui qu'à meilleur droit tout l'univers abhorre
> C'est la fourbe à mon avis.
>   ('L'Aigle, la Laie et la Chatte')

The fox on the other hand is given considerable charm; for all his immorality, he shows in fables such as 'La Cour du Lion' a supple skill which calls for our aesthetic appreciation. This contrast is characteristic of the total effect of the fables, which show the constant interweaving of a charming and witty use of words, rhythms, and images with a traditional, often hard, disillusioned common sense.

La Fontaine's fox is Molière's *fourbe*; the same ambiguities can be seen in both writers, but much more clearly in Molière, for Molière was of all writers the closest to Louis XIV in his best years, the most directly involved in the entertainment of the Court. Throughout his Paris career he depended on the patronage of the King, who helped him financially and protected him during the *Tartuffe* crisis. In return Molière developed for Louis and his festivities a new genre, the *comédie-ballet*, and in the accepted genres wrote for the Court a series of plays ranging from farces of the *George Dandin* type, which provide crude fun at the expense of provincials, peasants, and bourgeois, to heroic pastorals such as *Mélicerte*. *Mélicerte*, incidentally, contains a flattering portrait of the young King which may be compared with that in *Alexandre*—there is a similar one in Pierre Corneille's *Attila*, and all three were written soon after the 'gratifications' of 1663. In such plays, in fact in the greater part of Molière's theatre, serious worries are dismissed, the *fâcheux* are swept aside by the charming, amoral dance of the dissolute and elegant *marquis*, the *fourbes* and the *ingénues*, the Scapins and the Angéliques.

But then the revels will be broken by someone who refuses to play the game, a dupe perhaps who protests and makes us see the thoughtless dancers in a different and less charming light. *Amphitryon* is a good example. Essentially a Court entertainment, this is a comedy of great charm, written in beautiful *vers libres* and allowing the deployment of all the splendours of costumes and *machines*. It retells the old story in which Jupiter seduces the virtuous Alcmène by assuming the shape of her husband, Amphitryon. In 1668 'Jupiter' meant Louis XIV, and the moral of the story seems to be that, as Jupiter says:

> Un partage avec Jupiter
> N'a rien du tout qui déshonore. (III, x)

But alongside Jupiter we have Mercury, who has a similar but less dignified change of places with Amphitryon's valet Sosie. On his first appearance Sosie, who was originally played by Molière, complains about his servile position in a way which makes one think of Molière's obligation to write play after play at short notice to please his royal master. Between them, he and Mercury somewhat deflate Jupiter's charm, Mercury by his courtier-like cynicism:

> Lorsque dans un haut rang on a l'heur de paraître,
> Tout ce qu'on fait est toujours bel et bon;
> Et suivant ce qu'on peut être,
> Les choses changent de nom.   (Prologue)

and Sosie by his blunter comments:

> Le seigneur Jupiter sait dorer la pilule.   (III, x)

All this does not go beyond the sort of humorous licence allowed to a court jester; it does not amount to a serious criticism of the King or the Court, but the play is finally left suspended, the deceived Amphitryon remaining silent and Sosie moralizing:

> Sur telles affaires, toujours,
> Le meilleur est de ne rien dire.   (III, x)

Amphitryon is fairly typical of Molière's normal position; it is only occasionally that he gives more serious consideration to the rights and wrongs of Court and society life, notably in *Dom Juan* which gives us an attractive yet disillusioned picture of a 'grand seigneur méchant homme', and in *Le Misanthrope* where two possible meanings of *honnête homme* (honest man and social man) come into conflict. Molière's greatness in these two plays lies in the balance he holds between the two sides. Alceste's old-fashioned virtue compels some respect, or at any rate sympathy, though its motives appear unworthy and Alceste himself frequently ridiculous. Célimène and her small court have all the vices of an overcivilized society and all its charm.

Such were the tensions created for the writer by a system of government control over art and the powerful influence on literature of one particular section of society, the Court. La Bruyère's vision of this Court was shared in part at least by many of his contemporaries who were less moralizing and embittered than he:

Il y a un pays où les joies sont visibles, mais fausses, et les chagrins cachés, mais réels. Qui croirait que l'empressement pour les spectacles, que les éclats et les applaudissements aux théâtres de Molière et d'Arlequin, les repas, la chasse, les ballets, les carrousels, couvrissent tant d'inquiétudes, de soins et de divers intérêts, tant de craintes et d'espérances, des passions si vives et des affaires si sérieuses. (*Les Caracteres*, ch. viii)

NOTE

The best way to get to know the world of Louis XIV is to read memoirs of the period, in particular: Louis XIV, *Mémoires* (publ. 1928), Dangeau, *Journal* (publ. 1854–60, 19 vols.), Charles Perrault, *Mémoires de ma vie* (ed. Bonnefon, 1909), Primi Visconti, *Mémoires sur la cour de Louis XIV* (trad. Lemoine, 1909), Saint-Simon, *Mémoires* (Pléiade edition, vol. i, for the years 1691–1701), Spanheim, *Relation de la cour de France* (ed. Bourgeois, 1900), and the letters of Madame de Sévigné and La Princesse Palatine.

Among the most interesting or useful of subsequent accounts are: Voltaire, *Le Siècle de Louis XIV* (1751), F. Gaiffe, *L'Envers du Grand Siècle* (1924), P. Goubert, *Louis XIV et 20 millions de Français* (1966), J. Lough, *An Introduction to Seventeenth-Century France* (1954), H. Méthivier, *Louis XIV* ('Que sais-je?', 3rd edn., 1962), and R. Mousnier, *Les XVIᵉ et XVIIᵉ siècles* (3rd edn., 1961).

The various arts are discussed in greater detail in: A. Adam, *Histoire de la littérature française au XVIIᵉ siècle* (1948–62), A. Blunt, *Art and Architecture in France, 1500–1700* (1953), E. Magne, *Les Fêtes en Europe au XVIIᵉ siècle* (1930), and V. L. Tapié, *Baroque et classicisme* (1957).

For Molière, La Fontaine, La Bruyère, and Racine see notes to Chapters 7, 8, 9, and 11. Bossuet's funeral orations can be read in the Garnier edition. For his political ideas see *Politique de Bossuet* (ed. Truchet, 1966). The best edition of Boileau is that of Boudhors ('Les Belles Lettres', 9 vols., 1934–43).

There are records of music by Lully, Charpentier, and Lalande, and some of Quinault's opera libretti are included in his *Théâtre choisi* (best edition available: Fournel, 1882).

Most illuminating of all is a visit to Versailles.

7. Molière

MOLIÈRE criticism has been active in recent years, and a salutary change of emphasis has been claimed in the approach to his comedy. This change could be described briefly as follows: earlier critics tended to treat Molière's plays as vehicles for ideas, or to explain their genesis in terms of a dramatization of Molière's own personal predicaments; the emphasis was on the satirical and subjective (sometimes even 'tragic') elements; modern critics prefer to see the plays as self-contained aesthetic products which are best explored in terms of comic structure and technique, and of the theatrical rather than the primarily literary. The change has not perhaps been quite as radical as some of its practitioners make out; they have sometimes seemed to make too much of refuting what was bad criticism by any standards. Nevertheless, there has been a shift of emphasis, in line with the general trend of modern literary criticism, which rejects the approach through literary history and the author's 'intentions'. In addition to this, in the case of Molière, the writings of a number of men of the theatre, notably Louis Jouvet, have encouraged academics to reconsider their views with some reference to theatrical realities.

The gains from the change are obvious, but it has brought the risk of losses. The pronouncements of the actor, for instance, have a way of silencing what seems to be legitimate discussion—as when Jouvet rejects as irrelevant criticisms of Molière's endings, with the argument that they are 'de la plus fine convention théâtrâle', or writes rather touchily that no one who has seen *Dom Juan* acted will ever again complain of its incoherence. The incoherence (or suggestiveness) of a character is not dispelled by a single, perhaps spuriously coherent performance. Moreover, approaches which claim to avoid speculation and concentrate on the text sometimes bring back, under the guise of a new directness, another form of the intentional and the historical. To claim that Molière's concern was 'purely' theatrical is as doctrinaire as other unfounded assumptions about his aims. To say that he would not have dared to express views for which he could have been burnt is to ignore at least one firm fact: that if he wanted to avoid trouble he was singularly bad at doing so; so bad that the case for the rebel can be made as plausible as the case for the willing servant of popular taste and existing convention. The notion of 'pure' comedy itself is a dubious one at any level above that of simple farce; and it would seem an impoverishment—and a distortion—if such a controversial play as *Tartuffe* were finally rendered harmless and laid to rest, explained away totally in terms of some scheme of internal comic structures and techniques. Nor, when he complains that Alceste is not a fit subject for comedy, is it a complete answer to say that Rousseau lacks a sense of humour.

Another influence has taken Molière criticism in a somewhat different direction: the reaction against the approach to drama through character, occasioned by the excesses of the Bradleyan approach to Shakespeare which treated characters as real people whose pasts and motives could be rounded out and speculated on. Though sometimes suggestive, the move towards seeing the play as extended metaphor has not always led criticism in the way of unpretentiousness: where once critics talked about Molière's views on women or the Church, they are now likely to see the plays as dramatic projections of near-metaphysical . issues, such as 'the problem of identity', 'the nature of language', and, inevitably, 'appearance and reality'. This approach sometimes coexists un-expectedly with the 'theatrical' in a single critic; for though the actor is tied to some consideration of character, the insistence on the difference between the theatre and the real world, on the characters' having no existence off the boards, the redefinition of the play as not dramatized psychology but spectacle or ballet or poetry, these, perhaps, connive indirectly at the more extravagant metaphorical interpretations. In the following pages I intend to remain on the traditional middle ground between Molière the mummer and Molière the metaphorical poet; to treat him primarily as the creator of a comedy of character and a comic language which yield to fairly

conventional critical analysis; and to suggest, without going outside
the texts themselves, that the question: 'Molière pense-t-il?', which
stands so provocatively as a chapter-heading in R. Bray's *Molière*,
homme de théâtre, has not yet been finally settled in the negative.

The approach through character is certainly justified by Molière's
first masterpiece, *L'École des femmes* (1662). Here we have a central
character substantial enough for us to discuss in detail while remaining well clear of the Bradleyan fallacy. It is one of those plays which
look like the most sophisticated stage of a long tradition; yet a glance
at the known 'sources' proves it to be almost entirely original. At a
single stroke, in what is (after the semi-heroic *Dom Garcie de
Navarre*) his first five-act verse comedy, Molière has created a
character who is at once rounded and idiosyncratic, and a prototype
of the self-absorbed, presumptuous, vulgar figures who recur
throughout the mature plays. The theme of *la précaution inutile*
yields in prominence to the extended illustration of a comic state of
confusion and pretension. Indeed it is easy to overstate the importance of Arnolphe's final defeat, as though Molière were illustrating
some belief in a principle of ultimate justice, of the 'triumph of
nature' at work; such an undertaking might well trick him into
revealing the very habits of mind he pillories in Arnolphe. What we
have, rather, is a progressive self-revelation, in language so dense that
it would be worth quoting and commenting on verbatim. When we
know all there is to know Molière calls a halt with a well-known
comic device, and one with which he seems to suggest that it is
chance rather than rights that brings about such happy outcomes as
life affords.

In the opening scene exposition is skilfully fused with an introduction to Arnolphe's character; for love of exposition is actually part
of that character. Arnolphe is the man who delights in the relation
of his successful dealings with life, and the speech about the
tolerance of the local husbands, with its ready enumeration of their
varieties, is obviously (like the later speeches to Agnès about
marriage) a well-rehearsed set-piece. Arnolphe revels in his own
range, moving from the condescending to the sarcastic, from the
ostensibly open-minded ('Je crois, en bon chrétien, votre moitié fort
sage') to the archly allusive ('Mais je sais ce qu'il coûte à de certaines

gens'). And we begin to be alerted by odd collocations and transi-
tions, of which Arnolphe is himself unaware—for instance, from the
near-idyllic, to the brazen, to the pseudo-humble:

> Dans un petit couvent, loin de toute pratique,
> Je la fis élever selon ma politique;
> C'est-à-dire, ordonnant quels soins on emploîrait
> Pour la rendre idiote autant qu'il se pourrait.
> Dieu merci, le succès a suivi mon attente.

This is to be the central linguistic technique of the play, on which
Molière plays numberless variations, always significant even when,
as in the blend of moral superiority and prurience in the opening
remarks to Agnès, they are nearer the farcical mode. Agnès complains
of fleas in bed:

ARNOLPHE

Ah! vous aurez dans peu quelqu'un pour les chasser.

AGNÈS

Vous me ferez plaisir.

ARNOLPHE

Je le puis bien penser.

From the start the character has an almost Pecksniffian pomp and
nuance, and Chrysalde's bluff directness ('Ma foi! je le crois fou
de toutes les manières') contrasts neatly with the bogus judicious-
ness ('Il est un peu blessé sur certaines matières') which Arnolphe
maintains even when on his own. And in the following scene with
Horace, how indelicately, yet how credibly, Arnolphe steers the
conversation with the son of his old friend, quickly brushing aside
his polite comments on the architecture of the town! How comically
inconsequential, yet how natural in the man for whom precaution is
the supreme virtue, is his first reaction to Horace's revelation of his
love for Agnès—incredulous rage that Horace should be so imprudent
as to tell him! The realism of the whole scene has been questioned.
But Arnolphe's generosity goes quite naturally with his expansive and
patronizing manner. He belongs not to the semi-criminal world of a
Bartholo trying to cheat his ward—his fault is rather the opposite, that
of investing Agnès with the wrong sort of expectation. Similarly,

his precautions, though intensive, are restricted to identified dangers. Horace belongs to a world thought of through habit as friendly, and though Arnolphe's obsession with collecting material for his 'tablettes' (now frankly confirmed after the earlier hinting enumerations) makes him theoretically aware that Horace is 'de taille à faire des cocus', he still *sees* him not as a living threat but as he had once known him, 'pas plus grand que cela'. It is the counterpart of his failure to notice that Agnès herself has grown up, the product of his feeling of success in immobilizing the world around him. And so the way is prepared for his first intrinsically comic formulation of chagrin at life's ways:

> Aurais-je deviné, quand je l'ai vu petit,
> Qu'il croîtrait pour cela . . . ?

It is comic because for Molière, but even more for Arnolphe—though their valuations of it differ—'cela' is the natural and predictable way of all flesh.

Molière's achievement is perhaps at its most accomplished in the long speeches of Acts III and IV. Arnolphe's suffering is real, but our attention to his speech is never allowed to be other than critical. He continues to betray himself by his logic, his language, and his sentiments. In an essay in which he comments on Othello's shortcomings in tragic awareness, F. R. Leavis strikingly characterizes his remorse as 'an intolerably intensified form of the common "I could kick myself" '. Arnolphe defines his own emotion in precisely that way:

> . . . Ah, je crève, j'enrage,
> Et je souffletterais mille fois mon visage.

His response is at the level of chagrined irritation. And the one quality which could arouse our sympathy—his realization that he really cares for Agnès—is negated by the fact that he devalues it and considers it a nuisance ('Faut-il de ses appas m'être si fort coiffé?'). His logic is still comically self-justifying, as he seeks the causes of his misfortune anywhere but in the nature of the case. Agnès cannot be truly innocent:

> Elle a feint d'être telle à mes yeux, la traîtresse,
> Ou le diable à son âme a soufflé cette adresse.

The eloquent rehearsal of his troubles almost elicits from us a favourable response—but the very facility reminds us of the satisfaction with which he has always documented his case, and contains its own damning answer. Arnolphe is comic both in the extent to which he has changed his views, and in the extent to which they have remained the same. In the opening scene he implicitly denies the power of destiny, the gesture to 'le ciel' is a mere variant of self-congratulation; and as his worries increase gratitude is revealed, through the vulgarity of its expression, as no more than relief ('Grâce aux bontés du ciel j'en suis quitte à bon compte'). Now he is only too willing to appeal to heaven that 'mon front soit exempt de disgrâce', to abandon the proud claim to autonomy for a more consoling belief that it may be 'écrit qu'il faille que j'y passe'. But still there is no true humility, and Molière, by a well-judged stroke, wards off the threat of the tragic with an echo of the phrasing of the opening scene:

> Donnez-moi tout au moins pour de tels accidents
> La constance qu'on voit à *de certaines gens*.

Sarcasm blends with supplication, and our incipient sympathy is forfeited.

The climax of the play is the final scene with Agnès in which Arnolphe alternates abject self-abasement with the comic utterance and logic of wounded pride. Agnès works him up simply by replying in the light of nature. Asked why she wants to marry Horace and not him, she says that Horace actually makes marriage sound attractive, and not the austere duty she had been led to think: 'Ah! c'est que vous l'aimez, traîtresse' is Arnolphe's reply. Unheeding of her implicit admission, he throws the words at her at once as an accusation and a diagnosis. He expects that she will capsize at having been found out, and also that she will yield to his claim to have 'explained away' her unfair preference, to have convicted her of a partiality which does not give his expectations their legitimate due! As she retains her calm he can only rail: 'Pourquoi ne m'aimer point, madame l'impudente?' To such a point has the absurdity gone of man who wishes to introduce rights into a world of facts. And Molière's achievement is to have embodied the totally comic climax in a scene which is serious, dramatic, violent, and not a little frightening.

In *Le Misanthrope* (1666), the most important direct successor of *L'École des femmes*, we see the same techniques at work. Alceste's last speech to Célimène is at once impassioned pleading and preposterous effrontery. Like Arnolphe, he is irritated at the involvement of his emotions, aggrieved at the failure of life to collaborate with him in the realization of his ideals. When invited by Célimène to hate her, therefore, he reproves her for underestimating his difficulties—and refers to these in language more often to be found in admission of failure to love:

> Et quoiqu'avec ardeur je veuille vous haïr,
> Trouvé-je un cœur en moi tout prêt à m'obéir?

Unable to arm himself with this 'généreux mépris' he decides that the situation can only be saved by being made exemplary; and turning to his friends he invites them to watch him prove the very proposition which they have been trying to enforce on him throughout, and which only he could ever have contested:

> . . . que c'est à tort que sages on nous nomme
> Et que dans tous les cœurs il est toujours de l'homme.

The comic variant of tragic self-knowledge could hardly be more perfectly embodied. When he goes on to make his proposal-ultimatum, the desire to give to the particular the moral dignity of a general significance still persists: only by following him can she satisfy the requirements of justice 'dans *tous* les esprits', so that

> . . . après cet éclat, qu'un noble cœur abhorre,
> Il peut m'être permis de vous aimer encore.

The generalizing suggestion of the penultimate line (not 'I' but 'any honourable man') gives way to the confirmation in the last line that the plea is, basically, for help in achieving a minimum moral consistency.

I have ignored, for the moment, the problematic nature of the 'serious' comedies in order to illustrate their procedures. *George Dandin* (1668) is a remarkable achievement in that (except for moralists as strenuous as Rousseau) it avoids the problematical while still going well beyond the farcical. Dandin is a more immediately

comic version of Alceste, standing like him in bemused outrage
before a world in which he fails to get the treatment that abstract
justice demands. 'J'enrage de bon cœur d'avoir tort, lorsque j'ai
raison' is his colloquial echo of Alceste's more poetic complaints.
But moral issues are kept at bay by the data, as well as the tone, of
the play. Both sides are in the wrong, and Dandin admits his folly.
Moreover he, at least, is spared the tortures of real love. When
Alceste reviles Célimène with:

> Je voudrais qu'aucun ne vous trouvât aimable,
> Que vous fussiez réduite en un sort misérable

we feel that vitriol might not be safe in his hands; Dandin's natural
weapon however is the custard-pie: 'Il me prend des tentations
d'accommoder tout son visage à la compote, et le mettre en état de ne
plaire de sa vie aux diseurs de fleurettes.' Since his view of marriage
is at the level of vulgar maxim and mixed metaphor—'une chaîne à
laquelle on doit porter toute sorte de respect'—his desire for justice
goes no further than the ambition to convince his wife's parents of
her infidelity, a comically formulated wish to publicize his own
dishonour. Thus the comedy is legitimately narrowed in scope to the
consideration of Dandin's intellectual predicament: 'Est-il possible
que toujours j'aurai du dessous avec elle, que les apparences tourne-
ront toujours contre moi?' The answer, as with all the rhetorical
questions to which Molière's heroes seek a reassuring 'No, it's not
fair', is a resounding 'Yes', based, again, on considerations not of
justice but of fact. Dandin cannot win because he is stupid; but he
defines this norm as an endless series of exceptions, like the bad
games player who feels that he is never quite on his true form. For
the comic writer, form is the sum of individual performances. It is
a hard truth, and Dandin understandably sees suicide as the only
solution to life's injustice. But the cyclical structure of the play, with
its fluctuations of despair and hope, puts this threat firmly in
perspective: we may confidently imagine Dandin interpreting the
next situation more favourably, feeling that *this* time the parents are
arriving 'fort à propos', that now 'le sort ici me donne de quoi
confondre ma partie . . .'. Secure in this knowledge, we can relish
his expressions of bewilderment. When his wife makes blackmailing

threats of suicide herself he at first dismisses them, then begins to be convinced; and his conception of himself as universal victim makes him credit a motivation which (one would think) is beyond the bounds of normal psychological possibility. 'Ouais, serait-elle bien si malicieuse que de s'être tuée pour me faire pendre? ... La méchanceté d'une femme irait-elle bien jusque-là?' For Dandin, with women all things are possible, and psychological speculation is useless. But at least he is not put out by his emotions and decides, with his endearing peasant practicality, to resort to the empirical test: 'Prenons un bout de chandelle pour aller voir.'

Dandin stands between the philosophical comedy of Arnolphe and Alceste and the more overtly farcical mode which Molière never abandoned. Plays like *Les Fourberies de Scapin* (1671) contain superb comic utterance; the difference is that it is not backed up to the same degree as in the 'serious' comedies by the whole cumulative weight of evidence. Alceste's 'J'ai pour moi la justice et je perds mon procès', his 'Personne n'a, madame, aimé comme je fais' take their resonance from all that has gone before. For all their epigrammatic quality they are unobtrusively embedded in the character's speech. With Géronte's 'Que diable allait-il faire dans cette galère?' we are more conscious of the presence of Molière exercising his virtuoso's powers. In terms of provoking laughter and mocking human selfishness the mean, tyrannical Géronte is hardly inferior to the larger creations. 'Cinq cents écus! N'a-t-il point de conscience?' he exclaims on hearing the ransom demanded for his son, and forgetting in his self-pity that blackmail, by definition, excludes such refinements of valuation. It is a splendid scene, but the play remains (very enjoyably) episodic, an embroidery on the pre-existing, rather than the progressive creation of a substantial figure.

Harpagon is a similar case, and the notion of *L'Avare* (1668) as a 'study' of avarice seems altogether too solemn; it is, in fact, very much a repertory of Molière's comic techniques. The 'cassette' scene repeats the procedure of the 'galère'—a single comic repetition interspersed with subtler verbal variants: 'Il n'est pas question d'honneur là-dedans', Harpagon explodes in response to Valère's assurance, suspecting that restitution is being offered in terms of something less solid than money, and ignoring the normal equation of being upright and paying one's debts. The play is based on the simple conflict between Harpagon's desire to be loved and respected and his unwillingness to make the necessary gestures: a grosser variant of Alceste's unjustified claims on the world. This leads to the simple visual comedy of the ring scene and the linguistic techniques whereby Molière makes Harpagon reveal his values through his vocabulary, even when he is trying to be polished or delicately allusive:

> Mais Frosine, as-tu entretenu la mère touchant le bien qu'elle peut donner à sa fille? Lui as-tu dit qu'il fallait qu'elle s'aidât un peu, qu'elle fît quelque effort, *qu'elle se saignât* pour une occasion comme celle-ci? Car encore n'épouse-t-on pas une fille [note the attempt, like Alceste's, to put the personal on a general level], sans qu'elle apporte quelque chose.

Attempts to frame a general definition of Molière's comedy differ chiefly in the importance they allot to conscious pretension or imposture. For Bergson, comedy is what is done automatically, comedy of character is the spectacle of a man unconsciously revealing his own fixity. There *is* a moral element here in that unpretentiousness is counselled, in the manner of Chrysalde's warnings to Arnolphe, as the only way of avoiding ridicule. The banana skin is a cosmic injustice, but we lose all right to sympathy if it catches us in a posture of omniscience or superiority. But on the whole Bergson sees the comic character as the incurable *distrait* whose antics we are invited to relish. While this theory fits much of the discussion so far, it does not seem to keep Molière firmly in the world of 'ideas', from which I do not want to divorce him. A related theory is W. G. Moore's notion of the *mask*. He sees Molière as having revivified and transformed the existing convention whereby comic actors appeared in a mask giving them a (Bergsonian) fixity of character; for Molière the mask is not fixed but detachable, the important moment is when the mask slips to reveal the man underneath. This theory (though this is not its prime intention) would seem to allow the retention of some of the traditional views of Molière as social commentator, exposer of the abuses and pretences of his time. Perhaps, however, though convenient for my purpose, it puts a rather greater emphasis on conscious pretension or pretence,

on the existence of two 'layers' to character, on the structural aim of
exposure, than our experience of the plays justifies.

Is Argan in *Le Malade imaginaire* (1673), for instance, best seen
as a healthy man feigning illness—and does the attempt to expose
him loom large in the play? Certainly Toinette makes him forget
his ills and chase her—but this is no more than many invalids
could do under provocation. What perhaps interests Molière more
is the naturalness with which the comic character inhabits or returns
to his *persona*—in short his monolithic nature rather than his alleged
duality. The attempts to show Argan up are significantly fitful and
half-hearted. Toinette, *en médecin*, looks set to drive him to a confession through her threats, and we enjoy the sight of Argan torn
between respect for the profession and fear of real pain. But she
breaks off at the height of the act and our enjoyment is completed
in another way by the ease with which Argan slips back into the role
of 'illustre malade' with which Toinette had initially flattered him,
and excuses himself for not showing her out: 'Vous savez que les
malades [the general for the particular again] ne reconduisent pas.'
Our response here is surely not admiration (or amazement) at the
wit (or impudence) of an impostor; it is aesthetic pleasure at
Molière's making the character so perfectly and spontaneously
express his nature: the nature neither of the sick man, nor of the
healthy man pretending to be ill, but of the hypochondriac, a seam-
less, layerless type with its own internal logic.

Similarly with Bélise in *Les Femmes savantes* (1672) whose cast-
iron case that all the men love her seems proof against the assaults
of Ariste and Clitandre. Her replies may have the *appearance* of wit,
imposture, rapid improvisation:

ARISTE
De mots piquants partout Dorante vous outrage.

BÉLISE
Ce sont emportements d'une jalouse rage.

ARISTE
Cléonte et Lycidas ont pris femme tous deux.

BÉLISE
C'est par un désespoir où j'ai réduit leurs feux.

Yet the play as a whole proves that Bélise is not ready-witted. The semblance of wit is simply the operation of a one-track mind. In the same way Dandin's literal-mindedness, which fastens on to the single word and applies it to his case, gives what looks almost like a punning facility to his ripostes to his parents-in-law. Artistically, the conception gives Molière the best of two worlds—a surface wit and speed for which he gets the credit, combined with the portrayal of an almost sublime thickheadedness.

We do not, then, think of a calculating Bélise, congratulating herself, once on her own, on a neatly effected withdrawal. The language of offended *pudeur* ('Non, non, je ne veux rien entendre davantage' . . . 'Et de confusion j'abandonne la place') springs quite naturally to her lips. Yet it would seem equally misleading to describe her as *sincerely* believing herself loved. The parting lines have comic double meanings; they reveal a genuine, deeper 'confusion'. In terms of a hypothetical biography (if this may be temporarily permitted) Molière takes his characters at a point in their lives when they no longer consciously act a part. They live in a psychological no man's land between deception and self-deception; their former strategies have become indignant responses; their positions, when attacked, are automatically defended by blustering or retreat—but retreat neither into remorse nor into self-congratulation; the positions are repeatedly and nonchalantly resumed. The characters are at once, in their impermeability, perfect objects for aesthetic contemplation and perfect examples of *mauvaise foi*.

The notion of 'bad faith', of at least a historical responsibility on the characters' part for being what they are, suggests that their automatism need not preclude the presence of critical 'ideas'. Indeed, the opposite may be the case—and here we must consider the case of *Tartuffe*. *Tartuffe* (1669) has been consistently criticized—or welcomed—as a satirical and in some ways anti-Christian play; hence it is something of a test-case for the view of Molière as an ideologically innocent creator of self-contained comic structures. G. Michaut, in his *Luttes de Molière*, makes a case for a Tartuffe who is not an object of satire but simply an agent—a rogue like Scapin who precipitates the comedy of Orgon's character. This is to recognize an important structural point, but it hardly seems to do

justice to our total experience of the play. W. G. Moore goes a stage
further in both playing down satire and proposing Tartuffe as a
comic character himself, of the same kind as Alceste or Arnolphe.
Tartuffe too is the aspiring superman, laid low by the consequences
of his own sensuality. The comedy consists in the disparity between
the criminal's ambition and his performance, as revealed in alternate
droppings and resumptions of the mask of piety. The mask theory
clearly lends itself naturally to a play sub-titled *L'Imposteur*: 'He
wears the mask of piety, and that in itself is not a comic proceeding
unless or until it be shown to be . . . a mask, and not the man.'

The structural parallels proposed seem, however, to be open to
criticism. *L'École des femmes* and *Le Misanthrope* are explicitly set
up as anatomies of pretension—the heroes receive their warnings in
the opening scenes and we watch expectantly to see them justified.
By contrast, we know little of the precise nature of Tartuffe's
ambitions, which could well include Elmire as well as the *donation*.
The fact that he is transparent to every sensible character in the play
settles nothing—again there is little proof that he aims to fool them.
His prime aim is to exploit Orgon, and this is finally defeated not by
his sensual nature but by fortuitous intervention. In short, Tartuffe
remains a freer, more dangerous character than the other comic
heroes. Our relation to him is less one of knowledgeable domination,
our attention is less systematically directed and confined to his
internal contradictions; so that we too remain in another sense
'freer' to respond to any satirical or allusive elements. As for self-
revelation through speech, is not Tartuffe's tone perhaps more
unified than Moore allows? The only time he seems totally to 'drop
the mask' of lofty mysticism is quite late, in the conspiratorial
remark to Elmire that Orgon is 'un homme, entre nous, à mener par
le nez'; and the slight shock this gives us suggests a shift into the
over-emphatic on Molière's part rather than a lapse on Tartuffe's.
Similarly (always on the assumption, vital for Molière's 'innocence',
that Tartuffe is a pure impostor) the equation of such lines as 'Ah!
pour être dévot, je n'en suis pas moins homme' or 'Mais la vérité
pure est que je ne vaux rien' with Alceste's 'Personne n'a, madame,
aimé comme je fais' involves a rather inclusive use of the notion of
comic ambiguity. Since these are varyingly successful techniques of

trickery rather than self-revelation, their verbal ambiguity remains purely verbal, in that a criminal Tartuffe would not be wounded by our pointing out the deeper truth of his remark—as Alceste is by Célimène's acid rejoinder.

Yet, in so far as such responses can be analysed intellectually, we *do* seem at times, and in part, to be laughing *at* Tartuffe and not merely with him against Orgon or, more allusively, at recognizing a satirical portrait of a known social type. Is he, then, a pure impostor? One critic, in an attempt to define Tartuffe's essence, suggests that if we were to see him alone (which significantly we never do), he would not be congratulating himself on his strategic successes but fervently praying that Elmire should be made more favourable to his advances. Such an interpretation would be in line with our analysis of Bélise, and would suggest a possible link between Tartuffe and the preposterous and self-absorbed comic figures. And the parallel with Alceste just rejected would become exact if Tartuffe were not the impostor but the decadent, self-deceiving believer, desperately trying to reconcile his practice with his principles. Then indeed the comedy of 'Ah! pour être dévot . . .' would return with its full force. Now, while there is no textual support for the idea that Tartuffe was conceived by Molière as an 'ex-believer', the question 'Is Tartuffe sincere?', which has haunted Molière criticism, seems to be based on a genuine attempt to analyse our reaction to certain parts of the play. Michaut dismisses the question with outrage and accepts Molière's preface at its face value. Mauriac, in his *Journal*, while denying that this is what Molière has produced, allows that such a figure would be one of the profoundest comedy. Whatever Molière's aims, it seems impossible to deny that he produced, unconsciously perhaps, but willingly in a sense (he was willing to fight for his play), a figure much more problematic than Michaut allows. The stage direction 'Dès qu'il aperçoit Dorine' and Tartuffe's first, ostentatious appearance clearly point the distinction between man and part; but as the play progresses the distinction becomes much less clear. Was it that Molière was so keen an observer of the inveterate, the repetitive, the self-absorbed in human conduct that he almost unthinkingly conflated Tartuffe with the sort of comic character we have already discussed, in whom calculation is no longer a strong

factor? When Tartuffe is arguing with Cléante about his treatment
of Damis, we feel that he is really provoked by being opposed, not
merely tricking Cléante with borrowed theological subtleties. He
becomes, *momentarily*, a more ratiocinating variant of the blustering,
egotistical, middle-aged tyrant, in the cast of Argan or Harpagon;
and his parting 'Certain devoir pieux me demande là-haut' reminds
us of the built-in instinct to retreat of these totally self-absorbed
characters. Argan has his enemas and their effects, Harpagon his
money to inspect, Bélise her shocked *pudeur*—and Tartuffe his
devotions.

   Clearly, on such a reading, *Tartuffe* becomes not less but more
satirical in proportion as it comes in line with Molière's habitual
comic procedures; for instead of merely exposing an over-confident
criminal, it opens up a whole field of suggestion about the nature of
belief and its connections with self-deception. How far is such an
interpretation justified? In defining Tartuffe we must also examine
the other characters' attitudes to him. For his enemies he is an
offensive grotesque, laughable when not actively dangerous. But
their sense of him as a pure impostor is oddly fitful. In the scene just
discussed, for instance, Cléante argues quite seriously with him,
rather than accusing him of hypocrisy; we have almost a conflict of
two views of Christian duty, of which Tartuffe's is obviously seen
as selfish rationalization. In his preface Molère says that he has used
two preparatory acts so that there shall be no doubt that Tartuffe is
an impostor and not a caricature of a believer. But if this was his
aim, the execution is somewhat clumsy. For the attack on Tartuffe is
conducted on a very broad front. Dorine accuses him of hypocrisy—
but also of being an interferer and a kill-joy, in a way which makes
it clear that a 'sincere' puritan would be no more acceptable to her.
Accusations of hypocrisy and severity—logically mutually exclusive
—are used almost interchangeably to attack positions judged
absolutely unacceptable by criteria that pay scant attention to the
question of 'sincerity'. Is there perhaps, lurking behind these scenes,
a psychological axiom that all severity is, *ipso facto*, in some sense
hypocritical? The searing anatomy of prudery in both *Tartuffe* and
Le Misanthrope gives some support to this suspicion.

   Thus the blurring of the line between deception and self-deception, which at first appears to insulate the comic character from effective moral criticism, may in fact actually favour the introduction of 'ideas'. Indifference on the author's part to the nuances of subjective states itself constitutes a moral attitude. As their precise analysis is accorded less importance, objective standards can be more vigorously enforced. There is little to choose, socially, between an Orgon and a Tartuffe, the bigot and the hypocrite; the popular term 'cagot'— meaning both—is used by Damis of Tartuffe, and Molière makes no effort to dissociate himself from its presuppositions. Arnolphe, for Chrysalde, is 'fou de toutes les manières': and after that we shall hardly give his individual tenets sympathetic consideration.

The problematic nature of the serious comedies arises precisely from the rather automatic and generalizing way in which Molière associates character defects with the holding of views he disapproves of. Rousseau, in his *Lettre à d'Alembert*, attacks this levelling psychology as a wilful distortion on Molière's part: 'Le Misanthrope [meaning here the genuine idealist] et l'homme emporté sont deux caractères très différents ... Molière ne l'ignorait pas; mais il fallait faire rire le parterre.' Molière would probably have denied that they were 'très différents'. But only if the axiom: severity (or moral enthusiasm) equals hypocrisy (or bad temper) were provably true could he finally be cleared of propagating, for laughs, a mixture of worldly libertinism and social conformity; and of course it is not provably true, though Rousseau's easy acceptance of subjectively defined idealisms is further than most of us would go. In relation to the way in which we have appraised the comic techniques of the serious comedies, the charge against Molière could be phrased as that of dressing up the *worldly and aristocratic* critique of nonconformity and severity to look like the *philosophical* analysis of the quintessentially comic. Arnolphe and Alceste are—indisputably—comically confused about the nature of things. To 'complain' about being in love is as absurd as to complain when one's house has been struck by lightning. But when the representative of the nature of things is as provocative a creature as Célimène, we may feel that Alceste's powers of avoiding a comic formulation are put to an intolerable test. Could this just be social baiting in the guise of presenting a cosmic injustice which must be accepted if ridicule is to

be avoided? In *L'École des femmes* the character of Agnès provides
the problematic element. If Agnès *is* completely ingenuous, then
Arnolphe's reasoning:

> Elle a feint d'être telle à mes yeux, la traîtresse,
> Ou le diable à son âme a soufflé cette adresse

is comically uncomprehending; as is 'Peste! une précieuse en dirait-
elle plus?', provided that she is in no way a *précieuse*. But if we find
this ingenuousness incredible, if we can only believe in Agnès in
terms of a budding Célimène, then Arnolphe's puzzlement is more
excusable; he is up against a Molière who has weighted 'the nature
of things' with a psychologically impossible type. In such a world
Arnolphe and Alceste, for all their faults, are sorely tried; and Agnès
in particular receives all the prestige and benefit of the doubt that
youth, spontaneity, and 'nature' can be given against age, severity,
and notions of contractual obligation.

But Molière makes no concessions to the tragic view, which could
be defined as an admission of the right to cry out against the world
and the gods. On the one occasion in his plays when the gods
descend among men (on business not unconnected with the concerns
of Agnès and Célimène) there is little pity for their victim, whose
minor faults of character hardly justify their having picked him out.
Amphitryon remains silent as the play ends, perhaps because even
to call attention to him would risk upsetting the finely balanced
comic tone. Style must carry the day, and though there may be some
passing satire of the ways of the great, the burden of the play seems
to be that

> Un partage avec Jupiter
> N'a rien du tout qui déshonore

that to press one's alleged rights, or even to scrutinize one's human
situation too closely, is always to be ridiculous:

> Sur telles affaires toujours
> Le meilleur est de ne rien dire.

Bénichou is probably right, in social terms, in seeing Molière as an
aristocratic rather than a bourgeois writer who willingly flatters the
reigning 'Jupiter' at the expense of the more plodding virtues of

economy, prudence, and moral earnestness. Equally, he is not quite as shining an advocate of honesty and 'good sense' as some of his interpreters have claimed. 'La sincérité souffre un peu', Valère remarks of his own ruses at the beginning of *L'Avare* (another play which shocked Rousseau's patriarchal spirit); but the ends amply justify the means. In a world in which the rooted comic character can never be persuaded, only circumvented, the ethics of ruse must be endorsed from the start and coexistence rather than the triumph of principle must be the highest aim. Those who see Madame Jourdain's bourgeois honesty as an ideal set up against her husband's fantasies should notice that she nearly wrecks the whole scheme to defeat him (concocted by aristocrats and servants in league) by her slowness in the uptake.

But the opposition to the bourgeois spirit takes forms other than the narrowly social, and it is here that the positive and attractive sides of Molière's morality assert themselves. Precisely because the aims of the favoured characters are hedonistic and undogmatic, the circumventions that the pursuit dictates are on the whole practised unvindictively: the young trick their dreadful parents, but without the virulence that could come from a more principled desire to categorize or castigate human weakness. Argan and Jourdain are not humiliated, but flattered and dressed up and, to an undeserved degree, genuinely loved. And Molière has the generosity to give the comic butts themselves a robustness, a love of life, and even (though obviously the limits here are soon reached) an occasional glimmer of insight into the preposterousness of their own nature: 'Non, laissons cela. Je suis bilieux comme tous les diables; et il n'y a morale qui tienne', Jourdain exclaims, when offered lessons in moral philosophy. There is nothing *haïssable* here, and though Molière shares much of Pascal's and La Rochefoucauld's pessimistic psychology, and indeed at times seems to be dramatically illustrating the latter's *Maximes*, he stands temperamentally outside the contemporary debate on the nature of man. Rather, he looks forward to the next century's more practical, less metaphysically anxious concern for human well-being. The philosophy of coexistence, the good-humoured attention to the empirical situation—these have implications other than of facile sociability, and Bénichou is right in completing his 'aristocratic' interpretation by calling Molière's attitude a 'mélange de la hardiesse et de la conformité'. Sosie's 'Le meilleur est de ne rien dire' may counsel resignation to the monarchial *status quo*, but it also foreshadows Cunégonde's remark in *Candide* (apropos a similar misfortune): 'On ne meurt pas toujours de ces accidents.' Life is asserted in defiance of the ample grounds for philosophical despair. And one answer to Bray's question must be that if Molière does not, in the strictest sense, 'think', he prepares in a liberating and humanitarian way for others who do.

NOTE

JEAN-BAPTISTE POQUELIN, 1622–73, known as MOLIÈRE, was brought up in comfortable circumstances—his father became *tapissier ordinaire du roi*—but after a fairly complete formal education broke away to follow a theatrical career. After many years in the provinces he returned to Paris in 1658 as actor-manager-playwright. Though he established his troupe in royal favour his public life remained stormy: his *Tartuffe* and *Dom Juan* were temporarily banned and he was variously accused of incest, blasphemy, and ignorance of the rules of comedy. Nevertheless his theatrical activity continued uninterrupted until his death. Much Molière biography, especially that relating to his marriage and its possible dramatization in his plays, is purely speculative.

Works. After a few slight pieces, Molière's success as an author began with *Les Précieuses ridicules* (1659) and *L'École des femmes* (1662). In the next ten years he produced some twenty plays. They are not easy to categorize: the 'serious' five-act plays, *Tartuffe* (first version 1664, final version 1669), *Dom Juan* (1665), *Le Misanthrope* (1666), *L'Avare* (1668), and *Les Femmes savantes* (1672), all contain elements of farce; while 'lighter' pieces such as *Le Médecin malgré lui* (1666), *George Dandin* (1668), and *Les Fourberies de Scapin* (1671) are also important variations on the 'serious' themes. If any development is perceptible it is perhaps away from the 'serious' towards freer fantasies in which music and ballet play an important part: such are *Amphitryon* (1668), *Monsieur de Pourceaugnac* (1669), *Le Bourgeois gentilhomme* (1670), and *Le Malade imaginaire* (1673).

Editions. The best presentations of the complete works (including the disputed early farces, and containing useful explanatory material) are the Garnier edition, ed. R. Jouanny (2 vols., 1960), and the Pléiade edition, ed. M. Rat (2 vols., 1956). The single Intégrale volume, ed. P.-A. Touchard (1962), contains a text of Grimarest's *Vie de Molière* (1705), source of many Molière apocrypha (fuller text ed. G. Mongrédien, 1955). Relevant contemporary documents, including the important *Lettre sur l'Imposteur* can be found in the standard 'Grands Écrivains de la France' edition, ed. Despois and Mesnard (1873–1900).

Criticism. H. Bergson's theoretical *Le Rire* (1899) takes many examples from Molière. Among older studies E. Rigal, *Molière* (2 vols., 1908) is still useful; indispensable are G. Michaut, *La Jeunesse de Molière* (1922), *Les Débuts de Molière à Paris* (1925), and *Les Luttes de Molière* (1926), R. Fernandez, *La Vie de Molière* (1929) is much more than a biography. 'Moral' criticism of Molière is represented by J.-J. Rousseau, *Lettre à M. d'Alembert sur les spectacles* (1758, ed. M. Fuchs, 1948), F. Brunetière, 'La Philosophie de Molière', in *Études critiques sur l'histoire de la littérature française* (4e série, 1891), and F. Mauriac, *Trois grands hommes devant Dieu* (1930). P. Bénichou, *Morales du Grand Siècle* (1948) combines an approach through intellectual history with literary tact. The 'theatrical' approach is represented by W. G. Moore, *Molière, a new criticism* (1949), R. Bray, *Molière, homme de théâtre* (1954), and J. Guicharnaud, *Molière et l'aventure théâtrale* (1963). L. Gossman, *Men and Masks* (1963) ranges wide. Guicharnaud has also edited a Molière volume (1964) in the 'Twentieth Century Views' series, which gives a useful idea of recent trends in Molière criticism.

8. La Fontaine

Jupiter dit un jour: 'Que tout ce qui respire
S'en vienne comparaître aux pieds de ma grandeur...'

THESE opening lines of 'La Besace' (I. 7), which invite all living beings to parade before the King of the Gods, give some idea of the range of La Fontaine's inquiry in his *Fables*. His view is panoramic. His investigation delves down below the superficialities of behaviour to uncover fundamental facts about man; in doing this he seeks to encourage self-knowledge, to make us, in his own words, 'capables de grandes choses'. His observation is not bound by social limits, although these are important for him; it goes beyond the 'amour propre' diagnosed by La Rochefoucauld, and recognizes fear as 'la plus forte passion' (IX. 15) which seems to govern the impulsive responses of man. As we read 'La Besace' we do not think to challenge Jupiter's right to speak, or even to ask whether his command is a reasonable one, for La Fontaine is telling a story, or rather creating

Une ample comédie à cent actes divers,
Et dont la scène est l'univers.

(V. 1)

Like many other writers among his contemporaries, La Fontaine was convinced of the need to please his readers in order to arouse their attention and, not insignificantly, to ensure the worldly success for which he craved. Readers had to be persuaded into realizing truths about themselves, they had to be tricked into alertness, either through the wit and apparent nonchalance of the *Contes*, or by the fairy-tale atmosphere of *Psyché*. Recognizing the knowledge and the refined taste of his readers, La Fontaine worked in his *Fables* to create a form which would use their cultured talents and surprise them into discovery. Their profit and enjoyment was to come from the subtle art of telling a good story where the poet deliberately withheld detailed information, leaving 'quelque chose à penser' (x. 14). His stories, often already well known from Boccaccio, Aesop, and others, were touched up with his twin tools of variety and novelty; these gave his *Contes* and *Fables* a new look and also turned his reader's attention decisively towards the manner of telling the story, seeming to underplay its moral implications.

At first sight indeed it would seem that La Fontaine's desire to please worked against his will to teach. Pleasing involves a witty and judicious embroidery of the facts; moral intention usually requires a clear pointing of those facts. La Fontaine's task was to find some way of reconciling these two apparently contradictory aims. That he was acutely aware of the problem can be seen from the number of times the words *vérité* and *mensonge* appear as natural opposites throughout his work:

> L'homme est de glace aux vérités,
> Il est de feu pour les mensonges.
> (ix. 6)

But the very frequency with which these two words occur, juxtaposed in this way, suggests that La Fontaine wished to stress that they are not mutually exclusive: far from it. They are brought together so that the *mensonges* (the story) might delightfully cover up the truth, disguise it, but not distort it:

> Quand je songe à cette fable
> Dont le récit est menteur
> Et le sens est véritable . . .
> (v. 10)

In fact the very manner of the story sets forth its moral import. The covering-up process is necessary to interest and delight the reader, but penetrate the subtleties of characterization, speech, and rhythm, and you have discovered the truths that lie hidden as well as those expressed overtly by the moral tag which traditionally began or ended the fable.

Of course, the traditional ingredients of the fable-form facilitated La Fontaine's task. The reader of a fable automatically expects edification and entertainment; he accepts the human/animal parallel as naturally as he expects French classical tragedy to be written in alexandrines. And yet, in 1668, there was a good chance that the fable would not be seen as an adult form of art at all. So as not to insult his sophisticated readers, La Fontaine turned fables into *badineries* fit to delight any salon *galant*, but he assures us they are only *badineries* 'en apparence, car dans le fond elles portent un sens très solide' (preface).

In any comparison of men with animals it is usual to assume the superiority of the human element, but La Fontaine quickly destroys any such notion. He always shows the human/animal relationship as very complicated. Even in the titles La Fontaine gives to his animals, it is difficult to separate the animal and human content. 'Capitaine renard' (III. 5) for example might, for some readers, conjure up a picture of a fox with the particular characteristic of resourcefulness; for others, the human element 'capitaine' might be uppermost in the mind. When he compares the cat to the heroes Alexander or Attila, 'L'Alexandre des chats / L'Attila' (III. 18), he builds further complexities upon this already complicated relationship. The physical and mental attitudes of the cat are immediately seized by the comparison; we see it puffed up with its victories, swaggering with pride. The image of the two heroes, however, seems somewhat tarnished by the close proximity of feline cunning. La Fontaine has not suggested that the cat is superior, he has simply shown it to be like Alexander or Attila. It is our knowledge of these heroes' exploits and our observation of cats, brought together in this way, which upsets our normal notions of human beings and animals; and, as a consequence, the animal seems to gain in stature while the human is diminished.

The complexities suggested by simple juxtaposition are naturally enhanced when La Fontaine represents his animals actually performing specific actions. Let us take 'Les deux Coqs' (VII. 13) as a typical example:

> Deux coqs vivoient en paix: une poule survint,
>   Et voilà la guerre allumée.
> Amour, tu perdis Troie; et c'est de toi que vint
>   Cette querelle envenimée,

Où du sang des dieux même on vit le Xanthe teint!
Longtemps entre nos coqs le combat se maintint.
Le bruit s'en répandit par tout le voisinage.
La gent qui porte crête au spectacle accourut.
      Plus d'une Hélène au beau plumage
Fut le prix du vainqueur; le vaincu disparut.
Il alla se cacher au fond de sa retraite,
      Pleura sa gloire et ses amours,
Ses amours, qu'un rival tout fier de sa défaite
Possédoit à ses yeux. Il voyoit tous les jours
Cet objet rallumer sa haine et son courage;
Il aiguisoit son bec, battoit l'air et ses flancs,
      Et, s'exerçant contre les vents,
      S'armoit d'une jalouse rage.
Il n'en eut pas besoin. Son vainqueur sur les toits
  S'alla percher, et chanter sa victoire.
      Un vautour entendit sa voix:
      Adieu les amours et la gloire;
Tout cet orgueil périt sous l'ongle du vautour.
      Enfin, par un fatal retour,
      Son rival autour de la poule
      S'en revint faire le coquet:
      Je laisse à penser quel caquet,
      Car il eut des femmes en foule.

La Fortune se plaît à faire de ces coups:
Tout vainqueur insolent à sa perte travaille.
Défions-nous du Sort, et prenons garde à nous
      Après le gain d'une bataille.

The matter-of-fact, concise lines tell a complete story; and the speed with which these facts are outlined sets the slightly bantering tone which is the dominant note of the fable. A simple fight between two cocks is immediately made to seem a general war which is totally absorbing. Before we have a chance to supply for ourselves a detailed picture of the noisy strutting birds, La Fontaine has jumped on to a well-known human parallel, opening up huge historical perspectives with 'Amour, tu perdis Troie', simple yet ominous sounding words which evoke the scenes of battle and the clash of the heroes—Achilles and Hector—before the walls of Troy. Their resonant quality allows La Fontaine to step almost unnoticed on to an even more grandiose plane, reminding us of the wounds of Mars and Venus sustained in the service of love, the profound dangers of which are suggested through the adjective 'envenimée'. The entire range of being—stretching from animals to gods—is implicated in the omniscient narrator's detailed working out of the fable. Although La Fontaine appears to return sedately to the animal level of the story with 'Longtemps entre nos coqs le combat se maintint', and although this line seems to throw, retrospectively, a deflating light on the human and even divine elements, their interests have neverthe- less been stated, and this is important. The rhyme subtly reminds the ear of a connection, 'une Hélène au beau plumage' maintains the animal/human parallel. There is no need for La Fontaine to give an actual description of the fight. Human and divine levels of reference have already set the reader's imagination to work, and our literary knowledge on the one hand, and our fantasy on the other, are helped by further touches of quick characterization such as 'la gent qui porte crête'.

An elaboration of the loser's plight now occupies the poet's atten- tion, and the full force of the bitter adjective 'envenimée' is realized. Bantering, deflating tones, amused observation of animal habits give way to the tragic overtones of 'Il alla se cacher au fond de sa retraite'. For a time we forget that these words concern a cock, and we imagine some human counterpart, some beaten Antony driven into exile, as we listen to the depths of suffering suggested through general terms like 'amours', 'gloire', 'rival', 'défaite', and 'haine', terms which fleetingly recall the preoccupations of French classical tragedy, and which are here woven into a similar solemn rhythmic pattern. This tone of tragedy, however, is only momentary; before our sympathies are too deeply engaged we see again the silly cock, preparing for the fray, whipping up his courage with a sharpening of beak and a ridiculous, futile flapping of wings against the breeze. This sudden puncturing of the tragic tone is emphasized by a sharp interruption, 'Il n'en eut pas besoin'. Although we have been aware of the narrator throughout the poem, controlling the changes of rhythm and tone, constantly altering the focus, this is the first time he seems to be speaking in his own person, using his comment to switch attention to the fate of the proud victor. The latter is speedily disposed of. Embroidering on the adage 'Pride comes before a fall', La Fontaine fills in the detail with the precise 'Tout cet orgueil périt sous l'ongle du vautour'. His cruel end is not dwelt upon. Already the once vanquished cock has returned triumphant. Another lady-killer, oblivious to possible danger, he revels in the cries of admiration which greet him. But the words 'fatal retour' sound above the noise of the women, reminding the reader of an inevitable train of events which might well lead this second puffed-up bird to a similar sad and unexpected end. La Fontaine points a warning finger not only at a general animal and human situation where blind Fortune can strike unerringly; he also exposes areas of character which seem always to remain unalterable. At one and the same time he counsels lucidity and insight while affirming the difficulty of profiting from either. Ostensibly the elaboration of a simple story 'par quelques traits nouveaux' seemed only intended to bring alive the animals and humans involved, and make us laugh at the little drama love contrives. A closer look, however, reveals that it is precisely through the detail of these actions and the personalities they reflect that La Fontaine expresses his truths.

The serious implications of 'Les deux Coqs' do not obscure the fact that La Fontaine is also poking fun at the antics which love forces animals, humans, and gods to perform. Meaning in his *Fables* is often layered. Inside this poem, however, he has reduced all classes of the social hierarchy to one, obscuring the distinctions which normally separate animals and humans. They are depicted on the same plane, responding to events in the same ways with similar degrees of intensity. The parallel is made absolutely exact. As readers, we find it difficult to pinpoint the moments where the animal story takes on definite human overtones, or loses them, since we are too engaged in a world which we were invited to observe; only the narrator has the power to judge and to re-establish the real-life hierarchy.

'Les deux Coqs' shows La Fontaine at one of his kindest moments. Many other fables do not try to maintain this precarious and ambiguous balance between animals and humans. Instead, they seem to turn the animal/human relationship upside down. Then the animals are no longer representatives of man, but his observers, describing his world from their point of view. Looked at through their eyes, it can appear rich and new, infinitely attractive, but also dangerous ('Le Rat et l'Huître', VIII. 9), the greatest pitfall for them being, of course, man himself. Adopting man's own moral standards, animals relentlessly expose his weaknesses; his cruelty, for example, in 'L'Hirondelle et les petits Oiseaux' (I. 8), or his ingratitude in 'L'Homme et la Couleuvre' (X. I). The condemnation is by no means straightforward. If we consider these two fables we find a vast difference in tone between them. In 'L'Hirondelle et les petits Oiseaux', where man is seen as 'cette main qui par les airs chemine', the birds observe man, but their observation does not awaken them to a sense of their own danger in spite of the babble of the swallow. Here, La Fontaine's mockery and criticism are fairly evenly distributed between both man and animal: man's cruel inventions are displayed; the birds' blindness finds its own rewards. 'L'Homme et la Couleuvre' apparently presents a much more serious indictment of man. One after the other the serpent, the cow, the bull, and the tree all speak most forcibly against man and his appalling ingratitude. Their arguments are persuasive, their facts irrefutable. Much of the sting is taken out of their criticism, however, by the realization that their statements are only partial, severely limited by the character of each animal; and the criticism is tempered yet further by the knowledge that it is the serpent who has instigated the attack. We are inclined to dismiss their findings, however serious the tone, because we know that snakes are the most insidious of animals. And yet the facts go worrying on, the more so since the man peremptorily kills the snake in impotent rage, and because he protests so unreasonably: 'Je suis bien bon, dit-il, d'écouter ces gens-là.' Our complex and even puzzled reaction to such a poem is La Fontaine's way of turning our mind in upon itself, thus creating a moral tool out of ambiguity.

In the last books of the *Fables*, man is most frequently equated with wolf, for both are unscrupulous 'mangeurs de gens' (X. 3). There are times when even the rapacious wolf is presented as superior to man, as in 'Le Loup et les Bergers' (X. 5). This superiority is again presented much more ambiguously and probably more characteristically in 'Les Compagnons d'Ulysse' (XIII. 1). In this fable the poet deliberately turns upside down the traditional implications of the story. The magical transformation of human beings into animals is far from being the disaster suggested by the legend. From the outset Circe throws a knowing and malicious doubt upon the fact that Ulysses' companions would wish to recover their former shape: 'Mais la voudront-ils bien, dit la nymphe, accepter?' With a confidence, tantalizingly delaying the verb 'accepter', which is progressively undermined by the emphatic refusal of the animals to change their state, Ulysses confronts the lion, the bear, and finally the wolf. Although his arguments become more subtle at each confrontation, they have neither the insistent force of the animals' refrain 'Je ne veux point changer d'état', nor the powerful eloquence of the bear praising his form, or the wolf condemning man's behaviour to man:

> Si j'étais homme, par ta foi,
> Aimerais-je moins le carnage?
> Pour un mot quelque fois vous vous étranglez tous.

To the animals' speech La Fontaine has given the most persuasive power and yet, paradoxically, his own concluding comment to the fable—'Ils étaient esclaves d'eux-mêmes'—seems to contradict that power. Knowing the full force of the reader's conditioned reaction to the tale of Ulysses and his companions, the poet can use our expectations in order to control a very complicated response. Initially his comment is consoling; but we do not forget the animals' accusations. And as we consider this puzzling ambiguity it becomes clear that the struggle for animal or human moral superiority was not the main point of the story. It is a technique which brings two worlds together so that their interplay may provoke our reflection and help us to discover hidden facts about ourselves. Through the animal/human confrontation, La Fontaine seeks to destroy our equanimity and overweening confidence.

Such a degree of subtlety depends to a large extent for its success on the reader's willingness to play the game according to the poet's rules. While having to steer his way through understatement and complicated or ambiguous statement, the reader's intelligence is also challenged by constant and abrupt changes of tone and perspective.

In 'Le Lion et le Moucheron' (II. 9) different ways of describing the two animals explain what is going on in their minds and how they see themselves. In his own eyes the lion is 'Roi', for the fly he is a 'bête', for the narrator an undistinguished 'quàdrupède' or 'malheureux lion'; the insect is first 'excrément de la terre' to the lofty King of Beasts, to himself he is 'la trompette et le héros', the narrator sees him as an 'avorton de moucheron'; but the suffering lion, in his helpless agony, sees him as a figure of great proportions, an 'invisible ennemi'; he returns to his *insect* size only as he meets his doom in a spider's web.

Appreciation of the art of such story-telling relies on those fragile hints which could easily pass unnoticed were it not that La Fontaine felt assured of an alert and knowledgeable audience which could respond immediately to nuances of tone, shifts of rhythm, and swift changes of focus. The poet himself pops in and out of his narrative, consciously directing our response by loaded words such as 'censure' and 'haine', or by familiar self-appropriation of his characters, as in 'Notre souffleur à gages' (VI. 3), thus giving the impression that his own hand is planted firmly in the back of the West Wind, helping its effort. Now he conspicuously withdraws altogether, slipping in a nonchalant 'dit-on', designed to throw a further veil over the truth of what he recounts. Often such deliberate obscuring serves to concentrate our attention more particularly, as in 'Le Lion, le Singe et les deux Ânes' (XI. 5). As master of every available note of poetry (indeed the *Fables* can be seen as a synthesis of more than a century's poetic practice) he can switch from the direct speech of the fox, 'Bonjour monsieur du Corbeau' (I. 2), to the mock heroics of 'Le Phaëton d'une voiture à foin' (VI. 18) through to the easy flowing music of 'Sur les ailes du Temps la tristresse s'envole' (VI. 21). The grave, unctuous tones of the lion/king which flow on uninterruptedly,

> Mes chers amis,
> Je crois que le ciel a permis
> Pour nos péchés cette infortune
> ('Les Animaux malades de la peste', VII. 1)

betray his hollow confidence to all but the unfortunate donkey whose clumsy words, in contrast, tumble out full of nervous hesitations and the needless justifications which condemn him in advance:

> J'ai souvenance
> Qu'en un pré de moines passant,
> La faim, l'occasion, l'herbe tendre, et, je pense,
> Quelque diable aussi me poussant,
> Je tondis de ce pré la largeur de ma langue.

The trepidations of the donkey are well caught by the evershifting rhythms of the uneven *vers libres*. Searching his memory through the drawn-out alexandrine, 'La faim, l'occasion, l'herbe tendre, et, je pense', which leaves our curiosity in suspense, the stupid animal then rushes quickly through the next octosyllabic line with the daring suggestion that some devil might have been responsible for his sin, on to the final alexandrine whose even precision gives a concrete picture of the donkey licking his lips, succumbing to an extraordinary, yet legitimate, degree of temptation.

In this way, control of rhythm becomes the poet's main method of making us appreciate the timorous mental steps of the donkey. It would be easy to multiply examples to show the remarkable variations in speed of narrative and fluctuations of tone which La Fontaine achieves to catch our attention and keep our interest. The ponderous strokes of 'La Mort et le Bûcheron' (I. 16) betray the narrator's sympathy as well as the character's mental and physical burden:

> Un pauvre bûcheron, tout couvert de ramée,
> Sous le faix du fagot aussi bien que des ans
> Gémissant et courbé marchait à pas pesants,
> Et tâchait de gagner sa chaumine enfumée.

Here the main verbs are kept to the end of this long, winding sentence which struggles through a series of qualifying clauses, gaining in weight through repetition of similar sounds. There is the gay opening of 'Le Curé et le Mort' (VII. 11),

> Un mort s'en allait tristement
> S'emparer de son dernier gîte,
> Un curé s'en allait gaîment
> Enterrer ce mort au plus vite,

with its matching rhythms and parallel constructions, jokingly preparing us for a surprise; and then there is the lion/king's great joke:

> Et même il m'est arrivé quelquefois de manger
> Le berger
>
> (VII. I)

thrown into relief by the rudden change in rhythm, the unexpected
choice of the word 'berger' which happens to rhyme with 'manger',
giving it greater prominence. It is as though La Fontaine, aware of
his remarkable versatility, wants to dazzle with a series of sustained
virtuoso performances. These, for all their range and variety, do not
depart from the simplicity of style which seventeenth-century taste
and propriety demanded. One rarely has the impression that the
language is forced, that it is superfluous, or that the animals speak
out of character. In spite of the glitter of word play and the wit which
derives from terms well defined and carefully used, in spite of the
gaiety resulting from clever rhythms and a narrative delicately
handled, all the creatures' talk seems deceptively natural.

This engaging display of a poetic power which so rarely falters is
perhaps most apparent in those *Fables* where the reader is not
immediately involved in an obviously animal/human problem, where
in fact the human dimension has apparently dwindled into nothing-
ness, only perhaps faintly suggested by the animals' use of human
speech and reason, and where even the narrator has withdrawn to a
considerable distance from the poem, leaving the story to tell itself.
In a fable like 'Le Loup et l'Agneau' (I. 10) moral considerations
have apparently receded to give full rein to a show of artistic skill,
combining narrative power and poetic charm:

> La raison du plus fort est toujours la meilleure :
> Nous l'allons montrer tout à l'heure.
>
> Un agneau se désaltéroit
> Dans le courant d'une onde pure.
> Un loup survient, à jeun, qui cherchoit aventure,
> Et que la faim en ces lieux attiroit.
> 'Qui te rend si hardi de troubler mon breuvage ?
> Dit cet animal plein de rage :
> Tu seras châtié de ta témérité.
> — Sire, répond l'agneau, que Votre Majesté

Ne se mette pas en colère;
Mais plutôt qu'elle considère
Que je me vais désaltérant
        Dans le courant
Plus de vingt pas au-dessous d'Elle:
Et que, par conséquent, en aucune façon,
    Je ne puis troubler sa boisson.
— Tu la troubles, reprit cette bête cruelle;
Et je sais que de moi tu médis l'an passé.
— Comment l'aurois-je fait, si je n'étois pas né?
    Reprit l'agneau; je tette encor ma mère.
    — Si ce n'est toi, c'est donc ton frère.
— Je n'en ai point. — C'est donc quelqu'un des tiens:
        Car vous ne m'épargnez guère,
        Vous, vos bergers, et vos chiens.
On me l'a dit: il faut que je me venge.'
        Là-dessus, au fond des forêts
        Le loup l'emporte, et puis le mange,
        Sans autre forme de procès.

The moral tag appears disposed of in the first two lines of the fable. The finely balanced alexandrine gives this moral comment the flavour of a proverb; its import seems familiar and its expression is firm and authoritative. We accept it almost without thought, and certainly without question. Now the poet can get down to his demonstration or story, untroubled by any necessity to explain further. The main focus of the poem is to be on the *telling* of the story, a particularly difficult task since we know in advance that wolves gobble up lambs. We also know what lambs and wolves look like. La Fontaine has therefore consciously confined himself to relating a particular encounter. The lamb is simply introduced into a precise situation which itself recalls the traditional symbolism attached to that animal, that of innocence, mirrored in the quiet line 'Dans le courant de l'onde pure'. This tranquility is immediately shattered by the arrival of the wolf. Since he is hungry and looking for trouble we expect him to make a quick meal of the lamb. But this would round off the fable too quickly. This particular wolf is given vestiges of conscience: he wants to establish some kind of rational superiority over his prey, while reminding the lamb of his physical prowess through the clipped and harsh no-nonsense sound of 'Tu seras châtié de ta témérité'. Any sensible lamb would by now have skipped away out of the wolf's sight and hearing, but this pathetic little animal is riveted to the spot, overcome by a desire to compete with the wolf on the level of rational argument. His long answer starts hesitantly, and even obsequiously, flattering the wolf's strength with 'Votre Majesté'. As the unwieldy sentence continues, the lamb seems to gain confidence. He suggests a moment's reflection, provides mathematical proof of his innocence, and then resoundingly concludes 'par conséquent, en aucune façon'. The lamb, proud of his reasoning power, a victim of his own eloquence, has already become oblivious to the danger which confronts him. Even the laconic assertion 'Tu la troubles', which growls menacingly out, seems not to disturb him. The debate speeds up and changes direction as the wolf searches for more watertight reasons for eating up the lamb. Each argument is easily refuted—too easily. The sharper the lamb's reasoning power, the nearer he comes to death. But he does not perceive this danger, engrossed as he is in the argument; since he appears to be winning each sally with ease, it is natural that his thoughts should turn to his triumph. Meanwhile the wolf flounders clumsily around for some more reasons, which grow vaguer and less well founded at each charge; the lamb counter-attacks with increasing confidence, dismissing the awkward suggestions with an emphatic and almost rude 'Je n'en ai point'. Such a brusque dismissal is too much for the wolf. As hunger tears at his belly, he determines to have the last word—and the lamb. The rhythm of the verse speeds up markedly as the determined animal accumulates evidence against the lamb—evidence compiled from the imagined assurance of others, 'On me l'a dit'—and, before the unfortunate victim can crown this last series of vague blanket accusations with some deflatory quip, the wolf hurriedly adds: 'il faut que je me venge.' Vengeance is the honourable term he invents to disguise the natural hunger of a rapacious animal with a more sophisticated social conscience. The nasty process of gobbling up is hidden in the mysterious depths of the forest. La Fontaine never dwells on such unpleasantnesses; he leaves them to our imagination, hinting simply that the wolf has learned his lesson and gives the lamb no further opportunity to outwit him in talk.

Argument is obviously the dominant interest in this fable, as the word 'raison' in the first line warned us. At first we are a little disturbed by the uncharacteristic behaviour of the animals, but then, taken in by their determination to argue, we become absorbed in their talk. Only then do we remember that it is ironical for a wolf to indulge his pretensions by putting the lamb on trial, and finally understand that both animals are in some sense guilty. The lamb, unable to resist showing off his rhetorical skills, has indulged his eloquence, blurred his perception, and deserved his end. The wolf has, for the space of the story, put on a human skin, and herein lies his guilt, for he imagines himself better than he is and covers his actions with a veil of words and socially acceptable gestures. At the outset our sympathies are inevitably with the weakling, with the lamb who has no chance against his powerful neighbour. La Fontaine knows this, and in his story he has presented an unusually attractive wolf, and an over-confident lamb, to keep the weight of opinion evenly distributed between the two animals. Once again, his criticism is ambiguous. The animals are both guilty, but they are also attractive. Their vulnerability prevents us from covering them with too much blame. Though such an end seems out of all proportion to the crime, such ends are natural, just as such trials which hide hypocrisy are commonplace.

The word 'procès' standing out so conspicuously at the end of the fable takes our minds back through the whole pattern of argument. The word sounds hollow and unjust as we reflect on both the force and the inadequacy of the two animals' reasoning power. We are led back finally to the proverbial opening to the fable. These words now seem to mean much more than they did before. Initially we accepted them without challenge; they merely expressed a commonplace truth, one of our basic assumptions. Now we perceive what lies behind such assumptions. The faces of the animals recede into the background and all the human words they have been using, the terms 'raison', 'meilleure', 'procès', which operate in our human moral world, come to the fore; they transform the wolf into a human being of consequence who is sufficiently cultured to want to hide the surging waves of cruelty which lie beneath the surface. The lamb is any 'innocent' victim of power, greed, and injustice. The two animals

9. Aphorism and Portraiture

...re to express certain ideas in as brief and memorable a
...ossible is a long-standing human impulse. Evidence of its
...can be found in such things as early inscriptions, Egyptian
...ertain books of the Old Testament, or ancient Greek
... The most primitive purposes behind the formulation of
...ted statements probably had to do with the making of
...emonics and the creation of magic spells. Later purposes
...included the recording of disconnected empirical facts in
...stages of a science. An example of this latter type of collec-
...d be the 'medical' *Aphorisms* of Hippocrates which date
...fifth century B.C. Having begun with the famous dictum:
...short, the Art long, opportunity fleeting, experiment
...us, judgement difficult', they continue with many pithy
...f an informative and analytical kind on such subjects as diet
...se.

...chapter, however, we are concerned only with the very
...ted kind of brief statement which has achieved distinct
...atus and is used as a vehicle for character analysis or the
...n of insights into moral experience. There is general agree-
...t this kind of aphorism reached a unique degree of perfec-
...venteenth-century France. It is true that it flourished in
...rters in the eighteenth century, and collections of aphorisms
...s have occasionally been published in more recent times,
...rked decline in the quantity of striking aphorisms set in
...e eighteenth century. A question immediately arises, there-
...o why this upsurge took place, when and where it did,
...enteenth century. Various answers have been given. The
...f aphorisms can be related to a literary tradition going back
...e of emblems and 'devices', or to that moral writing of an

talk as we would imagine wolves and lambs would talk, if only they had the power of speech. Yet, what these particular animals say in this situation is totally uncharacteristic of the personalities normally attributed to them. The wolf's ruthlessness is tempered by conscience, the lamb's innocence contaminated by over confident talk. This is La Fontaine's way of giving us profitable pleasure. He blurs our black and white notions of animal characteristics and simultaneously removes the absolute casing we always set around moral values. What began as a simple fable story, whose main attraction seemed to be the ingenious dressing up of Red Riding Hood in a new guise, suddenly gathers moral resonances of a scope at first unsuspected. The detailed pattern of the fable leads us straight to a rethinking of our basic assumptions: as in most of La Fontaine's fables, truth and aesthetic pleasure are inseparably linked.

In the long run, it is the pleasure which stays uppermost in the mind. However unpleasant some of the discoveries are that we make about ourselves in reading the *Fables*, these are always tempered not only by the attractive way in which we find them out, but also by the poet's own indulgent smile. His admonishment can, as we have seen, be sharp, his observations uncomfortably acute, yet the temptations we succumb to are either natural or as delectable as the moon which seemed to the fox and the wolf some luscious creamy cheese ready to be eaten (IX. 6). Life has its bad moments, life in society is particularly fraught with them, but the fox's gay panache provides a marvellously attractive way out. His virtually uncrushable resilience, his wit and irresistible ingenuity are the best antidotes to social exposure. These qualities of the fox, together with his clarity of perception, are reflected on the aesthetic level on every page of the *Fables*. For La Fontaine this way of story-telling 'c'est proprement un charme' (I. 5). Just as this art discloses truth, so it provides the means to counteract truth's most unsavoury aspects.

An acute insight which could cut through the outward manifestations of human behaviour needed not only an artistic gift to make the truth attractive, it also required some means of escape. No doubt it is for this reason that in his other works, where the urge to enlighten his contemporaries is much diminished La Fontaine's own personal taste seems to dwell most particularly upon those states of

feeling and those forms of art where the edges of pain and pleasure
are softened. In *Psyché* and in his operas he tries to create charmed,
intimate atmospheres where he can indulge his oft expressed desire
to dream and to sleep. But even in Arcadia, drowsiness of mind
cannot be maintained for very long. La Fontaine the person might
wish to indulge his laziness, but the conscious artist and observer
of man constantly intrudes.

A final reason why readers are willing to accept and appreciate
La Fontaine's diagnosis of themselves lies in the fact that his
observations are so personalized. In 'La Laitière et le pot au lait'
(VII. 10) he is painting himself, his own power of self-deception.
His dreams are often shattered by the harshness of reality, but his
resilience allows him to dream again. Ultimately it is the poet's
constant presence in his *Fables* offering proof of such understanding and indulgence, as well as his poetic skill, which gives us
confidence and makes our minds turn willingly in upon themselves.

NOTE

JEAN DE LA FONTAINE, 1621–95, was born at Château-Thierry where he was
educated until 1635 when he probably went to Paris. There he followed a fairly
orthodox career; he tried and abandoned the Oratory (1641–2), read law (1645–7),
married (1647), and bought several offices at Château-Thierry which he held
precariously. From 1654 he lived in Paris and devoted himself increasingly to
writing, protected and supported first by the tax-farmer Fouquet, then by the
Duchesse d'Orléans, and later by Madame de la Sablière. He was acquainted
with most of the important literary and scientific figures of his time, many of
whom have written appreciatively of his talents. Although these did not bring
him any marked royal favour, he was elected to the Académie Française in 1684.
He died piously.

Works. La Fontaine tried his hand at almost every literary genre, publishing his
first comedy, *L'Eunuque*, in 1654 and destroying his last on his death-bed in
1695. His *Fables* were published in three lots, the first six books in 1668, the
next five in 1678, and bk. xii in 1693. His reputation had been established with
the *Contes et Nouvelles*, 1665 and 1666, and he showed further versatility with his
hybrid novel *Les Amours de Psyché*, 1668. Other works include operas: *Daphné*
(1682), *Galatée* (1682), *Astrée* (1691), and an incomplete tragedy *Achille*; heroic
and scientific poems: *Adonis* (1669), *Poème du Quinquina* (1682), and miscel-
laneous command pieces like *Le Songe de Vaux* (1671).
Editions. The most useful *Œuvres complètes*, with considerable critical apparatus,

containing biography, bibliography, and notes,
2 volumes: vol. i, *Fables, Contes et Nouvelles*, e
(1959); vol. ii, *Œuvres diverses*, ed. Pierre Clarac
are so numerous that it seems superfluous to
except perhaps the recent Garnier edition, ed. G.
ing since it reproduces many original illustration

Criticism. Indispensable general works on the *F*
La Fontaine: Fables (1960) and *O Muse, Fuyante*
La Fontaine (1962); Margaret Guiton, *La Fonta*
P. Clarac has provided the most authoritative b
et l'œuvre (1947, augmented edn. 1959), whic
P. Wadsworth's *Young La Fontaine* (1952). Par
discussed in G. Couton's *La Poétique de La Fo*
La Fontaine (1959); in F. Gohin's *L'Art de La*
and in the edition he prepared jointly with H. B
de la Sablière (1938). There are stimulating (b
tions by Taine, *La Fontaine et ses Fables* (1853)
tions de La Fontaine (1938), and illuminating
La Fontaine' (1774, published in vol. i of hi
Adonis in *Variété I*, and by J. C. Lapp on the
gence' in *L'Esprit créateur*, iii 3, 1963.

aphoristic kind to be found, in a wider context, in the plays of Corneille and Racine. Again, we know that the aphorisms of Tacitus were collected, indexed, and widely read between 1580 and 1650 and probably stimulated emulation as well as interest. It has been claimed, too, that the aphorism or the maxim often represents the sophistication by an urban or court society of traditional peasant wisdom. In general terms, I think we can say that the whole phenomenon is intimately connected with the coexistence of both a highly refined literary culture and a very concentrated aristocratic society. In fact, the aphorism goes hand in hand with the aristocratic and intellectually inclined salons of seventeenth-century Paris.

These salons had two divergent effects. They began by institutionalizing social activity, but in time they also exposed it to sharp moral analysis. As a result of the first of these effects, many collections of maxims, particularly prior to 1660, were essentially sets of recipes for worldly success within a highly conformist framework. Moral behaviour and certain agreed social rituals were closely identified. Vestiges of this kind of writing can be found in La Rochefoucauld's 'Réflexions diverses', appended to his *Maximes*, particularly in the sections headed 'De la société', 'De la conversation', and 'De l'air et des manières'. Yet eventually, and no doubt inevitably, the very uniformity of this behaviour in its public manifestations led to speculation about the different motives operating in various individual instances. One result was the emergence of much more critical and analytical collections of aphorisms. These collections often contained a very rigorous assessment of human nature at variance with earlier social assumptions. This is the period, indeed, when the emphasis shifts from Corneille's heroic view of man to Racine's explorations of human weakness.

If the content of seventeenth-century aphorisms was affected by contemporary salon life, it is equally true that their form was encouraged by these salons which created a restricted and intimate atmosphere raising discussion or conversation to the level of a minor art. Verbal expression—both spoken and written—was valued for its qualities of elegance, accuracy, and conciseness. It became, in the formulations of the aphorists, one of the most authentic and penetrating creations of this highly artificial society and a mirror of some of its own worst faults. Furthermore, a well-established and highly appropriate linguistic tradition lay to hand. This tradition has to do with the singular richness of the French language where the vocabulary of human feeling and motive is concerned. There is considerable justice in Matthew Arnold's remark, on the subject of the French aphorism, that 'at least half the merit ought to go, not to the maker of the saying, but to the French language'.

So far I have treated the terms 'aphorism' and 'maxim' as though they were synonymous. Strictly speaking, one ought to differentiate between them by saying that the maxim goes further than the aphorism. Both formulate what is claimed to be a general truth, but the maxim goes on to recommend or imply a rule of conduct arising from this truth. In his famous fragment: 'Le cœur a ses raisons, que la raison ne connaît point', Pascal presents us with an aphorism. But when La Rochefoucauld writes: 'Comment prétendons-nous qu'un autre garde notre secret si nous n'avons pu le garder nous-mêmes', he has offered us a maxim. Again, both the aphorism and the maxim differ from the epigram since, in the most strict sense of the term, an epigram need only be true of an individual case or in a particular polemical context. According to this definition, La Bruyère created an epigram when he wrote: 'L'on est plus occupé aux pièces de Corneille; l'on est plus ébranlé et plus attendri à celles de Racine.'

In practice, I doubt whether these distinctions are really useful. Apart from the fact that many writers have not observed such differences in the terminology they themselves have used, clear lines of demarcation are often almost impossible to draw when one is presented with a particular brief saying. Even at a more general level, distinctions are difficult. For example, most aphorisms imply consequences for behaviour, and thus veer towards the maxim, by the very fact of making a general judgement about life and human experience. In this chapter, therefore, I shall not observe the classification indicated above. I shall use the word 'aphorisms' to include 'maximes', 'pensées', 'réflexions', 'sentences', and what were known in England, in earlier centuries, as 'apophthegms', 'laconics', and 'sentiments' respectively.

It is easy to underestimate the value of the aphorism. Systematic wisdom, by contrast, is widely admired and discussed because of the learning it presupposes, the intellectual skill which it reveals, and the closely linked chains of argument on which it depends. But very often the over-all system aimed at distorts the interpretation of details, or the systematizing design removes the whole rational structure from the sphere of concrete individual experience. It is on this latter point that an aphorism, or collection of aphorisms, can be so valuable and revealing. One of its most striking features is, in fact, the capacity to embody in literary form a momentary insight or the consequences of a fragmentary, but authentically lived, experience. The systematic treatise leans heavily on abstractions and buys coherence at the cost of those variations or exceptions which remain a stubbornly irreducible element in living. The collection of aphorisms takes a different direction, is fundamentally open-ended in a way the system is not, and therefore embodies more closely the discrete and discontinuous features of existential reality. This is the distinction between 'Methods' and 'Aphorisms' made by Bacon in *The Advancement of Learning*: '. . . Aphorisms, representing a knowledge broken, do invite men to inquire farther; whereas Methods, carrying the show of a total, do secure men, as if they were at the farthest.'

The aphorism, then, rests on empirical knowledge or 'knowledge broken'. It is the result of individual experience and a sharp scrutiny of human behaviour. It is predictable that La Rochefoucauld should write: 'Il est plus nécessaire d'étudier les hommes que les livres' and that La Bruyère should describe his *Caractères* as a portrait of his public, 'ce portrait que j'ai fait de lui d'après nature'. But Bacon's comment above also points to an important effect which the aphoristic form produces. By its very nature it opens up further possibilities and prompts further thought. Normally, the brief and pregnant saying achieves concision at an apparent cost—for instance, at the expense of sufficient qualification. But the very concision highlights the need for qualification or definition. Most readers are immediately aware of this and they consequently treat individual aphorisms less as completed truths than as valuable starting-points for further exploration in the direction of truth. This is the effect of a maxim such as the following by La Rochefoucauld: 'Le plus grand effort de l'amitié n'est pas de montrer nos défauts à un ami, c'est de lui faire voir les siens.' On reading this sentence various different points may strike us. To begin with, we may well be surprised that La Rochefoucauld did not seize on the revelation of *our own faults* to another person as the most difficult exercise of friendship. We may then decide that if this would be a very exacting task for some individuals it would be less so for others. And if we found it very exacting, might this not indicate that the friendship in question was less perfect, less satisfactory than we had supposed? Should one not be able to reveal the worst of oneself, as well as the best, to a genuine friend? At this point another line of thought can arise. May it not be that our friend is already much more accurately aware of our faults than we seem to have been assuming? We believe we know both his faults and his virtues. Is there any good reason for thinking him more obtuse in his assessment of us? Gradually, therefore, as we give more thought to the reciprocal demands of friendship we see more force in La Rochefoucauld's remark. We may indeed agree that it is more difficult to reveal our friend's faults to him than it is to reveal our own once we have reminded ourselves sufficiently sharply of the essentially two-way nature of friendship. In short, this particular maxim not only makes a practical point with which we may come to agree after some thought; it requires us, by the same token, to speculate further beyond the immediate limits of its own formulation to the nature of friendship as such.

All this amounts to saying that the aphorism puts an idea in such a way as to prompt re-examination of the author's assumptions—and our own. We read a particular statement and find that our response to it—sometimes even our understanding of its point—requires reconsideration of a whole set of assumptions and implications. This effect of making us look twice, and look critically, at a statement is most obviously achieved, I think, by the antithetical form of aphorism. When La Rochefoucauld writes: 'Il y a du mérite sans élévation, mais il n'y a point d'élévation sans quelque mérite', the nature of the formulation requires us to examine the terms 'mérite' and 'élévation' in two different and partly contrasting mental contexts. In doing so, we bring more than one set of criteria to bear and are able to clarify our minds more effectively as a result.

The concentrated and sharply focused nature of the individual aphorism causes it to surge up before us and appear, momentarily at least, to arrest systematic thought. With a collection of aphorisms this effect is even stronger. The non-systematic genre of the aphorism seems to appeal to writers whose own thought avoids closely knit, deductive patterns of thinking. Pascal, La Rochefoucauld, and La Bruyère, for example, are all thinkers who treat the claims of rational thought with considerable scepticism. Pascal writes: 'Il n'y a rien de si conforme à la raison que ce désaveu de la raison.' La Rochefoucauld boldly asserts: 'L'esprit est toujours la dupe du cœur.' La Bruyère tells us: '. . . il y a peu d'hommes dont l'esprit soit accompagné d'un goût sûr et d'une critique judicieuse.' In a word, one of the several apparent paradoxes built into the aphorism as a form is the fact that it attempts to make a statement of general validity while also emphasizing the atomistic nature and often conflicting characteristics of human experience. In so far as it aims at the universal, it is careful to do so through the medium of the individual. It treats the specific as the only means of access to the universal.

Clearly, then, the most successful aphorisms have a number of distinct virtues. They bring to light, and focus in a remarkable way, impressions and experiences which till then we had only imperfectly grasped. They contain a mechanism which obliges us to reconsider and clarify further the concepts with which they deal. They start from the basis of lived experience in their formulation of generalized statements. This formulation is such that the aphorism possesses the double appeal of particularly felicitous verbal expression and highly concentrated thought. And yet, despite such qualities, the aphorism also has its faults and dangers as a genre. There is the temptation, lying in wait for all writers of maxims, which Lord Chesterfield described as the preference for 'the prettiness to the justice of a thought, and the turn to the truth'. It is easy, in fact, to sacrifice some part of the truth in the interests of an extremely concise or striking phrase. The aphorist faces the daunting task of conveying truth without resort to qualifying clauses. Arising from this last point we may say that all significant general propositions about human behaviour—and most aphorisms are highly condensed general propositions of this kind—involve some measure of inaccuracy or non-applicability. No doubt it was an awareness of this problem which prompted La Rochefoucauld, apparently encouraged by Mme de Sablé and Mme de La Fayette, to modify some of his maxims by replacing 'toujours' by 'souvent', etc. A further difficulty arises for the writer of aphorisms in that the truism or the well-worn commonplace can sometimes receive undue attention if tricked out with sufficient verbal skill. And occasionally even as accomplished an aphorist as La Bruyère can produce a remark which now seems resoundingly obvious, as when he writes: 'Celui-là est riche qui reçoit plus qu'il ne consume; celui-là est pauvre dont la dépense excède la recette.' Finally, despite its starting-point in existential experience, the generalizing aim of the aphorism is instrumental in producing an abstract picture of man. The aphorism has strong 'essentialist' tendencies which place human nature outside time, and to this extent, though it inevitably reflects seventeenth- or eighteenth-century doctrines of man, it is at variance with those considerations of 'historical situation' or 'economic factors' to which contemporary thought pays a great deal of attention.

The appearance of a pirated edition in Amsterdam prompted La Rochefoucauld to publish his own version of the *Maximes*. They appeared at the very end of 1664 (with the date 1665) and four further editions were issued during his lifetime: in 1666, 1671, 1675, and 1678. To each edition La Rochefoucauld made alterations, and rather more additions than omissions, so that by 1678 the number of maxims had grown from just over 300 to more than 500. In terms of mere bulk it still remained a slight work, yet no book has demonstrated more acutely or more disturbingly the traditional French gift for sceptical dissection of the springs of human conduct.

Inevitably, La Rochefoucauld's *Maximes* give rise to two contrasting reactions—as indeed they did during his own lifetime. One set of readers has regarded his account of human beings, and particularly of the disproportion between what they may seem to be and what they actually are, as an accurate picture of human sinfulness and the state of the human heart untouched by God's grace. Thus a contemporary (no doubt a Jansenist) wrote: 'On pourrait dire que le chrétien commence où votre philosophie finit.' The opposite reaction was expressed by Mme de La Fayette in a letter: 'Quelle corruption

il faut avoir dans l'esprit et dans le cœur pour imaginer tout cela!'
This latter statement echoes the view of a majority of readers who
have found in La Rochefoucauld a traducer of human nature, a
sterile and destructive thinker, a bitter, sardonic misanthropist. In
support of their view they can point to such 'cynical' aphorisms
as 'Nous nous consolons aisément des disgrâces de nos amis
lorsquelles servent à signaler notre tendresse pour eux', or 'On
pleure pour avoir la réputation d'être tendre; on pleure pour être
plaint; on pleure pour être pleuré; enfin on pleure pour éviter la
honte de ne pas pleurer'. However, before convicting La Rochefoucauld of sheer perversity we must investigate rather more closely his
own intentions in the *Maximes* and the background against which
they were written.

La Rochefoucauld's general conclusions about human behaviour
are summed up by a formula which began, with rather different
wording, as a maxim in the first edition and was then omitted until
1675 when it returned as the epigraph to the whole collection. It
reads: 'Nos vertus ne sont le plus souvent que des vices déguisés.'
A number of readers might accept this statement provided the
qualification 'le plus souvent' is adequately interpreted and emphasized. Self-inspection, let alone the scrutiny of other people, may
convince us, for instance, that 'Nous avons tous assez de force pour
supporter les maux d'autrui', or that 'La pitié est souvent un sentiment de nos propres maux dans les maux d'autrui'. La Rochefoucauld reaches his conclusion after a voyage of exploration to what he
calls 'le pays de l'amour propre', also defining 'amour-propre' as
'l'amour de soi-même et de toutes choses pour soi'. Egotism, pride,
self-love, and hypocrisy are among the chief landmarks which he
describes. Indeed, he goes so far as to say: 'Dieu a permis, pour
punir l'homme du péché originel, qu'il se fît un bien de son amour-
propre pour en être tourmenté dans toutes les actions de sa vie.'
This statement—almost unique in the *Maximes* because of its
reference to God and the doctrine of original sin—throws considerable light on La Rochefoucauld's assumptions. He is not only offering us what the 1665 preface calls 'un portrait du cœur de l'homme';
the same preface says of the *Maximes* that 'ce qu'elles contiennent
n'est autre chose que l'abrégé d'une morale conforme aux pensées de

plusieurs Pères de l'Église'. The preface of 1666 is even more explicit. It states that the author of these aphorisms 'n'a considéré les hommes que dans cet état déplorable de la nature corrompue par le péché et . . . ainsi la manière dont il parle de ce nombre infini de défauts qui se rencontrent dans leurs vertus apparentes ne regarde point ceux que Dieu en préserve par une grâce particulière'. The last phrase is particularly significant. La Rochefoucauld is not attempting to give us a fully rounded portrait of human nature which would include the saint as well as the sinner. He is working in the dimension of the unregenerate only and excluding from consideration the capacities of man when illuminated and aided by divine grace.

There is a clear lack of correspondence here between La Rochefoucauld's theoretical remarks about what Pascal called 'la misère de l'homme sans Dieu' and the noticeable absence of theological terminology or allusions in the *Maximes* themselves. Even if he works from very similar assumptions to those of Pascal in the *Pensées* (and we know that he had repeated theological discussions with many Jansenist friends and acquaintances including Arnauld and Jacques Esprit), his immediate aim is different. The evidence suggests that La Rochefoucauld's purpose was primarily to refute the concept of *vertu païenne*, the idea that to follow the promptings of one's nature is an adequate guide to the moral life. Thus, for example, he writes in a letter to Père Thomas Esprit of his aim 'de prouver que la vertu des anciens philosophes païens, dont ils ont fait tant de bruit, a été établie sur de faux fondements'. Not only did he oppose the doctrine of 'suivre nature'. He rejected the assertion that natural virtue as practised by a Socrates, a Cato, or a Seneca is really more impressive and more genuine than the ethics imposed by Christian dogma. In fact, although the *Maximes* appear to be making the point that virtue is non-existent, they are strictly only claiming it to be contrary to the spontaneous promptings of our nature. It is in this context that we should see the repeated emphasis on self-interest, on the fact that emotion ultimately rules the intellect, on the contrast between the appearance and the reality of conduct, on the deceptive nature of what appears to be self-knowledge.

In the end, the *Maximes* collectively emphasize two general propositions: (i) that man is not naturally virtuous, and (ii) that he is seldom effectively rational. If we ask why La Rochefoucauld gave such prominence to these two judgements on human nature, a number of possible answers suggest themselves. Those who think La Rochefoucauld's picture to be an accurate one will simply ascribe it to his own individual insight and penetration. The more historically minded will perhaps point rather to his experience of the Fronde and the French Court. On this interpretation the *Maximes* are strictly relevant to a particular society at a particular moment in time. They are the fruit of reflexion on the savagery of civil war and the strategic self-seeking which formed a normal part of daily life at Versailles. Others again will point to somewhat different social and political implications in these ideas. They will emphasize the opposition implied to despotic rulers, the light thrown on Machiavellian behaviour, and the general antagonism (also shared in different ways by Pascal and La Bruyère) to contemporary aristocratic assumptions about man. Finally, those less sympathetic to La Rochefoucauld's conclusions will see his *Maximes* as one more facet of a seventeenth-century moral pessimism, ultimately deriving from Christianity, which found its most familiar expression in the life-denying assertions of Jansenism.

Whatever one's reactions, however, the *Maximes* contain a series of psychological insights which cannot be ignored or dismissed. There is the ring of experience behind such a remark as 'Quand on ne trouve pas son repos en soi-même, il est inutile de le chercher ailleurs'. There is the modern appreciation of the quasi-identity of supposed emotional opposites in many sayings such as '. . . on est souvent ferme par faiblesse, et audacieux par timidité', or 'Si on juge de l'amour par la plupart de ses effets, il ressemble plus à la haine qu'à l'amitié'. Again, there is a dynamic psychology, a sense of the changing, protean aspects of personality, in such statements as 'Le caprice de notre humeur est encore plus bizarre que celui de la fortune'. Not least of all, there is the marvellous bringing together of psychological insight and perfectly condensed statement in such a well-known maxim as 'L'hypocrisie est un hommage que le vice rend à la vertu'.

La Bruyère, in common with the other two major aphorists and moralists of seventeenth-century France, Pascal and La Rochefoucauld, is mainly concerned with the scrutiny of human conduct. However, in addition to the writing of aphorisms, he is associated more particularly with incisive character portraits. At first sight it might seem that aphorism and portraiture are only connected in the sense that both literary forms were practised at the same period and both are products of a relatively small, intimately organized, and highly self-conscious society. Yet the relationship between them is more organic than this. It is clear, for example, that the maxim which concentrates on conduct is a character study in a nutshell, or contains the germ of a portrait. Thus when La Rochefoucauld writes: 'La simplicité affectée est une imposture délicate', this aphorism could obviously be given more body or colour by a few additional sentences showing how the behaviour of an individual, imaginary or real, illustrates this truth in several different situations. In other words, the portrait as practised by La Bruyère and others can be, in essence, an extension and exemplification of an initial maxim. The maxim containing the germ of the portrait need not necessarily come first, of course, and in the following brief example from La Bruyère it provides in fact the final, clinching sentence:

Celui qui, logé chez soi dans un palais, avec deux appartements pour les deux saisons, vient coucher au Louvre dans un entre-sol n'en use pas ainsi par modestie; cet autre qui, pour conserver une taille fine, s'abstient du vin et ne fait qu'un seul repas n'est ni sobre ni tempérant; et d'un troisième qui, importuné d'un ami pauvre, lui donne enfin quelques secours, l'on dit qu'il achète son repos, et nullement qu'il est libéral. Le motif seul fait le mérite des actions des hommes, et le désintéressement y met la perfection.

A related point here is the fact that an aphoristic style of writing can greatly enliven a character portrait. Epigrammatic sentences make it more vivid while also conveying the impression that the individual traits described are inseparable from certain more universal characteristics. The effect obtained can be illustrated by the first two sentences of La Bruyère's description of the Maréchal de Villeroy to whom he gives the pseudonym of 'Ménippe':

Ménippe est l'oiseau paré de divers plumages qui ne sont pas à lui. Il ne parle pas, il ne sent pas; il répète des sentiments et des discours, se sert même si naturellement de l'esprit des autres qu'il y est le premier trompé, et qu'il croit souvent dire son goût ou expliquer sa pensée lorsqu'il n'est que l'écho de quelqu'un qu'il vient de quitter.

One final aspect of the connections between aphorism and portraiture has to do with the genesis of the *Maximes* and the *Caractères*. As regards the former, some of La Rochefoucauld's contemporaries have claimed that many of his maxims are the distillation of his observation of the habits and characteristics of certain prominent members of French society. A 'key' to the *Maximes* was even compiled along these lines. To this extent, therefore, they are the result of a narrowing movement from portraiture to aphorism. Conversely, La Bruyère's *Caractères* represent a broadening movement from the pithy saying to the more extended moral portrait. This broadening took place progressively during the eight years separating the first edition of 1688 from the ninth edition of 1696, the last to be published in La Bruyère's lifetime. The *Caractères* were originally a collection of maxims and epigrams, not very different from La Rochefoucauld's work of twenty-four years earlier. Partly on this account, no doubt, and also encouraged by the great success of his own book, La Bruyère used the fourth edition of 1689 to add to his original aphorisms a considerable number of more extended portraits as well as further maxims. Succeeding editions, up to and including the eighth, were expanded along the same lines.

La Bruyère was thirty-five years old when La Rochefoucauld died. He was twenty when the latter's aphorisms were first published. It is not certain that he met La Rochefoucauld, but he was undoubtedly very familiar with the *Maximes*, as indeed he was with Pascal's *Pensées*. He leans heavily on both these predecessors as regards the ideas he discussed and even, frequently, in his general approach to their formulation. He shows a similar misanthropy. He emphasizes man's subjection to his passions, his contradictions, his hypocrisy, his self-love. It is usually said, therefore, that La Bruyère's use of portraiture side by side with his aphorisms was a means of giving the appearance of novelty to what were already familiar moral judgements. I think there is some justice in this claim, but it should not blind us to the fact that La Bruyère's emphases are different and distinctive because of his own temperament and social circumstances.

Pascal and La Rochefoucauld were two kinds of natural extremist. La Bruyère, on the contrary, was essentially a man of moderation and considerable human sympathy alongside his sharp, satirical gifts. There is a kind of tolerant misanthropy, foreign to both his predecessors, in much of his work: 'Ne nous emportons point contre les hommes en voyant leur dureté, leur ingratitude, leur injustice, leur fierté, l'amour d'eux-mêmes, et l'oubli des autres: ils sont ainsi faits, c'est leur nature, c'est ne pouvoir supporter que la pierre tombe ou que le feu s'élève.' It is perhaps not too fanciful to suggest that we have here that avoidance of precipitate judgement and reverence for humane moderation which characterize the bourgeois mind of the period and which are also evident, for example, in Molière. La Bruyère was very conscious of his middle-class origins—particularly so in the service of the Condé household—and even his more severe statements lack the *grand seigneur* tone and the often harsh condescension of La Rochefoucauld.

Because of the vantage-point which his origins gave him, La Bruyère shows a greater sense of social diversity than either Pascal or La Rochefoucauld. The various classes and social groupings of his day make a much more differentiated appearance in his work. This has two main results. In the first place, the *Caractères* give us a more lively feeling of 'period'. Secondly, they ultimately lead to a number of political considerations. Where the sense of period is concerned, these aphorisms and portraits convey a remarkable sense of lived historical reality. Not only do we have sketches of many notable figures of the period; we also have details of fashion and behaviour which range from discussions of high heels and make-up to the way in which certain distinguished ladies use the seclusion of a private oratory in order to read their lovers' letters.

As regards political considerations, La Bruyère has often been praised for his sense of social justice. He shows an awareness of the desperately poor and indeed sub-human existence of the peasants:

L'on voit certains animaux farouches, des mâles et des femelles, répandus par la campagne, noirs, livides et tout brûlés du soleil, attachés à la terre qu'ils fouillent et qu'ils remuent avec une opiniâtreté invincible; ils ont comme une voix articulée, et quand ils se lèvent sur leurs pieds, ils montrent une face humaine, et en effet ils sont des hommes. Ils se retirent la nuit dans des tanières, où ils vivent de pain noir, d'eau et de racines; ils épargnent aux autres hommes la peine de semer, de labourer et de recueillir pour vivre, et méritent ainsi de ne pas manquer de ce pain qu'ils ont semé.

At the other end of the social scale, again, La Bruyère is sharply conscious of the shortcomings of the nobility and of the suffering and injustice brought about by an administration of self-seeking financiers and officials. Unlike Pascal or La Rochefoucauld, he emphasizes the social and economic, as well as the moral, consequences, even if he hardly proposes specific social and economic solutions. The passage on the peasantry above is humane, not revolutionary, and in general La Bruyère's reactions are coloured by his bourgeois misanthropy. In the last resort, he shows a middle-class respect for established authority, as when he writes: 'Si toute religion est une crainte respectueuse de la Divinité, que penser de ceux qui osent la blesser dans sa plus vive image, qui est le Prince?' Indeed, his sense of fallen human nature causes him to renounce all hope of significant social reform: 'Je mets au-dessus du grand politique celui qui néglige de le devenir et qui se persuade que le monde ne mérite pas qu'on s'en occupe.'

   These last two quotations bring us to a point where La Bruyère again differs from La Rochefoucauld, but comes closer to Pascal. Religious conviction plays an explicit role in his work and he even claimed, in the preface to his *Discours de réception à l'Académie française*, that the first fifteen chapters of the *Caractères* are a preparation for the final chapter in which atheism is refuted and divine providence affirmed. His general religious orthodoxy, however, in no way prevents him from seeing, and saying, that many pay lip service to a religion which they exploit for purely secular ends, just as he also notes the hypocrisies inherent in much court religion. The affirmative side of La Bruyère's religious ideas may be exemplified by the remark 'L'impossibilité où je suis de prouver que Dieu n'est pas me découvre son existence'. His strictures on the social conformist in religion are summed up thus: 'Un dévot est celui qui sous un roi athée serait athée.' The implications for the social attitudes of his religious thinking are present in his striking penultimate aphorism: 'Les extrémités sont vicieuses et partent de l'homme: toute compensation est juste, et vient de Dieu.'

The *Caractères* contain several references to style and form to which La Bruyère attributed something approaching moral value. He was very much the artist, working constantly at his book in order to find a clear and lasting expression for his ideas and observations. His handling of language ranges, in fact, from the verbal concentration of some of his best aphorisms to the varied, calculated, but often vigorous style of the portraits (for example, the passage on the peasants quoted above). He is still worth reading not only as a social and historical witness but as a skilful exponent of the resources of language.

NOTE

FRANÇOIS, DUC DE LA ROCHEFOUCAULD, 1613–80, was involved during the early part of his life in intrigues against Richelieu and Mazarin. During the civil war of the Fronde (1648–53) he was severely wounded. Having retired from active public life he wrote an account of his experiences (*Mémoires*, 1662) and frequented in particular the Jansenist-inclined salon of Madame de Sablé. He was associated with Madame de Sévigné, and especially with Madame de La Fayette, during the composition and later revisions of his *Maximes* (1664).

JEAN DE LA BRUYÈRE, 1645–96, was a bourgeois by birth. Through his friend and patron Bossuet he became tutor to the grandson of the Prince de Condé. He achieved fame through a single book, *Les Caractères* (1688), the full title of which reads: *Caractères de Théophraste traduits du grec, avec les caractères ou mœurs de ce siécle*. La Bruyère entered the Académie Française in 1693, though not without opposition. Towards the end of his life he wrote some undistinguished and posthumously published *Dialogues sur le quiétisme*.

(Biographical and bibliographical details for PASCAL are in the Note to Chapter 4, pp. 64–5.)

Modern editions. The major edition of La Rochefoucauld remains that by D. L. Gilbert and J. Gourdault in the 'Collection des Grands Écrivains de la France' (4 vols., 1868–83). The Pléiade edition (1957) by L. Martin-Chauffier and J. Marchand is more manageable but contains inaccuracies and omissions. The best working edition of the *Maximes* is a recent one in the 'Classiques Garnier' collection edited by J. Truchet (1967).

In the case of La Bruyère also, the most complete edition is by G. Servois in the 'Collection des Grands Écrivains de la France' (7 vols., 1865–1922). There is a Pléiade edition (1951) by Julien Benda, and R. Garapon edits the *Caractères* in the 'Classiques Garnier' series.

Criticism. Useful full-length studies of La Rochefoucauld include R. Grand-saignes d'Hauterive, *Le Pessimisme de La Rochefoucauld* (1914), E. Magne, *Le Vrai Visage de La Rochefoucauld* (1923) and W. G. Moore, *La Rochefoucauld, his Mind and Art* (1968). On La Bruyère, three books should be noted: E. Magne, *La Bruyère* (1914), G. Michaut, *La Bruyère* (1936), and P. Richard, *La Bruyère et ses 'Caractères'* (1947). Some of the best writing on both authors is to be found in vols. iv and v of A. Adam, *Histoire de la littérature française du XVIIᵉ siècle* (1948–56) and in A. J. Krailsheimer, *Studies in Self-Interest* (1962). There is also a suggestive analysis of La Rochefoucauld's ideas in P. Bénichou, *Morales du Grand Siècle* (1948).

10. Prose Fiction

THE subject-matter and quality of the bulk of prose fiction in any period are related to the nature and demands of its public. In France in the seventeenth century there was a rapid extension of literacy: through the expansion (mainly by the teaching religious orders) of secondary education, usually centred on grammar, rhetoric, and the classic texts of the ancient Graeco-Roman world, a considerable proportion of the commercial middle classes, on whom increasing wealth conferred some social and even political importance, began to acquire second-hand some of the cultural values of the administrative and legal upper middle classes and of the aristocracy. Thus the reading public for prose fiction was constituted not only, as was the case in the sixteenth century, of members of what we might call the ruling classes and the intellectual élite, but also of elements of the independent bourgeoisie. What did they read for entertainment?

Principally they read romances, distantly descended from the verse romances of chivalry of the later Middle Ages through works such as the *Amadis de Gaule*. The *Polexandre* of Gomberville, for example, the publication of which began in its definitive form in 1632, is basically the story of the improbable adventures of a knight in speciously exotic settings, and it implies the ethos of a feudal society which had long since disappeared as a living force from the France of everyday reality; moreover, it includes elements of magic. That is to say, it is a literature built on literature. Similarly, the three best-known novels of La Calprenède, *Cassandre*, *Cléopâtre*, and *Pharamond*, which began to appear respectively in 1642, 1646, and 1661, recount ostensibly authentic deeds of exemplary heroic figures from the mistily historical past. These works are often repetitious, imprecise, and vague in their presentation of the physical events they describe, slackly written with a superabundance of personification and clichés. *Cléopâtre*, for example, opens as follows: 'Les ombres de la nuit n'avaient pas encore fait place à la lumière, quand le triste Tyridate, éveillé par ses cruelles inquiétudes, et ne pouvant attendre la clarté du jour, sortit de sa solitaire demeure, pour promener son corps languissant, et ses amoureuses pensées sur le rivage d'Alexandrie.' And a little later, he describes a ship on fire: 'C'était un grand feu qui sortant du milieu des ondes, semblait ne s'élever dans le ciel, que pour y chercher comme dans son centre ordinaire un asile contre ses ennemis qu'il suivait.'

Yet here and there these novels contain passages of psychological perception, paragraphs of analysis of, for example, the scale of values of the married woman, that help us to understand why even so intelligent and sensitive a reader as Madame de Sévigné found them fascinating: 'Le style de La Calprenède', she writes to her daughter, Madame de Grignan (12 July 1671), 'est détestable, et je ne laisse pas de m'y prendre comme à de la glu.' But then she adds: 'La beauté des sentiments, la violence des passions, la grandeur des événements, et [as for the heroes] le succès miraculeux de leur redoutable épée, tout cela m'entraîne comme une petite fille.'

Much, indeed, in these works appeals to the adolescent element in the reader (even to the sadistic element), as does much in their modern progeny: the central female character of one of the novels of Mademoiselle de Scudéry, *Le Grand Cyrus*, is frequently abducted but always escapes unscathed, and *Polexandre* contains descriptions of what could be called James Bond-type barbarities. As successive instalments of these immensely long romances appeared (*Cassandre* ran to ten volumes, *Cléopâtre* and *Pharamond* to twelve each), they were discussed in the salons by the cultured women of the aristocracy and by the *bourgeoises* assimilable to them (not all the *précieuses* were *ridicules*), eager to identify those of their illustrious contemporaries who figured, as it were in disguise, in these compilations of adventure and exquisitely rare sentimental situation which corresponded to their public's dreams, aspirations, and fantasies. By the 1660s these centred more often than not on the civil wars of the Fronde: it was then that the *Parlement* and the feudal nobility were submerged as political forces by the superior power of autocratic monarchy working through a centralized and more rational administration—the *Parlement* until the Revolution of 1789, the aristocracy for ever. Many of the first readers of these novels could have said with Madame de Sévigné (writing once again to her daughter): 'Pour les sentiments, . . . ils sont d'une perfection qui remplit mon idée sur les belles âmes. Vous savez aussi que je ne hais pas les grands coups d'épée . . .' (15 July 1671).

It was not always, however, at the price of extensive romanticized swashbuckling that fiction presented subtlety of feeling. There was another type of novel that, although often as long, paid less attention to vigorous adventure and more to the careful, evaluative delineation of sentiment. This had its roots in another tradition, more clearly linked to classical antiquity, the tradition of the *pastorale*, set in an imagined golden age of quiet bucolic communities and exploring the amorous tensions of highly self-conscious men and women wearing the conventional fancy dress of shepherds and shepherdesses. The immediate ancestors of the French pastoral novel were three internationally known foreign works of the preceding century: *La Diana enamorada*, in prose and verse, by the Spaniard Montemayor (1542); *L'Aminta*, a dramatic poem by the Italian Torquato Tasso (1572); and, inspired by the latter, a pastoral tragi-comedy by Tasso's compatriot Guarini, called, significantly, *Il pastor fido* (1585).

The great example of the type in France is *L'Astrée*. Its author, Honoré d'Urfé, is of an earlier generation than that of the other French writers we have mentioned, and this may explain in part the relative absence from his novel, which began to appear in 1607, of deeds of military valour: the conflict that he had lived through—the Wars of Religion—had been considerably more serious and sanguinary than that of the Fronde, and there are some experiences that are better forgotten than romanticized. Another reason is that he is clearly more interested in ethics and ideas than in violent events, unlike Gomberville and La Calprenède; also, he is an incomparably better psychologist than they, and his narrative of the trials and tribulations that have to be endured by the faithful shepherd Céladon (whose name, like that of Tartuffe, soon achieved in literary society the status of a generic noun, such was his symbolic significance) in order to qualify for marriage to the shepherdess

Astrée, daughter of a Druid in an imagined fifth-century Gaul, contains discussions of sexual attitudes that are still of interest today in the assumptions they make about the nature of the gregarious human animal. Throughout, too, we can see implied (and sometimes stated) a steady belief in a particular conception of love that helps to give the work philosophical coherence. This conception is usually known as platonic, because it derives ultimately from the notion of Plato that behind the world of appearances, constantly changing, in which we live—and which the unthinking take to be the only world—there is a world of immutable essences, or fixed ideas, which the truly human being tries to manifest, in however pale an imitation, in the actions of his own living. (He tries, for example, to be just, because the concept of Justice is beautiful.) In other words, the only concrete things worth having are those which correspond to acceptable abstractions. Plato had little to say, however, about relations between men and women, and it would be more accurate to refer to the conception of love we find in *L'Astrée* as neoplatonic, since it came down to us through the writings of Plotinus, who re-thought some of the notions of Plato in the light of the moral revolution brought about by the spread of early Christianity. He produced some doctrines proclaiming love as a stimulant to honourable conduct and high endeavour, and woman as a creature of eminent dignity, love of whom for men was an approximation to the love of God for human beings. These doctrines reappear at intervals in one form or another in the subsequent course of the history of European literature: in the *amour courtois* of the Middle Ages, in Dante, in Petrarch.

It is not, then, surprising that *L'Astrée* was one of the most popular works of prose fiction of its time in the salons, recommending itself as a much more suitable manual of civility than the novels of Gomberville or La Calprenède (which it anticipated and outlived) to the intelligent women of the upper classes in their attempt to impose some kind of discipline on a society demoralized by the Wars of Religion of the second half of the sixteenth century. Unlike these works, *L'Astrée* is not so much concerned with the gratification of fantasy as with the elaboration of a dignified code of manners, and to the visitors to the Hôtel de Rambouillet d'Urfé's novel became a kind of reference work, crystallizing conflicts and problems far transcending the particular localized circumstances in which the text presents them. Nor is *L'Astrée* simply an exemplary romance, a mirror of politeness: there is moral and psychological realism in the presentation of the gaily sinister figure of the 'bad' shepherd, Hylas; there is no attempt to suggest that the devil does not exist, and his advocate is allowed to speak. And if some passages of the work are long-winded and diffuse, it is in the main well-written: the words correspond adequately to clear and unambiguous concepts.

Most of the writers of the seventeenth century whom we now think of as great and characteristic were familiar with *L'Astrée*, which they admired chiefly, it would seem, for the authenticity of its notations of moral feeling. They included Madame de La Fayette, to whom historians and critics ascribe, on fairly sound evidence, at least a major share in the authorship of a handful of works of prose fiction: *La Princesse de Montpensier* (anonymous, 1662); *Zayde* (published under the name of Segrais, a novelist of her acquaintance, 1670); *La Princesse de Clèves* (anonymous, 1678); *La Comtesse de Tende* (posthumous, 1724), and two other works: the *Histoire de Madame Henriette d'Angleterre* (the daughter of Charles II—Madame de La Fayette was her lady-in-waiting and confidante; published posthumously, 1720), and the *Mémoires de la Cour de France pour les années 1688 et 1689* (posthumous, 1731).

Whether Madame de Lafayette did in fact write all or part of these is really of minor importance: in the discussion and evaluation of literature what matters first and foremost is the texts themselves, and the four fictional works listed are all of high quality, while one of them (*La Princesse de Clèves*) is a masterpiece. But the moral system implied in them is related to that of *L'Astrée*, and it is interesting that there were *L'Astrée* reading parties at Madame de La Fayette's house, and that one of her acquaintances, Mademoiselle de Scudéry, had been a passionate reader of *L'Astrée* in her youth.

Mademoiselle de Scudéry perhaps played some small part in the literary education of Madame de Lafayette, since she was herself a talented writer (publishing usually under the name of her brother, Georges, the dramatist who crossed swords with Corneille in the *Querelle du Cid*). She wrote romances, of some distinction, which form a kind of amalgam of Gomberville, La Calprenède, and d'Urfé. In the main she depicts great, exemplary figures (representing by a tacit convention known contemporary persons) taking part in events of a melodramatic or sentimental kind in a shadowy setting of prestigious antiquity, as in the work of the 'heroic' novelists. But here the melodrama is less frequent and the element of adventure tends to be replaced by that of analysis and discussion (see, for example, *Artamène ou Le Grand Cyrus*, which began to appear in 1649 during the Fronde). It is one of the romances of Mademoiselle de Scudéry, *Clélie* (whose publication began in 1654), that contains a most revealing document showing the increasing preoccupation of intelligent Frenchwomen of the century with the search for truth, security, and stability in love relationships, which they hoped to achieve through the application to the movements of the emotions of an analytical approach, associated with Descartes in that it is based on the establishment of clear and distinct ideas. This is the 'Carte du Tendre', and this map of the 'Kingdom of Tenderness' is much more than a skittish conceit. It is a topographical schematization of the attitudes and actions to be avoided or adopted by couples travelling down the river of 'Inclination' towards the uncharted lands of marriage. Too much time spent, for example, in the villages of Tiédeur or Légèreté can lead them to the shores of Le Lac d'Indifférence, while going through Perfidie and Orgueil can bring them to La Mer d'Inimitié. On the other hand, the two main highways lead, through stages like Constante Amitié and Bonté to one of the twin towns of Tendre sur Reconnaissance and Tendre sur Estime, the recommended embarkation points for the connubial journey to the Terres Inconnues. Love is not thought of, in this kind of literature, as a favour lightly granted or as a sensational enjoyment to be gained by trickery or lies, but as a vital moral experience engaging the whole person—and for life. What we have here, presented allegorically, is a principle of medieval romance—the notion of the knight having to *deserve* his lady (a principle, in whatever form, of considerable social value)—but with much more attention paid to the observable psychology of the human being, particularly the woman.

It is in this respect perhaps more than in any other that the 'romance' tradition differs essentially from that of another kind of love fiction, also widely read but understandably less popular in the salons, that pays more attention to the male amorous chase, tends to present women predominantly as objects to be conquered, and sometimes, in addition, suggests that they are monsters of duplicity. This tradition also has its roots in the Middle Ages—in the *fabliaux*, in the continuation by Jean de Meung of the *Roman de la Rose* (in which the troubadour-like idealization of love and women of the first part is replaced by a cruder, more cynical attitude), and in Boccaccio's *Decameron*. To this tradition of masculine 'common sense' and impatience must be related also the so-called 'realist' stream of fiction, criticizing by implication, satirizing, and sometimes burlesquing the more obvious departures from verisimilitude of the sentimental, pastoral, and adventure novels. Sorel, for example, followed his *La Vraie Histoire comique de Francion* (1623), the adventures of a young gentleman in his brushes with the Parisian world of education and the law (a world ruled by the dogma of pedantic schoolmasters and the ferocious cynicism of corrupt judges, a world which the author scrutinizes, and condemns, by the light of reason), with *Le Berger extravagant* (1627), which mocked characteristic aspects of *L'Astrée*; Scarron (the first husband of Madame de Maintenon, who became the second wife of Louis XIV) applied, in *Le Roman comique* (1651–63), the structure and techniques, and often the language, of a 'heroic' novel to the un-heroic material of the day-to-day social and financial troubles of a travelling theatre company; Furetière, in *Le Roman bourgeois* (1666), using a similar approach, offered a panorama of life in lower-middle-class urban society that is brutally opposed to the system of values implicit in the works of d'Urfé and his successors. Furetière has no sympathy for his characters, no wish to understand them, to explain them: his attitude is deliberately non-analytical, and he goes as far as to tell the reader bluntly (as indeed did Scarron before him) that he has no idea of what went on during such and such an interview, because he was not present. In its pseudo-objectivity *Le Roman bourgeois* qualifies for consideration as the first 'anti-novel'.

A non-analytical approach is to some extent characteristic also of yet another (and more important) type of fiction of the time, the *nouvelle*, essentially a 'long short story', a 'tale', a concise, rapid, striking, chronological presentation of *events*, *actions*, 'what *happened*', always dramatic, often surprising, sometimes inconsequential, sometimes tragic. The story of Floridor, for example, in the *Nouvelles françaises* of Segrais (1656), uses the same material as Racine's *Bajazet*, and indeed may have been one of the dramatist's sources. As was the case for the pastoral novel, the prototype for the *nouvelle* was non-French—the Italian *novella*, best represented by the tales constituting the *Decameron*. Through translation and imitation, however, there had developed a native tradition that tended to take as its central character a woman in love, often in dangerous, if domestic, circumstances—perhaps because the author of the best-known French collection, the *Heptaméron* (1559), was a woman, Marguerite de Navarre, the sister of François Ier.

If mention has been made of all these types of fiction, and at some length, it is because the enduring masterpiece of the seventeenth century in this field, *La Princesse de Clèves*, contains, sublimated and exploited, elements of all of them: the greatest formal originality of its author is to have created a dynamic living synthesis of already-existing material and devices. Like the long romances of the time, it is set in the past, but it is not the remotely vague past: it is a *known* past, and a *French* past, with overtones of nostalgic value for contemporaries: the period of the Valois kings only about a hundred years before, the period during which the *Heptaméron* was written, the period used by Segrais for some of his *Nouvelles françaises*.

Like *L'Astrée*, *La Princesse de Clèves* is the story of a passion, but its development is recounted far more succinctly: it has none of the tiresome digressions characteristic of the structure of the 'heroic' novel, the so-called '*tiroirs*', inset tales which tend to begin with some variant of the formulas 'that reminds me' or 'let me explain to you how I came to be here', tales which sometimes open out one from another like the sections of a telescope and which interrupt the main narrative for so long that the reader sometimes forgets what the main narrative was about. An earlier work which there is evidence for ascribing to the author of *La Princesse de Clèves*, *Zayde* (1670), does contain some '*tiroirs*' (*Zayde* is clearly an 'apprentice-piece', containing as it does, in addition, such cliché situations as a rescue from shipwreck, like those in *Polexandre* and *Cléopâtre*, and love for a Moorish girl, as in Mademoiselle de Scudéry's *Almahide*, the first part of which appeared in 1660), and it is evident that in the intervening eight years an artistic lesson had been learnt. Although *Zayde* is already itself shorter than *Almahide*, *La Princesse de Clèves* is shorter still—only five times the length of the author's earlier *nouvelle*, *La Princesse de Montpensier*, which runs to about thirty pages—so that attention is concentrated on the predicament of the main characters and on their resultant emotions. In other words, the author had learnt to present the essential material of a novel through the medium of the *nouvelle*. There are certainly some 'episodes' in the *Princesse de Clèves* centred on subsidiary 'historical' characters, but they are all related to the main protagonist herself—the princess—and all have a function in her own decisions as mirror, temptation, or warning, and they are thus psychologically, dramatically, and structurally *organic*, and therefore justifiable. Similarly, the delineations and discussions of states of mind, which bear some resemblance to those of *L'Astrée*, are in the *Princesse de Clèves* not only considerably shorter, but are also either the result of significant action or a preparation for it. In the same way, the 'adventures' that figure in the *Princesse de Clèves* are 'reasonable'—all of them possible, most of them likely, and, again, having a direct bearing on the feelings and decisions of the characters: the first meeting, at a court ball, of the princess and the man with whom she is to fall in love, a lost letter, a fall from a horse, a walk in a forest ending in an accidental overhearing of a confession from the princess to her husband. Like her friend Madame de Sévigné, the author of the *Princesse de Clèves* is clearly a very rational person, but she also sees that there is much in the world that is irrational, and she is fascinated by it. (There is a moment in the *Princesse de Montpensier* when the author says of the un-looked-for encounter of two lovers: 'Cette aventure . . . leur parut une chose de roman.')

For all the glamour of its setting, the *Princesse de Clèves* is really, like Racine's *Bérénice*, a domestic tragedy. The young Mademoiselle de Chartres is brought to court by her widowed mother and married to the eligible Prince de Clèves. In the general run of romances, marriage, or at any rate some form of capitulation, terminates the narrative: the ending, that is to say, is happy. 'God's in His heaven—all's right with the world!' In the *Princesse de Clèves* marriage is the beginning of tragedy. This was not, historically speaking, an innovation. There had been works of fiction that dealt with the plight of the woman married to a man she did not love: most notably, in the immediate past, the same author's *Princesse de Montpensier* (1662), and the story of the Maréchal de Bellegarde, forming the second volume of *Les Désordres de l'amour* by Madame de Villedieu, which appeared in 1675 and may have been one source of some of the subject-matter of the *Princesse de Clèves*. But the theme was sufficiently unusual to cause comment, even without the particular treatment and emphasis that mark the *Princesse de Clèves* as a work of art of deep and disturbing significance. The story of the Maréchal de Bellegarde, although its author is clearly interested in psychology, concentrates attention on the melodramatic aspects of the situation and on the problems of the unhappy marriage in the contemporary world, while the *Princess de Clèves* is equally clearly concerned with more than this. If it is true that the heroine marries Clèves partly because of the ambitious promptings of her mother in a society in which partners are chosen for dynastic, financial, or class reasons, it is equally true that the problems arising for her out of this marriage transcend the day and age because they are rooted in characteristics of human nature which do not appear to have changed since the seventeenth century: she becomes fond of her husband, she feels gratitude and respect towards him, and she would like to be able to return the passionate love he shows for her, not only because her mother has taught her that this is socially desirable in a married woman, but because of a strong sense of personal dignity. The author of the *Princesse de Clèves* is aware of the *complexity* of human relationships and values, and she knows that we are sometimes faced by problems not easily solved, if at all.

Clèves, unlike the traditional figure of the husband in the 'eternal triangle', is neither a villain nor a fool. He too has high principles and noble intentions: he knows that his wife does not love him, and gives her to understand that, if ever she were to fall in love with someone else, he would be capable of advising her as if he were not her husband—that is, dispassionately. The principle is put to the test, and it fails: the princess confesses to him that she is in danger of falling in love, and this knowledge, together with the apparently well-grounded suspicion that he has in fact already been deceived, kills him. (Once again, *Zayde* shows us the author working towards the tragic irony of this situation in the episode of Alphonse and Bélaisre, a study of pathological jealousy that causes a husband to lose the love of his wife and to kill his best friend.)

The man towards whom Madame de Clèves is attracted, the Duc de Nemours, is no more of a villain than her husband (although considerably less admirable). They are well suited to one another from all conceivable social and 'natural' points of view, and the widow is now free to accept his offer of marriage. But she rejects him. In the best of all possible worlds, she renounces what happiness of a conventional kind it could offer her, without any reference to the idea of God, or indeed to any philosophical idea of established acceptability, but for reasons which, however tinged with meta-physic they may be, are profoundly, authentically human. It is here, in the deliberately 'unhappy' ending, that the *Princesse de Clèves* is most essentially distinct from the love fiction that immediately preceded it, and looks forward to our own time, for her mother's indoctrination is only one factor, and of minimal importance, in the heroine's decision. By the time she comes face to face with Nemours as a free agent, she has evolved from the naïve, inexperienced girl entering for the first time the sophisticated world of the court into a firmly disillusioned adult, dismissing her lover for ever with no other power than her own inner resources. This is not a case of 'society crushing the individual', but of the individual woman making up her mind to refuse a permanent relationship with a man towards whom she is attracted, because of the relative inadequacy of that man, and of men in general, measured against her absolute conception of love. For the princess, a love relationship must be perfect or it is degrading, and she has learnt that it is possible to be sexually drawn towards someone whom one does not altogether admire. Nemours has great charm. He is not a criminal, nor even a scoundrel, but he has made love successfully to many women, and there is no conclusive evidence that he really is the reformed character he claims to have become: there is a strong risk that, as the princess herself says, she might see him become for others what he has already become for her: 'Je vous croirais toujours amoureux et aimé et je ne me tromperais pas souvent. . . . Je ne sais même si j'oserais me plaindre. On fait des reproches à un amant; mais en fait-on à un mari, quand on a à lui reprocher de n'avoir plus d'amour?'

This is a risk that she is not prepared to take, because the confirmation—or even the suspicion—of her lover's infidelity would expose her to what she considers the most terrible of all mental tortures, experienced once before during the night when she had believed Nemours to be deceiving her, namely jealousy.

Jealousy is a passion, one of the dynamic emotional forms in which the ego blindly and irrationally asserts itself either against others or, if no contact can be made with an adversary, against itself, and always, in either case, destructively. The theme of the destructive, anarchic power of passion runs through the *Princesse de Clèves*, as it does through the tragedies of Racine, like a *leitmotiv*. In taking her decision to reject Nemours, the princess may seem to be acting like a heroine of Corneille, but there is no question in the novel of a renunciation of the present in order to safeguard an optimistically viewed future. What Madame de Clèves is giving up, it would seem, is a whole sector of life itself, because it stains the white radiance of eternity by being inextricably bound up with the passions, and the final situation of her choice could be described in the words used of themselves by corpses in one of the *Operette morali* of Leopardi: 'Joyless indeed, but safe'. Or if this is a victory for neoplatonism, it is a Pyrrhic victory, since it involves self-mutilation. The case for renunciation is, however, strongly argued: Nemours, we are told, does in time forget even this, his one apparently sincere relationship; and the indictment of passion is persuasively presented. Passion is responsible for the death of the heroine's husband (the only man close to her whom she respects): firstly because without his own passionate love for her he would not have become a victim of the jealousy that causes him wrongfully to suspect her and that kills him; secondly because, paradoxically, it is *fear* of passion that causes her to involve him in the problem set by the growth of her infatuation with Nemours, a problem that many women might be prepared to solve alone; thirdly because the indiscretion of Nemours that apparently justifies the husband's suspicion is a direct result of the intensity of the lover's feelings for the princess. And since for a woman to admit to a man that she loves him is to give him power over her, the princess, as a free individual (free socially, also, now that she is a widow), is careful to make a formal statement of her love to Nemours only after she has decided not to see him again.

It is not only in its psychology and attitude to the passions—that is, in its vision—that the *Princess de Clèves* is outstanding, although it is principally in these respects that the work adds a dimension to prose fiction (unlike the satirical, erroneously-named 'realist' novels of the time, which in the last analysis are functions of the conventions they mock). The impression that the characters are serious persons trying to impose their will and a rational pattern on forces by definition beyond their control (hence the personification of the passions as if they had an independent existence of their own, penetrating the life of the individual without his consent) is communicated, as in the plays of Racine, by an extensive use of monologue, often self-analytical ('What do I feel? Who am I? What must I do? What do I think of myself?') that ushers the reader into the heart of the matter and involves him willy-nilly, through the first person singular, in the predicaments of the protagonists. And the effect of the style in the narrow sense is parallelled and reinforced (again, as in the plays of Racine) by the *structure*. In much the same way as in, for example, *Phèdre*, passion working through the protagonist's reactions to events brings about other events which ultimately precipitate the death of the man she loves, so in the *Princesse de Clèves* there is a tightly related series of happenings and reactions to them that forms, as it were, a mechanical spiral staircase down which the prince and his wife are moved to their individual realization of the tragic nature of certain aspects of the human condition. The princess, for example, attracted towards Nemours, begins to tell her mother, who asked for her complete confidence, first less than the whole truth, and subsequently positive lies; then her mother's death makes it difficult for her not to turn for help in her inexperience to her husband, with disastrous consequences; and his death, which forces her to take her final decision in responsible isolation, in its turn increases her sense of guilt. Moreover, some of the events of the *Princesse de Clèves* have a *symbolic* importance which transcends the face value of the physical actions described and the precise semantic indications of the words used, so that the sensitive reader, aware of their relationship to other events, perceives that they possess a significance in the economy of the work considered as a whole. The scene, for example, in which the princess and Nemours try to reconstruct from memory the missing letter is, we realize, the only occasion on which the pair are ever fully gay and unconstrained together, and this, we see on reflection, is because of the presence of Clèves, which makes the meeting at least socially guiltless. In other words, the author may be suggesting through this scene—although this is not *stated*—that passion and innocence are incompatible. After all, what is really in question in the *Princesse de Clèves* is not the details of the destiny of a particular woman in specifically seventeenth-century conditions (still less sixteenth-century, since the author was clearly *using* history, not writing it), but the nature of love and of sexual relationships and the viability of the whole concept of marriage, the problems of which are still with us.

The *Princesse de Clèves* is perhaps the first work of prose fiction to provide a really adequate imaginative focus for the sympathetic study of these problems in depth. Its precise formal, literary influence is difficult to assess. It was certainly held up by critics for the next hundred years or so as a model of the *roman d'analyse*. At least one great novelist of world rank, Stendhal, claimed frequently that it was his aim in his own work to emulate its structural and stylistic virtues, and there are elements of its moral vision and subtlety of analysis discernible in such works as the *Histoire d'une Grecque moderne* (1741) of the Abbé Prévost, Jean-Jacques Rousseau's *La Nouvelle Héloïse* (1761), André Gide's *La Porte étroite* (1909) and *La Symphonie pastorale* (1919). It certainly helped to establish the notion that the novel should be as well written and as serious in its intentions as, say, tragedy; that it should display the qualities of precision, astringency, understatement, and delicacy of expression that are prized by the reader who is intelligent and sensitive; and that it should be capable of serving as well as other genres as a vehicle for a poetic vision of life. Perhaps we can say that the

Princesse de Clèves is one of the sources—and one of the most important—of what was to become, with the addition of much more detail of behaviour and environment, the great tradition of the European novel that reaches its climax two centuries later with Tolstoy's *Anna Karenina*.

NOTE

HONORÉ D'URFÉ, 1567–1625, took part in the civil Wars of Religion on the losing side (that of the Catholic *Ligue*). During subsequent exile in Savoie, then an independent state, he composed the long pastoral romance, *L'Astrée*, set in his native region of the Forez (part of the Loire valley west of Lyon). Part iv of this was published posthumously in 1627 by his secretary, Baro, who in the same year also brought out a conclusion of the work based on d'Urfé's notes. D'Urfé was also the author of two pastoral dramatic poems, *Sireine* and *Sylvanire*.

MADELEINE DE SCUDÉRY, 1607–1701, was one of the most popular novelists of the century and a well-known figure in Parisian literary society. A highly intelligent feminist, she never married. A graduate of the Hôtel de Rambouillet, she held Saturday gatherings in her own salon, where she was known as Sapho (the famous poetess of Greek antiquity), the name under which she appears in a self-portrait in *Le Grand Cyrus*.

MARIE-CATHERINE-HORTENSE DESJARDINS, 1640–83, known as MADAME DE VILLEDIEU, was a tempestuous and talented blue-stocking whose imagination bears comparison with that of George Sand in the nineteenth century, but who was socially less fortunate. She was one of the first to try to fuse the form of the *nouvelle* and the essentially significant content of the novel.

MARIE-MADELEINE PIOCHE DE LA VERGNE, COMTESSE DE LAFAYETTE, 1634–93, was the daughter of a military engineer who became tutor to a young relative of Richelieu; her mother's side of the family included scholars and doctors. After the birth of her two sons, her husband spent a good deal of time looking after his estates in the Auvergne, while she remained in Paris, handling the legal side of the family affairs. She was known in salon circles for her sober and judicious intelligence, and for her friendships with Madame de Sévigné, to whom she was related by marriage, and the Duc de La Rochefoucauld, whom she saw nearly every day for the last fifteen years or so of his life, and who is believed by some critics to have had a hand in the composition of at least some of the works ascribed to her. (Her married name usually appears nowadays in the form 'La Fayette'. She herself, however, spelled it as one word.)

Modern editions. The Vaganay edition of *L'Astrée* in five volumes (1925–8) is excellent, but an adequate idea of the tone of the work can be obtained from the volume of extracts in the 'Classiques Larousse' series. *Romanciers du XVIIe siècle*, in the Pléiade series (1958), includes the best-known 'realist' works, and has an outstanding introduction by A. Adam. The *Romans et nouvelles* of Madame de Lafayette, ed. É. Magne (1958), contains all her fiction in one volume. The best school edition to date of *La Princesse de Cleves* is that by K. B. Kettle (1967).

Criticism. The best all-round study in a small compass is still A. Le Breton's *Le Roman au dix-septième siècle* (1890), which offers sound discussions of all the major works. Dorothy McDougall's *Madeleine de Scudéry, her romantic Life and Death* (1938) is good, in spite of its title, while *The Life and Works of Marie-Catherine Desjardins* by B. A. Morrissette (1947) is the definitive work on its subject. On *La Princesse de Clèves*, the first (and contemporary) appraisal— Valincour, *Lettres à Mme la Marquise*** sur le sujet de la Princesse de Clèves* (ed. A. Cazes in the 'Chefs-d'œuvre méconnus' series, 1925)—is still worth reading, while a handy and intelligent coverage of most aspects of the life and environment of the author is offered by B. Pingaud in his *Madame de Lafayette par elle-même* (1959).

11. Racine

'LA principale règle est de plaire et de toucher', Racine wrote in his preface to *Bérénice*. The terms are rather vague, but they set Racine clearly in the rhetorical tradition of literature, according to which a writer or speaker will set out to please or move an audience, his ultimate aim being to persuade or instruct them. It may be that in Racine persuasion and instruction, which are not mentioned in the preface to *Bérénice*, are no longer the guiding purpose—I shall return to this point later. But whatever the ultimate aim of the tragedian, the spectators are asked above all to let themselves be moved: 'qu'ils se réservent le plaisir de pleurer et d'être attendris.'

'Il n'y a que le vraisemblable qui touche dans la tragédie.' This was not an original opinion in Racine's day. Most theorists would have agreed with Boileau that 'L'esprit n'est point ému de ce qu'il ne croit pas' (*Art poétique*, iii). Given certain conventions of the theatre—that alexandrines represent prose, for instance—the audience was to be shown an action and characters in which it could believe. Criteria naturally changed as spectators became more sophisticated; what had been acceptable to one generation seemed ludicrous to the next. It was easy for Racine to mock plays containing 'un grand nombre de jeux de théâtre, d'autant plus surprenants qu'ils seraient moins vraisemblables' and 'une infinité de déclamations, où l'on ferait dire aux acteurs tout le contraire de ce qu'ils devraient dire' (first preface to *Britannicus*).

In particular, in Racine's generation, the criterion of verisimilitude was held to demand a certain simplicity of plot. The unities of time and place, which in their turn were founded on verisimilitude, made it difficult for a playwright to present a complicated chain of events and physical actions without damaging the illusion of truth. Yet in spite of the demands of the theorists, simplicity of plot was far from universal in Racine's time. The big box-office success of the century was Thomas Corneille's *Timocrate* (1656); in this play a plot of extreme deviousness must have submitted the audience's belief to a heavy strain, but they seem to have loved the suspense and surprise of it.

Timocrate, it is true, was a tragi-comedy and was written in the decade before Racine started writing, but the popularity of this sort of play did not suddenly cease in 1660. Nevertheless Thomas Corneille, who followed public taste rather than creating it, was writing more simply by 1672 (*Ariane*). This was due above all to the influence of Racine, who had largely abandoned suspense and surprise as dramatic weapons.

Hardly ever in his tragic theatre do we find a case of disguise or mistaken identity, which are at the heart of plays of the *Timocrate* variety—Racine keeps such tricks for his comedy *Les Plaideurs*. In tragedy he prefers 'une action simple, chargée de peu de matière' (first preface to *Britannicus*). As often as not the outcome will be known in advance to the spectator with some knowledge of the Bible or classical antiquity, but even where it is not, it is usually made to follow with what looks like necessary logic from the initial situation. The audience's emotion, which is so important to Racine, will come not so much from a fascinated attention to the development of the plot as from involvement in 'les intérêts, les sentiments et les passions des personnages' (first preface to *Britannicus*). According to traditional rhetorical theory the vivid simulation of violent emotion by the actor will create similar emotions in the audience:

> Que dans tous vos discours la passion émue
> Aille chercher le cœur, l'échauffe et le remue.
> (Boileau, *Art poétique*, iii)

In practice it is very hard to generalize about the reactions of different spectators in the theatre, but while there may not be total 'identification' with the actor, at least one can say that the spectator tends to react to the emotions presented in the same way that he might react to tense emotional situations surrounding him in his everyday life, with a mixture of sympathy and fascination.

It has often been said that Racine's theatre is one of litotes, euphemism, or civilized understatement. This is only part of the truth. It is true that frequently in his plays we are made to feel the presence of passions which the characters themselves are not openly expressing and may not be even be aware of, but this is only possible because such moments are surrounded by others, just as numerous, in which emotion is directly and often violently expressed. Not of course that emotion is ever conveyed in the shouts, groans, and disjointed prose of everyday life—no-one in Racine's day questioned the assumption that tragedy is a noble genre which must be written in verse of the elevated style. Sometimes Racine may come near to the messiness of life, as when Mathan becomes distraught:

> Avant la fin du jour . . . on verra qui de nous. . .
> Doit. . . Mais sortons, Nabal.
>
> (*Athalie*, III. v)

but always it is what the seventeenth century called 'le beau désordre'; the apparent incoherence does not impair the form. In the example quoted above the alexandrine remains intact and the sentence, though interrupted, is still quite clear. But beauty or clarity of form does not necessarily mean understatement. Often in fact the patterns and rhythms of the alexandrine heighten the effect of direct expression, as in Hippolyte's declaration of love;

> Depuis près de six mois, honteux, désespéré,
> Portant partout le trait dont je suis déchiré,
> Contre vous, contre moi, vainement je m'éprouve:
> Présente, je vous fuis; absente, je vous trouve;
> Dans le fond des forêts votre image me suit;
> La lumière du jour, les ombres de la nuit,
> Tout retrace à mes yeux les charmes que j'évite;
> Tout vous livre à l'envi le rebelle Hippolyte.
>
> (*Phèdre*, II, ii)

Here the emotion is given a form which might almost be described as operatic, but this increases rather than diminishes its power to affect an audience. One of the secrets of Racine's art lies in the mastery with which he varies the manner in which the passions are expressed.

In Act IV, scene 5 of *Andromaque* the Greek princess Hermione confronts Pyrrhus, the king of Epirus, who has just deserted her for his captive Andromaque, provoking her to plot his assassination. It is amply clear when the scene opens what this confrontation means to her. She does not need to say anything for us to feel how his words wound her. But at first her reply remains calm on the surface; she preserves her dignity and her true emotions are only apparent in the ferocity of her irony, which is on the verge of hysteria as she accuses him:

> Vous veniez de mon front observer la pâleur,
> Pour aller dans ses bras rire de ma douleur.

Pyrrhus is eager to keep the conversation to the formal tone which she has adopted; deliberately misunderstanding her, he wounds her unforgivably:

> Rien ne vous engageait à m'aimer en effet.

This is too much for her. The dignified mask drops and with passionate *tutoiement* she breaks out in breathless enumeration of the proofs of her love. Only after twelve lines does she regain control and return to the formal *vous* and the measured rhythms of her earlier speech—but again, as his eyes look momentarily away in search of Andromaque, the rhythm changes and the *tu* reappears in a fierce cry:

> Vous ne répondez point? Perfide, je le voi,
> Tu comptes les moments que tu perds avec moi.

Her speech gathers momentum in a series of imperatives until she sweeps off with the violent threat:

> Va, cours. Mais crains encor d'y trouver Hermione.

In this scene, which makes its impact through the communication to the audience of Hermione's love, hate, and wounded pride, these emotions are in turn half-concealed and violently expressed. It is perhaps more usual for such shifts to occur from one scene to another. Here the typical pattern is that a monologue or a speech to a *confident* openly expresses the passions of a character who subsequently attempts to conceal them and preserve the appearances of polite, rational conversation.

In Act III, scene 4 of *Mithridate* the ageing king has been left alone to brood on the accusation that his favourite son Xipharès is his rival for the love of Monime. His short soliloquy is characteristic of Racine's technique of monologue—in these plays people are left alone not to sing or philosophize but to wrestle with their personal problems. As I have said, Racine resorts less than many of his contemporaries to keeping his audience guessing at the outcome of the plot; instead we are made to participate in the uncertainty, irresolution, and alternating hopes and fears of the *characters*. It is this which makes Racine's monologues so intensely dramatic.

Thus Mithridate is no sooner alone than he drops the public mask of the trusting father and noble king, and the somewhat pompous language that goes with it. Now there are none of the formal periods built of several clauses, each of which is an alexandrine; instead the alexandrine is broken and insistent questions and exclamations give open, though still somewhat stylized, expression to Mithridate's real emotions:

> Je ne le croirai point? Vain espoir qui me flatte!
> Tu ne le crois que trop, malheureux Mithridate.
> Xipharès mon rival? et d'accord avec lui
> La Reine aurait osé me tromper aujourd'hui?

The monologue progresses in sudden jumps with changes of direction and interruptions in the logical flow as Mithridate searches desperately for a way out:

> Non, ne l'en croyons point. Et sans trop nous presser,
> Voyons, examinons. Mais par où commencer?
> Qui m'en éclaircira? Quels témoins? Quel indice?
> Le ciel en ce moment m'inspire un artifice.
> Qu'on appelle la Reine. Oui, sans aller plus loin,
> Je veux l'ouir.

Here again one notices the striking use of short sentences to break up the potentially chanting rhythm of the alexandrine. This is the

sort of scene in which the audience is put directly in touch with the
feelings of the characters on stage.

It is followed, as is usually the case in Racine, by a scene where
emotion is betrayed rather than deliberately expressed. Mithridate,
whose reputation is largely built on cunning, attempts to discover
Monime's real feelings, which she is anxious to conceal. From the
preceding monologue and previous scenes we know perfectly well
what the protagonists feel and we are prepared to catch the slightest
hint of these feelings; as they converse, at first in polite and formal
language, we watch with fascination for one of them to crack. In
particular we notice the contrast between the insincere and beautiful
shape of Mithridate's first words:

> Enfin j'ouvre les yeux, et je me fais justice.
> C'est faire à vos beautés un triste sacrifice,
> Que de vous présenter, Madame, avec ma foi,
> Tout l'âge et le malheur que je traîne avec moi.

and the barely concealed fury of his last lines:

> Non, Madame, il suffit. Je vais vous l'envoyer.
> Allez. Le temps est cher. Il le faut employer.
> Je vois qu'à m'obéir vous êtes disposée.
> Je suis content.

A similar but more rapid change is seen in Monime when she has
been lured into revealing her hidden love for Xipharès and suddenly
sees Mithridate's expression change:

> Si le sort ne m'eût donnée à vous,
> Mon bonheur dépendait de l'avoir pour époux.
> Avant que votre amour m'eût envoyé ce gage,
> Nous nous aimions. . . . Seigneur, vous changez de visage.

It is reported that Racine taught the actress La Champmeslé to
mark Monime's alarm by raising her voice an octave on 'Seigneur'.

In a scene of this sort much of the audience's emotion is due to
the confrontation of characters on stage. A large proportion of
Racine's scenes are scenes of debate and conflict. In this, of course,
Racine does not depart from the normal pattern of his time; in
Pierre Corneille's theatre, for instance, most of the excitement comes

from the splendid verbal battles. But, without making any excessive distinctions, it is clear that the nature of the verbal battles differs in these two playwrights. Whereas a scene such as that between Flaminius and Laodice (*Nicomède*, III. ii) is a debate in which we admire the aggressive eloquence of the debaters, in scenes such as that between Agrippine and Néron (*Britannicus*, IV. ii) our attention goes beyond the excellent debate to what it reveals of the relation between mother and son, their ability to dominate or wound one another. As Néron coolly insults his mother:

> Mais si vous ne régnez, vous vous plaignez toujours

one realizes that this emancipation of the son marks a critical stage in the life-and-death struggle of these two monsters. It is this, rather than dazzling eloquence, which makes Racinian dialogue so gripping.

The same assault on the audience's emotions which we have seen in the expression of the passions can be seen too in the ordering of the Racinian play as a whole. Unity of action, strictly interpreted, ensures that nothing distracts the audience's attention from the tragic situation: 'les plus belles scènes sont en danger d'ennuyer, du moment qu'on les peut séparer de l'action, et qu'elles l'interrompent au lieu de la conduire vers la fin' (preface to *Mithridate*). The plays do not depend for effect on numerous exciting events, but there are just enough changes of fortune (usually arising naturally from the characters rather than coming in from outside) to keep the audience's feelings constantly engaged. The alternation of scenes of polite dispute, solitary deliberation, violent conflict, and rapid action prevents the monotony which might come from too great a concentration on a single action acted out among three or four people. And usually the aim is that the audience's emotions should grow more intense as the play proceeds:

> Que le trouble, toujours croissant de scène en scène,
> A son comble arrivé se débrouille sans peine.
>
> (Boileau, *Art poétique*, iii)

Bérénice, for instance, starts in a low key with the minor character Antiochus, through whom most of the necessary (and quite leisurely) exposition of past events is done. Nevertheless we are put in touch with his feelings from the second scene onwards and these feelings are given moving if tranquil expression in his confession of love in Act I, scene 4. But when he is gone and Bérénice takes the centre of the stage, the emotional pitch rises with the vivid evocation of her adoration of Titus. The other main character, Titus, has been kept in reserve for the beginning of Act II—this was standard practice in the seventeenth century. Again the act begins in a low key, but we move rapidly from Titus's public face to his private feelings. Then Bérénice enters and painful confrontation takes the place of heroic deliberation. Titus comes near to breaking down—his incoherence is the most powerful indication so far of his emotion:

TITUS

Non, Madame. Jamais, puisqu'il faut vous parler,
Mon cœur de plus de feux ne se sentit brûler.
Mais. . .

BÉRÉNICE

Achevez.

TITUS

Hélas!

BÉRÉNICE

Parlez.

TITUS

Rome. . . L'Empire. . .

BÉRÉNICE

Hé bien?

TITUS

Sortons, Paulin: je ne lui puis rien dire.

(II. iv)

The act ends, like the two subsequent ones, on a note of questioning which heightens the audience's attention and anxiety.

The following acts show a similar pattern of build-up to a key scene of confrontation, and in each act the tension and the passion are greater than in the previous one. Possibly there is a certain drop in intensity after the great scene between Titus and Bérénice (Act

IV, scene 5); certainly nothing thereafter matches the passionate eloquence of this scene, but the audience is involved in the tension of the search for a *dénouement* and Racine is right to say that the heroic and painful ending 'renouvelle assez bien dans le cœur des spectateurs l'émotion que le reste y avait pu exciter'.

All I have said so far points to a Racine setting out to stir his audience's emotions with a vigorous but simple action played out by characters whose passions are realistically expressed. This is the 'psychological drama' side to Racine and it has in the past (though less so in recent years) received its fair share of admiration. However, the most rapid reading of a Racine play reveals that there is a great deal here besides psychological drama, a great deal which might well be condemned if psychological drama were Racine's only aim. One thinks of passages such as the 'récit de Théramène' in *Phèdre*, criticized by Fénelon as undramatic in its ornate splendour. Compared with contemporary dramatists (Quinault, Pradon, Thomas Corneille, Boyer) Racine is notable for his dynamic presentation of character. But as one looks back three centuries and compares Racine's tragedies with the sort of realistic play which has been written since his day, it is obvious that the movement and the passion which I have examined are balanced by a more static decorative or solemn element.

At its simplest this is something which Racine shares with all his contemporaries. For all tragedians of his time tragedy was not only a dramatic presentation of action and character, it was also a piece of fine writing, a poem. This double face of the play is shown in the term normally given to it, 'poème dramatique', and is clearly expressed in *La Pratique du théâtre* (1657) of the Abbé d'Aubignac. D'Aubignac, while giving great weight to *vraisemblance* ('tout ce qui paraît affecté en faveur des spectateurs est vicieux'), is unable to ignore the importance of the poem aspect of plays. Thus he expounds the compromise between passion and beauty: 'par l'ordre des choses qui se disent, on réforme ce que la Nature a de défectueux en ses mouvements; et, par la variété sensible des figures, on garde une ressemblance du désordre de la Nature.' Similarly, in the preface to *Bérénice*, alongside 'la violence des passions', Racine speaks of the need for 'la beauté des sentiments' and 'l'élégance de l'expression'.

Alexandre le Grand is perhaps the play of Racine's in which this elegance is most apparent. From the first scene of the play we find the Indian prince Taxile talking to his sister in this way:

> Vous pouvez, sans rougir du pouvoir de vos charmes,
> Forcer ce grand guerrier à vous rendre les armes;
> Et sans que votre cœur doive s'en alarmer,
> Le vainqueur de l'Euphrate a pu vous désarmer.
>
> (I. i)

Now, although it might be possible to see this as a fairly realistic piece of persuasive talking, it is evident that a great deal is 'affecté en faveur des spectateurs'. In the first place the rhythm of the verse has a somewhat banal nobility about it; this sort of quatrain linked by an 'et' at the beginning of the third line is to be found everywhere in the tragedy of the period. Then there is the ingenious play on the traditional metaphor of the war of love; in a conceit typical of this play the conquering warrior is in his turn conquered by love. And finally there are the elegant periphrases, 'ce grand guerrier' and 'Le vainqueur de l'Euphrate'. These contribute to the glorification of the godlike Alexandre which dominates the play. Very much in the manner of Quinault, Racine not only conforms to the models of worldly elegance of speech, but also plays his part in the deification of Louis XIV and contributes to the myth of the hero who is perfect in love and war.

In Racine's subsequent plays the elegance persists, though generally in a subdued form, but the glossy world view which it had supported in *Alexandre* is reversed. Heroes and heroines are rarely paragons of perfection and the world they live in does not allow the easy victories of *Alexandre*. So the elegance becomes a mask, concealing where possible the realities of violent passion and mutual destruction. *Mithridate* is perhaps the play nearest to *Alexandre* in its elegance of language and its vision of humanity, but even here, as we have seen, the formal beauty of Mithridate's speech in Act III, scene 5 is simply a trick to deceive Monime. This is the world of the outwardly splendid and inwardly immoral and unhappy court

described for us by La Bruyère in *Les Caractères* ('De la Cour').
The elegance is the gilt frame to a cruel Goya portrait.

But by the static element in Racine's tragedies I do not mean
simply this surface elegance which he shares to a large extent with
his contemporaries. I mean also the way in which, in these dramas of
movement and passion, we are kept constantly aware of the total
shape and perhaps also the significance of the action. We are inside
it, yet we can see it from a distance, in its wider context. Often this
happens in isolated lines which create a kind of verbal tableau effect.
Thus someone may refer to himself in the third person; from the
beginning of *Andromaque* we are presented with the traditional
friendship of Orestes and Pylades as Oreste says:

> Qui 'leût dit, qu'un rivage à mes yeux si funeste
> Présenterait d'abord Pylade aux yeux d'Oreste?
>
> (I. i)

Or else a line in apposition, almost in parentheses, will give a
memorable definition of a character's situation; in the first few lines
of *Iphigénie* Agamemnon's servant Arcas reminds him in a typically
Racinian apposition that he is 'Roi, père, époux heureux, fils du
puissant Atrée' (I. i). These words take their place in the attempts of
Arcas to find out what is worrying Agamemnon, but for the audience
they may stand slightly apart and remind us of Agamemnon's
unalterable situation. He is the King and the Father, normally two
enviable roles, but now imposing on him the unbearable task of
ordering his daughter's sacrifice for the good of the community.
More than this, he belongs to the bloody line of Atreus—his wife
will bring this home to him later in the play:

> Vous ne démentez point une race funeste.
> Oui, vous êtes le sang d'Atrée et de Thyeste.
> Bourreau de votre fille, il ne vous reste enfin
> Que d'en faire à sa mère un horrible festin.
>
> (IV. iv)

And finally he is an 'époux heureux', an ironic hint to a knowledgeable audience of his future fate—to be murdered by his wife and her
lover.

In this and other such lines Racine evokes a vast expanse of space and time surrounding and influencing the apparently limited dramatic world governed by the unities; in *Iphigénie* it is the past history of Agamemnon's family, Greece, the seas, Troy, the future deaths of Achilles and Agamemnon and even the young avenger Orestes, still a babe-in-arms. And ruling over this world we dimly perceive the cruel gods. Although Agamemnon is 'Du sang de Jupiter issu de tous côtés (I. i), he is forced to admit—in another line which stands out—that 'Les Dieux depuis un temps me sont cruels et sourds' (II. ii). All these references combine to give the characters an almost statuesque grandeur which modifies our perception of them as individuals racked by passion—and thus changes the nature of our emotional response. Racine was fully conscious of the advantages he got from using well-known figures from history or legend—in the preface to *Phèdre* he talks of 'les ornements de la fable, qui fournit extrêmement à la poésie'. And when in *Bajazet* he takes a subject which has not the associations of an ancient story, he attempts to compensate for this disadvantage by constant allusions to the stifling atmosphere of the Sultan's palace, the ever-present menace of the absent Sultan, and the past history of the Ottoman empire. He hopes that the exotic local colour will compensate for the lack of historical distance since (as he says in his preface) 'les personnages tragiques doivent être regardés d'un autre œil que nous ne regardons d'ordinaire les personnages que nous avons vus de si près. On peut dire que le respect que l'on a pour les héros augmente à mesure qu'ils s'éloignent de nous.' Although they must be real to us, the heroes and heroines of tragedy must not be too familiar.

Our participation in the emotions and conflicts of the characters on stage is tempered not only by their heroic stature, but also by our knowledge of their fate. Except in *Bajazet*, we are witnessing the re-enactment of great actions that have long ago been recorded and fixed for all time, the death-struggle of the sons of Oedipus, the murder of Pyrrhus, the murder of Britannicus, the separation of Titus and Bérénice, the death of Mithridates, the sacrifice of Iphigenia, the deaths of Hippolytus and Phaedra. Racine may reinterpret these old stories, may even alter them in part (for example, by having Hermione die at the end of *Andromaque*), but only in *Iphigénie*, with the invention of the 'heureux personnage d'Ériphile' to rescue Iphigénie, does he radically change the basic action. Not that the other tragedies all end in disaster for all those involved. Sometimes, indeed, victims are snatched from the jaws of catastrophe; Monime in *Mithridate* is the most flagrant example. But more usually, while we may partly share the uncertainty of the characters and their hopes that success, happiness, or escape may still be possible, we are half-conscious all the time that there can be only one outcome.

So too are the victims—eventually. The characteristic Racinian pattern is that of *Oedipus the King*, where the characters' ignorance or self-deception gives way to blinding recognition of the truth. It is the gap between our and their recognition of what comes to be seen as their destiny that provides the scope for the dramatic irony which is so powerful an element in Racine's tragedies; one of the most striking examples of this is the scene in *Bajazet* (v. vi) where Atalide is still pleading for her lover's life when we know that he has been sent to his death. Again and again this theme of self-deception appears:

ORESTE. Je me trompais moi-même.   (*Andromaque*, I. i)

HERMIONE. Je crains de me connaître en l'état où je suis.

    (*Andromaque*, II. i)

BÉRÉNICE. Hélas! pour me tromper je fais ce que je puis.

    (*Bérénice*, III. iii)

TITUS. Mon cœur se gardait bien d'aller dans l'avenir
    Chercher ce qui pouvait un jour nous désunir.

    (*Bérénice*, IV. v)

This life-loving blindness makes possible the hope and the action on which the drama depends, but all these actions are played out against a backcloth of tragic vision. Abandoning illusions, Titus has attained this vision of his destiny when he solemnly announces to Bérénice: 'Mais il ne s'agit plus de vivre, il faut régner' (IV. v). Eventually Bérénice joins him in his recognition of the inevitable and with a supreme tableau effect they take up their positions for eternity:

Adieu: servons tous trois d'exemple à l'univers
De l'amour la plus tendre et la plus malheureuse
Dont il puisse garder l'histoire douloureuse.

(v. vii)

Sooner or later there is nothing left to fight for; the victims have died, the killers have killed or been killed, the ritual has been accomplished. Out of the dramatic to and fro of emotion and action has emerged the final tragic pattern, a pattern which now seems inevitable and may perhaps even be seen as willed by some supernatural force.

In this respect it has often been noted that there is a certain evolution in Racine's tragedies. Of the two elements, the dramatic and the ritual, which I have somewhat artificially separated, the first seems to predominate in most of the early tragedies—in these plays our attention is focused above all on the immediate actions and passions of the very human protagonists. But after *Mithridate* the solemn ritual element gains in force. It asserts itself above all in *Phèdre*, which can certainly not be played simply as psychological drama. If we compare this play with (say) *Britannicus*, we notice a rather greater solemnity of language and a much increased sphere of reference. In particular the action is permeated with the presence of the gods, Venus, Neptune, Minos, the Sun—or at least there is constant reference by those on stage to their all-powerful will. So, superimposed on the wayward movement of emotion and the apparent changes of circumstances which spring from Thésée's reported death and unexpected return, we feel—and Phèdre feels—the presence of a divine will which can make all human endeavour futile: 'Minos juge aux enfers tous les pâles humains' (IV. vi).

The play may begin with Hippolyte's hope of escape, but from her first to her last appearance Phèdre knows that she is doomed. In her initial dialogue with Œnone we can hear clearly the confrontation of the dramatic and the ritual; to Œnone's insistent questioning she replies with a solemn invocation:

Noble et brillant auteur d'une triste famille,
Toi, dont ma mère osait se vanter d'être fille,
Qui peut-être rougis du trouble où tu me vois,
Soleil, je te viens voir pour la dernière fois.

(I. iii)

Against her better judgement she allows Œnone to persuade her to live and to act, but she can never really hope; constantly her thoughts return to her guilt and the anger of the gods. And it is this awareness of tragic destiny which gives her the great stature of a sacrificial victim, setting her above the level of Hippolyte, Aricie, and Thésée, whose themes are escape, lawful love, and enterprising activity. We hope with them and fear for them, but all our hopes and fears and agitations are finally subordinate to the vision which we share with Phèdre.

So in *Phèdre* the ritual element is strong. But even so, Racine has not openly announced the action of his play at the beginning (as Euripides does in his version of the story). Nor are these gods in whom we or a seventeenth-century audience could fully believe— they are perhaps just 'les ornements de la fable'. Their recurring names cannot reduce the dramatic elements of the play to insignificance. In fact in *Phèdre* the balance is marvellously kept between psychological drama and ritual tragedy. It is only in the religious plays, *Esther* and *Athalie*, that the dramatic is submerged by the ritual, particularly in *Esther*. In *Athalie* Racine generates strong emotions with his fairly sympathetic treatment of the wicked queen and his skilful handling of the conspiracy. As a human drama of this sort *Athalie* was much admired in the eighteenth century. But this human drama is constantly seen as controlled by a god, who cannot now be considered as a mythological ornament since he is, in Racine's view, the true God, in whose providential plans the audience must rejoice. In particular the lengthy choruses between the acts introduce a note of oratorio which relegates the elements of psychological drama to second place.

For the most part, however, the particular quality of Racine's tragedies lies in the combination of the two elements I have spoken of, the dynamic and the static, the dramatic and the ritual. It is perhaps this combination which makes the plays so difficult to stage today, since producers and actors may be tempted into either an exaggeratedly psychological or a monotonously liturgical version, or perhaps a haphazard mixture of the two. At all events the emotion which Racine was so bent on producing in his audience springs not simply from 'la violence des passions' which I examined in the first part of this chapter. Racine came nearer to defining it when he spoke (again in the preface to *Bérénice*) of 'cette tristesse majestueuse qui fait tout le plaisir de la tragédie'. Here, however, the accent seems to be too heavily on the static element. Bringing the two together I should say that the emotion aroused by Racine's tragedies is essentially a pleasurable combination of excitement and awe.

Finally, to return to the terms used at the beginning of this chapter, one may ask what aim of instruction or persuasion (if any) Racine serves by moving and pleasing his spectators in this way. To a twentieth-century audience this may seem a rather pointless question, but it is one which worried people in the seventeenth century. The theatre was under spasmodic fire from strict Christians, who pointed to the corrupting influence of the vivid depiction of such passions as love and ambition (which dominate Racine's plays). Indeed Racine had at the beginning of his theatrical career broken with his former Jansenist schoolmasters of Port-Royal over this issue, when the Jansenist Nicole had described the novelist or the dramatist as 'un empoisonneur public'—with no special reference to Racine. In his vicious reply Racine completely fails to meet the challenge and concentrates on the ridiculous side of the Jansenists' literary ambitions. Subsequently, in his prefaces, he never refers to the moral justification of tragedy. Never, that is, until the preface to *Phèdre*; here, aiming at a reconciliation with Port-Royal, he bravely attempts an orthodox moral interpretation of his play:

Les moindres fautes y sont sévèrement punies. La seule pensée du crime y est regardée avec autant d'horreur que le crime même. Les faiblesses de l'amour y passent pour de vraies faiblesses. Les passions n'y sont présentées aux yeux que pour montrer tout le désordre dont elles sont cause; et le vice y est peint partout avec des couleurs qui en font connaître et haïr la difformité.

Leaving out of consideration *Esther* and *Athalie*, which are clearly designed to edify, can one reasonably see any clear moral position in *Phèdre* and the earlier plays? It is a delicate question and one which has divided critics. Nowhere in these plays is there a character who can be taken as the author's mouthpiece—even to the doubtful extent of a Molière *raisonneur*. There are very few of the maxims which Renaissance dramatists sprinkled freely over their tragedies, and those which there are are simply part of the characters' dialectical armoury. Racine is well hidden and one is tempted to say that he is neutral. Nevertheless, although we are left free to judge as we choose, it seems to me difficult to resist the impression that in such plays as *Britannicus* or *Bajazet* certain actions or qualities—such as deceit or cruelty—are to be seen as evil. No convincing moral is drawn from these plays, but they would tacitly demonstrate to Racine's audience the corruption of the world and in particular that world which is represented by the palace, a place of arbitrary cruelty, boundless egoism, and total untrustworthiness. (They may demonstrate something different to another audience in another age.) These plays (and *Andromaque*) provide a good illustration of the self-destroying fury of the damned as it is seen in *King Lear*:

> If that the heavens do not their visible spirits
> Send quickly down to tame these vile offences,
> It will come,
> Humanity must perforce prey on itself,
> Like monsters of the deep.

And then there are the virtuous, or at any rate the relatively virtuous. Often they too, like Cordelia, are carried away in the destruction of the damned (Hippolyte, Britannicus), or else they may survive (Junie, Aricie), or even conquer (Andromaque, Xipharès, Monime), but whatever happens to them it is clear that Britannicus and Xipharès are morally superior to Néron and Pharnace. I do not think it can be argued that Racine's plays are morally neutral.

Even so, our first reaction to Phèdre is not to judge her character or her actions. It would be absurdly limiting to view Racine's plays— or any tragedy—solely through the categories of right and wrong. Their value is not to be found primarily in the confirmation (or denial) of orthodox moral standards, nor indeed in the conscious or unconscious illustration of any particular vision of the world, but rather in the audience's emotional participation in the imitation of great actions. Of course these imitations probably express certain views of the world—not a single view, however, since it is impossible to find a single explanatory principle which will embrace with equal success *Alexandre* and *Phèdre*, *Bérénice* and *Athalie*. Indeed it is noticeable that successive commentators tend to pick on different plays as the essential Racine and exclude others from an arbitrary canon based on a supposed single world view.

Naturally we all create our own Racine. As a recent critic says, one of Racine's outstanding qualities is the transparency which makes it possible to see so much in him. One can equally well define the subject of *Phèdre* in terms of Jansenist theology and morality, the tragic vision of a certain social group in seventeenth-century France, the Baroque perception of the disorder of the universe, the psychology of the passions, Freudian psychoanalytic theory, or such metaphorical themes as the struggle of light and dark or the hunting out of the monster. All these interpretations are worth having; this is not the place to judge between them or to add another. In any case the precise formulation of the central theme of a given play or of Racine's theatre as a whole is of secondary importance. What really matters is that Racine's art enables us both to experience the passions generated by his tragic action and to contemplate it in its wholeness. Racine was right to stress the emotion, if by emotion we understand both the excitement and the awe; it is this, rather than the presentation of any theme or world view, which gives value to Racine's tragedy.

NOTE

JEAN RACINE, 1639–99, remains elusive as a man, but his career is well known. Born of a bourgeois family in La Ferté-Milon (Aisne), he became an orphan soon afterwards and was brought up by his grandmother and then at various Jansenist schools. After vainly attempting to make a career in the Church, he devoted himself to literature; his plays led him to quarrel with his former Jansenist masters and paved his way to worldly success. In 1673 he became a member of the Académie Française and in 1677, together with his great friend Boileau, official historian to Louis XIV. From then on he devoted himself to his official duties, which brought him ever-increasing royal favour, to his family (he was married in 1677), and to the God of the Jansenists, whose cause he now embraced again.

Works. The essential works are nine tragedies, *La Thébaïde* (1664), *Alexandre le Grand* (1665), *Andromaque* (1667), *Britannicus* (1669), *Bérénice* (1670), *Bajazet* (1672), *Mithridate* (1673), *Iphigénie* (1674), and *Phèdre* (1677); two religious plays, *Esther* (1689) and *Athalie* (1691); and the comedy *Les Plaideurs* (1668). Racine also composed official odes, epigrams, official history, academic discourses, religious poetry (in particular the *Cantiques spirituels* of 1694), religious history (the *Abrégé de l'histoire de Port-Royal*), and an anti-Jansenist pamphlet (*Lettres à l'auteur des Imaginaires*, 1666).

Modern editions. The standard complete edition, now somewhat dated, is that of P. Mesnard in the 'Grands Écrivains de la France' series (2nd edn., 1885, 10 vols.). Many subsequent editions of the plays (for example, the quite satisfactory Garnier edition, 1960) are based on Mesnard. The best edition for most purposes is that of R. Picard (Bibliothèque de la Pléiade, 1950–2, 2 vols.), which has thoughtful notices on individual plays. Editions of the plays by P. Mélèse (1951) and G. Truc (1929–30) reproduce the spelling and punctuation of the 1697 edition, the last complete edition in Racine's lifetime.

Criticism. There is a useful introduction by P. Moreau, *Racine* (2nd edn., 1956). Among the best of much general criticism are E. Vinaver, *Racine et la poésie tragique* (1951), J. C. Lapp, *Aspects of Racinian Tragedy* (1956), J. D. Hubert, *Essai d'exégèse racinienne* (1956), and O. de Mourgues, *Racine* (1967). On Racine's life see *La Carrière de Jean Racine* (2nd edn., 1961) by R. Picard, who has also produced an invaluable collection of contemporary mate. al relating to Racine in his *Corpus Racinianum* (1956, supplement in 1961). Racin 's tragedies have been suggestively related to his age by L. Goldmann, *Le Dieu caché* (1955) and P. Butler, *Classicisme et baroque dans l'œuvre de Racine* (1959). Aspects of Racine's dramatic art are studied by G. May, *Tragédie cornélienne, tragédie racinienne* (1948), J. Scherer, *La Dramaturgie classique en France* (1950), B. Weinberg, *The Art of Jean Racine* (1963), and P. France, *Racine's Rhetoric* (1965). Stimulating chapters on Racine will be found in M. Raymond, *Génies de France* (1942), G. Poulet, *Études sur le temps humain* (1949), and J. Starobinski, *L'Œil vivant* (1961).

12. Towards the Enlightenment

FOR the historian of ideas, the reign of Louis XIV marks the victory of intellectual and artistic orthodoxy. At every point the royal administration supervised the thoughts and taste of the royal subjects. The universities were institutions in which orthodox doctrine in law and theology was taught. The Académie des Sciences, founded by Colbert in 1666, aimed at guiding scientific debate along acceptable lines. Art was controlled from above, much of it under the patronage of Charles Le Brun acting in the name of the King. Finally, the royal palace of Versailles dominated the artistic life of France by the patronage which the Court was able to purvey. It was difficult for any artist to resist being drawn into the machine.

Such is the weight of the official evidence that this state of affairs tends to be accepted as inevitable. The sources used by historians are drawn from administrative archives in which the official view is taken for granted. The reign comes to be associated with the virtues of order and coherence, which in turn were based upon the un-questioning self-confidence of the regime. A more recent interpreta-tion, however, suggests that this confidence was a façade behind which lay anxiety and self-doubt. On this view, eloquently expounded by Paul Hazard, orthodoxy between 1680 and 1715 faced a crisis as severe as it experienced in the nineteenth century under the impact of the ideas of Darwin. Thus the seemingly confident attitudes of Louis XIV's reign were really defensive. Versailles now appears as a rhetorical gesture by a regime which needed reassurance. Perhaps even the Revocation of the Edict of Nantes sprang out of fear. Perhaps also the regime's obsession with intellectual orthodoxy rested upon a need to prevent doubt spreading.

What was happening in France during this period was part of the general European phenomenon in which scientific discovery and new historical methods acted as dissolving agents upon the traditional foundations of Christian belief. At first, it is true, the revolutionary discoveries of Copernicus, Galileo, and Kepler, and the critical historical approaches of the Renaissance, had remarkably little influence in France outside a small coterie of intellectuals. The organization of the Church, backed by the monarchy, slowed down where it did not prevent the dissemination of new ideas. But intellectual ferment first in Holland and then in England presented an increasing challenge during the second half of the century.

The challenge was most obvious in the implications of scientific discovery for Aristotelian philosophy, and hence for orthodox theology. As it existed in France during the seventeenth century, orthodoxy had come to terms with the science of an earlier period. A Christian synthesis was taught in the seminaries and universities in which the Bible and Aristotelian science had been reconciled with extraordinary ingenuity. Christian dogma was defined in Aristotelian terms. The presence of Christ in the Eucharist was defined as 'transubstantiation', a notion which rested upon an Aristotelian distinction between substance and accident. The relationship between soul and body was defined in terms of matter and form, a unity which after death was broken up to be restored at the General Resurrection.

The world of nature was looked at in ways which supported this point of view. Evidence of divine purpose was seen throughout the cosmos. The sun and stars were created for man. The seasons had been created by God for man. The Bible as the source of scientific knowledge, as well as of moral and doctrinal revolution, taught that the world as it now stood had been created for man 4,000 years before. In addition, the divine hand was to be discerned in matters of daily life or of direct human experience. Portents were accepted as a sign of God's displeasure. Comets were regarded as a warning of disaster. It seemed natural and appropriate for God to intervene in the working of the universe which he himself kept in existence.

This synthesis also had social implications. There was a hierarchy in the world which reflected and justified the social hierarchy. From the vegetables and animals up to disembodied intelligences—the angels—stretched a Great Chain of Being. Its elements were not connected by evolution but were distinct and separate creations in themselves. The divine principle of hierarchy was also illustrated in the serried ranks of angels clustered around the throne of the Almighty. The universe was in fact a kingdom on the grandest scale.

The first full-blooded attack on this synthesis of reason and revelation began in 1637 when Descartes published his *Discours de la méthode*, followed up in the 1640s by fuller expositions, including the *Principia Philosophiae*. René Descartes was born in 1596, son of a gentleman in Touraine. As such it was understandable that he should first be educated by the Jesuits and secondly take up a military career. The surprising fact about him was that he should be interested in philosophy, which was normally reserved for clerical academics in the universities. This was one habit among many which he was to change. The layman interested in philosophy was to become much more common, as a result of Descartes's writings.

A man of extreme caution, Descartes had no wish to lay himself open to charges of heresy, though this was one of the risks of taking up philosophy outside the schools. The persecution of Galileo by the ecclesiastical authorities in Italy made him pause, and seems to have been decisive in turning him towards the free atmosphere of Holland, where he lived from 1629 after giving up his military career. The *Discours* was first published in Holland.

The *Discours* in effect was a devastating criticism of the scholastic approach in philosophy (a term, we should remember, which included science as well as ethics and metaphysics). An orthodox philosopher brought up in the scholastic tradition automatically tried to prove his case by referring to traditional authorities, especially Aristotle, Augustine, and Aquinas. He also used a technical vocabulary derived ultimately from Aristotle. Descartes regarded this dependence on tradition as doing a disservice to the cause of truth. Indeed he regarded it as a root cause of the prevailing scepticism in so many circles.

In place of scholasticism, Descartes proposed to substitute a new method of reasoning which, by going back to first principles as he conceived them, would clear the ground for progress. This reasoning hinged upon the use of methodic doubt, but doubt was not an end in itself. It was a means by which the philosopher removed ill-founded conclusions from his path. This method led Descartes to be attacked as a sceptic, but he himself regarded his role as providing an answer to scepticism. He believed that his method could be used by men of average intelligence, and he summed up its principles under four headings which all could understand. This also was in contrast with the technical approach of scholastic logic. He set out the four rules of his method as follows:

Le premier était de ne recevoir jamais aucune chose pour vraie, que je ne la connusse évidemment être telle: c'est-à-dire, d'éviter soigneuse-ment la précipitation et la prévention; et de ne comprendre rien de plus en mes jugements, que ce qui se présenterait si clairement et si distincte-ment à mon esprit, que je n'eusse aucune occasion de le mettre en doute.

Le second, de diviser chacune des difficultés que j'examinerais, en autant de parcelles qu'il se pourrait, et qu'il serait requis pour les mieux résoudre.

Le troisième, de conduire par ordre mes pensées, en commençant par les objets les plus simples et les plus aisés à connaître, pour monter peu à peu, comme par degrés, jusques à la connaissance des plus composés; et supposant même de l'ordre entre ceux qui ne se précèdent point naturelle-ment les uns les autres.

Et le dernier, de faire partout des dénombrements si entiers, et des revues si générales, que je fusse assuré de ne rien omettre.

This in itself was provocative enough, but Descartes went further. He used his method to provide a rival synthesis to Aristotle's. Descartes did away with the Aristotelian notion of spheres moved by higher intelligences and replaced it with a universe in which the planets were moved round by swirling vortices of matter. He also replaced the Aristotelian theory of matter by one in which matter was composed of particles, though he was careful to avoid the term 'atom' because of its association with Lucretius and atheism. The Cartesian universe was in fact a vast machine operating according to mathematical laws. Even animals were machines in this world. Where Aristotle's favourite analogy had been organic (the oak grow-ing from a seed), Descartes adopted the machine.

This approach was revealed most dramatically in Descartes's view of man. The human body, being composed of matter, was a machine, a conclusion which Harvey's discovery of the circulation of the blood was held to substantiate. What saved Cartesian man from being a machine was the fact of thought. A man's thoughts pointed to the existence of a spiritual side in his nature—his soul. Thus Descartes's tag 'Cogito, ergo sum' ('I think, therefore I am') was both an answer to the sceptics and a religious affirmation involving belief in the existence of the soul.

Descartes's idea of God was equally distinctive. In the orthodox universe, divine purposes were constantly in evidence. In the Cartesian world, moving according to mechanical laws, God did not intervene. Hence the traditional proofs for the existence of God had no basis. Instead Descartes turned to a more satisfactory proof, as he thought, in which he argued from the human idea of infinite perfection to the fact of divine existence. In this, as in his theory of methodic doubt, and his proof of the existence of the soul, Descartes saw himself as cutting the ground from underneath the sceptics.

Descartes realized that his views were bound to give rise to debate in conservative quarters, but he did not doubt his own orthodoxy and he expected support from enlightened churchmen. The violent reaction in French orthodox circles surprised and dismayed him. But if it surprised him it need not surprise us. Cartesianism was something more than an academic exercise. Descartes did not frame a political philosophy (unlike Hobbes), but there were anti-hierarchical implications in his mechanistic world view. The structure of hierarchy disappeared to be replaced by a world of *parts*. Moreover, for the Cartesian there was no scope for miracles outside the Scriptures, an outlook which was bound to alarm the French authorities in the heyday of the counter-Reformation. Equally subversive in the eyes of orthodox theologians were the implications of his philosophy for Christian teaching on the Eucharist. Descartes claimed to be able to define the doctrine of the Eucharist adequately in terms of his own philosophy, but this was not good enough for the theologians. In rejecting Aristotelianism, Descartes seemed to them to be rejecting the definitions so painfully arrived at in the Council of Trent.

Thus on social and religious as well as scientific grounds the authorities tried to prevent the spread of Cartesianism. In this they were not alone. In Holland, England, and Scotland, the 'new philosophy' was regarded with hostility by many Protestant theologians. In France, however, the defences of orthodoxy were more formidable still. In particular the Jesuit order, backed by the Crown, was totally committed to the defence of scholasticism in the universities. The order had taken its stand against the new discoveries in Galileo's lifetime and it fought them with the same discipline and vigour which it brought to the campaigns against Jansenism. Indeed, to some eyes, the Cartesians were Jansenists in disguise. The Oratorians, bitter rivals of the Jesuits, came under criticism for their Cartesian sympathies and were forced to dismiss suspect professors from some of their colleges.

The authorities made determined efforts to crush the new philosophy and in certain areas they were successful. In the universities, for example, professors were required to follow the Ancients as against the Moderns, though to some extent compromise textbooks began to be used, in which the old was blended with the new. The informal literary circles of the salons were more difficult to control and it was here, from the 1680s, that the new philosophy became fashionable. The battle of Ancients and Moderns was fought here and won by the Moderns. Eventually the Jesuits admitted defeat and came over to Cartesianism, unfortunately just as Newtonian physics had undermined its scientific basis.

The human instrument by which popularization of the ideas of Descartes took place from the 1680s onwards was Bernard le Bovier de Fontenelle, a member of a *robe* family in Normandy. Fontenelle, nephew of Corneille, was a man of wide interests ranging from opera and drama to philosophy and science. He was not an original mind but, in his ability to communicate the ideas of others to a wider audience, he may be regarded as anticipating the role of the *philosophes* in eighteenth-century France. Like them he was a popularizer, in the sense that he reached beyond the academic field to the salons of the bourgeoisie. His most famous book, *Entretiens sur la pluralité des mondes*, published in 1686, ran into nearly thirty editions before he died, and it also sold well outside France in translation.

Fontenelle's achievement was to raise informally questions which had been debated in a lengthy and technical manner for a century and more. The *Entretiens*, between a cultivated *marquise* and a gentleman, discuss the question whether the planets are inhabited. Superficially a conversational piece in a salon, this raised by implication the uniqueness of Christian revelation, and the infinity of the universe. Fontenelle also accepted as true the Cartesian hypothesis that the world is a machine. Nature was organized on mechanical principles, but the actual machinery was hidden and this had led earlier philosophers into misconception:

Mais ce qui, à l'égard des philosophes, augmente la difficulté, c'est que dans les machines que la nature présente à nos yeux, les cordes sont parfaitement bien cachées, et elles le sont si bien, qu'on a été longtemps à deviner ce qui causait les mouvements de l'univers. Car représentez-vous tous les sages à l'opéra, ces Pythagore, ces Platon, ces Aristote, et tous ces gens dont le nom fait aujourd'hui tant de bruit à nos oreilles; supposons qu'ils voyaient le vol de Phaéton que les vents enlèvent, qu'ils ne pouvaient découvrir les cordes, et qu'ils ne savaient point comment le derrière du théâtre était disposé. L'un d'eux disait: 'C'est une certaine vertu secrète qui enlève Phaéton.' L'autre: 'Phaéton est composé de certains nombres qui le font monter.' L'autre: 'Phaéton a une certaine amitié pour le haut du théâtre; il n'est point à son aise quand il n'y est pas.' L'autre: 'Phaéton n'est pas fait pour voler, mais il aime mieux voler que de laisser le haut du théâtre vide'; et cent autres rêveries que je m'étonne qui n'aient perdu de réputation toute l'antiquité. A la fin, Descartes et quelques autres modernes sont venus, qui ont dit: 'Phaéton monte, parce qu'il est tiré par des cordes, et qu'un poids plus pesant que lui descend.' Ainsi on ne croit plus qu'un corps se remue, s'il n'est tiré ou plutôt poussé par un autre corps; on ne croit plus qu'il monte ou qu'il descende, si ce n'est pas l'effet d'un contre-poids ou d'un ressort; et qui verrait la nature telle qu'elle est ne verrait que le derrière du théâtre de l'opéra.

The conversations stretched over six evenings, in the course of which the *marquise*'s partner tried to disabuse her of the Ptolemaic assumptions in which she had been brought up. The stars, he told her, were not unchanging. They too were subject to the same laws as the rest of the universe. The old distinction between the perfection of the lunar world and the imperfection of the sublunar regions was false and the reasoning of the Ancients on this point, as on so much else, was awry:

Toute cette masse immense de matière qui compose l'univers est dans un mouvement perpétuel, dont aucune de ses parties n'est entièrement exempte, et dès qu'il y a du mouvement quelque part, ne vous y fiez point, il faut qu'il arrive des changements, soit lents, soit prompts, mais toujours dans des temps proportionnés à l'effet. Les anciens étaient plaisants de s'imaginer que les corps célestes étaient de nature à ne changer jamais, parce qu'ils ne les avaient pas encore vu changer. Avaient-ils eu le loisir de s'en assurer par l'expérience? Les anciens étaient jeunes auprès de nous. Si les roses qui ne durent qu'un jour faisaient des histoires, et se laissaient des mémoires les unes aux autres, les premières auraient fait le portrait de leur jardinier d'une certaine façon, et de plus de quinze mille âges de roses, les autres qui l'auraient encore laissé à celles qui les devaient suivre, n'y auraient rien changé. Sur cela elles diraient, 'Nous avons toujours vu le même jardinier, de mémoire de rose on n'a vu que lui, il a toujours été fait comme il est, assurément il ne meurt point comme nous, il ne change seulement pas.' Le raisonnement des roses serait-il bon? Il aurait pourtant plus de fondement que celui que faisaient les anciens sur les corps célestes; et quand même il ne serait arrivé aucun changement dans les cieux jusqu'à aujourd'hui quand ils paraîtraient marquer qu'ils seraient faits pour durer toujours sans aucune altération, je ne les en croirais pas encore, j'attendrais une plus longue expérience. Devons-nous établir notre durée, qui n'est que d'un instant, pour la mesure de quelque autre? Serait-ce à dire que ce qui aurait duré cent mille fois plus que nous, dût toujours durer? On n'est pas si aisément éternel. Il faudrait qu'une chose eût passé bien des âges d'homme mis bout à bout, pour commencer à donner quelque signe d'immortalité.

Fontenelle's *Entretiens* were by no means original. He depended a great deal upon a treatise by the Englishman John Wilkins, who published *Discovery of the New World* in 1638 (it was translated into French in 1656). But Wilkins himself was indebted to Campanella (1568–1639), who in turn owed a great deal to Galileo (1564–1642). Thus the line which Fontenelle represents stretches back beyond Galileo and even as far as Bruno (c. 1550–c.1600) and Nicolas of Cusa. The figure of Cyrano de Bergerac writing in the mid-seventeenth century must also be added to the story. In fact, the success of the book was not due to its originality but to its apparent originality in the France of Louis XIV. It says much for the efficiency of the controls exercised upon intellectual movements in France that Fontenelle's modest treatise should achieve such celebrity. With a certain literary grace he provided a setting for ideas which were commonplace in England and other countries. In this also he resembled the *philosophes* of the eighteenth century.

Where Fontenelle failed to anticipate the Enlightenment was by his refusal to come to terms with the discoveries made by Isaac Newton, published in the *Principia* (1687). Throughout his life Fontenelle remained committed to Cartesian ideas, which he made in effect into the criterion of a new orthodoxy. In 1697 he was appointed permanent secretary of the Académie des Sciences, a post which gave him influence in promoting the Cartesian cause, and it was not until after his death that Newtonian ideas made headway in France—with the publication of Voltaire's *Éléments de la philosophie de Newton* in 1738.

If we take Descartes as representing the scientific challenge to orthodox interpretations of God, man, and nature, we may look upon Spinoza as the historical challenge to orthodox interpretations of history. More accurately, perhaps, we may see Spinoza as applying the Cartesian approach of methodic doubt to areas which were held to be sacred. History to the orthodox mind was divided into sacred and profane. There was an analogy here with the orthodox view of nature. The Bible, with its inspired authorship, was as free from fault as the stellar world of Aristotle. It was in addition an infallible source of knowledge about nature. Spinoza took a more sceptical view of the sacred text, and perhaps it is not too fanciful to see him as the historian's Galileo, applying the telescope to the Scriptural moon and displaying its imperfections to the world.

Baruch de Spinoza (1634–77) was born into a Jewish family in Amsterdam and was brought up in a scholarly Rabbinical atmosphere. Around the age of twenty he faced a religious crisis, was excommunicated by the synagogue, and took refuge with a group of dissenters first in Amsterdam and later at Leiden. He earned his living as a lens-grinder, but his early training enabled him to deal at first hand with problems of biblical scholarship. The first fruit of his work was the *Tractatus Theologico-Politicus*, published anonymously in 1670.

Spinoza's *Tractatus* never achieved the popular appeal of Descartes's *Discours de la méthode*. Nevertheless it had an enormous impact on contemporary thought, often indirectly, thanks to orthodox attempts to refute it. The reaction of the churches was one of horror. The book was banned even in Holland, and its influence in France was confined to clandestine routes. But there can be little doubt that Spinoza was one of the fathers of the Enlightenment. He forged the weapons against orthodox interpretation of the Old Testament which were later popularized by the *philosophes*. Spinoza, like them, advocated toleration and expounded a simplified version of Christianity in which dogmas were left on one side.

Spinoza's most revolutionary contribution was his analysis of the Pentateuch (the first five books of the Bible) attributed without question to Moses by every church authority. By analyzing the text, Spinoza showed that the Pentateuch was a compilation made many centuries after the death of Moses. He points out, for example, that certain place-names mentioned in Genesis were not styled by the names they had in Moses' lifetime but by others which they were given subsequently. And he argues that Moses merely wrote certain short accounts which were incorporated by the compiler within his version of the Pentateuch, the general framework of which was post-Mosaic. Spinoza wrote: 'It is thus clearer than the sun at noonday that the Pentateuch was not written by Moses but by someone who lived later than Moses', and he suggested that the only individual mentioned in the Bible who could have been the compiler was Ezra.

Spinoza's discussion of prophecies and miracles was equally radical in its implications. He looked upon prophets as men 'endowed with unusually vivid imaginations and not with unusually perfect minds'. It followed that the prophets should not be taken literally, since they 'perceived nearly everything in parables and allegories, and clothed spiritual truths in bodily forms, for such is the usual power of imagination'. What certitude they possessed was moral, not mathematical.

The nature and style of prophecy varied according to the personality of the individual prophet: 'God had no particular style in speaking, but, according to the learning and capacity of the prophet, is cultivated, compressed, severe, untutored, prolix or obscure.'

Some of the prophets were ignorant and could make mistakes: 'For instance, nothing is more clear in the Bible than that Joshua, and perhaps also the author who wrote his history, thought that the sun revolves round the earth, and that the earth is fixed, and further that the sun at a certain period remained still.' Spinoza goes on to question the accuracy of knowledge of Solomon, Noah, Abraham, Jacob, Ezekiel, Samuel, Jeremiah, and even Adam whom the Church thought was a perfect man. After this list few, if any, prophets were exempt from the charge of ignorance.

On miracles, Spinoza put the unusual argument that if they existed they were likely to lead to atheism. In his view we are led to knowledge of the existence and providence of God by contemplating the unchanging order of nature. Hence: 'Miracles in the sense of events contrary to the laws of nature, so far from demonstrating the existence of God, would, on the contrary, lead us to doubt it, where otherwise we might have been absolutely certain of it, as knowing that nature follows a fixed and unmoveable order.' Moreover, many phenomena, which can easily be explained as natural, were considered to be miraculous by the unlearned.

As the *Tractatus* goes on, Spinoza makes clear that he regards the biblical text as being both corrupt and full of errors of fact. Hence what is essential for the student of the Bible is knowledge of Hebrew and the ability to understand the style in which the Scriptures were written. 'We are at work', Spinoza wrote, 'not on the truth of the passage, but solely on its meaning.' Despite this the main message of the Bible remains. It is a message of utter simplicity which the scholars have distorted into a web of false subtleties. The Bible teaches the doctrine of true religion with piety and obedience as its over-all lesson. In contrast, the object of human reason is to reach truth and wisdom. Between reason and revelation there is no contact, philosophy and theology do not mix. Hence Spinoza denounces the very notion of scholasticism: 'The sole object of such commentators seems to be to extort from Scriptures confirmation of Aristotelian quibbles and their own inventions, a proceeding which I regard as the acme of absurdity.'

The revolutionary character of the *Tractatus* may be seen clearly
if we contrast it with the book which was in effect the classic statement of the orthodox point of view, Bossuet's *Discours sur l'histoire
universelle*. Bossuet, who acted as tutor to the Dauphin, originally
wrote the *Discours* for the benefit of his pupil, but it was published
in 1681 and reprinted before Bossuet's death in 1704. In it, he
attempted to sketch the history of the human race, leading up,
naturally, to the establishment of the French monarchy.

Bossuet made the orthodox assumption that the Bible is the
source of all truth:

> Quel témoignage n'est-ce pas de sa vérité, de voir que dans les temps
> où les histoires profanes n'ont à nous conter que des fables, ou tout au
> plus des faits confus et à demi oubliés, l'Écriture, c'est-à-dire, sans
> contestation, le plus ancien livre qui soit au monde, nous ramène par tant
> d'événements précis, et par la suite même des choses, à leur véritable
> principe, c'est-à-dire à Dieu qui a tout fait; et nous marque si distincte-
> ment la création de l'univers, celle de l'homme en particulier, le bonheur
> de son premier état, les causes de ses misères et de ses faiblesses, la
> corruption du monde et le déluge, l'origine des arts et celle des nations,
> la distribution des terres, enfin la propagation du genre humain, et
> d'autres faits de même importance, dont les histoires humaines ne parlent
> qu'en confusion, et nous obligent à chercher ailleurs les sources certaines.

His hero was Moses. He tells us that Moses was the author of the
Scriptures: 'Ce grand homme, instruit par tous ces moyens, et
élevé au-dessus par le Saint-Esprit, a écrit les œuvres de Dieu avec
une exactitude et une simplicité qui attire la croyance et l'admiration,
non pas à lui, mais à Dieu même.'

Finally God was the real author of the Scriptures which were
inspired by him and preserved in textual purity over the ages:

> C'est ainsi que s'est formé le corps des Écritures saintes, tant de
> l'Ancien que du Nouveau Testament; Écritures qu'on a regardées, dès
> leur origine, comme véritables en tout, comme données de Dieu même,
> et qu'on a aussi conservées avec tant de religion, qu'on n'a pas cru
> pouvoir sans impiété y altérer une seule lettre.

If Spinoza was correct, however, the magnificent structure so
eloquently constructed by Bossuet had no real foundation. Bossuet

rested his case upon tradition and the constant teaching of the Church throughout the centuries. Spinoza in contrast returned to the text, backed by a knowledge of Hebrew which Bossuet did not possess. Here in essence was the conflict between the Ancients and Moderns, with each side using different criteria for truth. In Spinoza's intellectual world, the authority of Augustine counted for nothing. What mattered was the evidence available, and here Spinoza's knowledge of the scriptural text was superior to that of Bossuet or indeed of any of the Church Fathers.

When seen against the background of Spinoza's criticisms, Bossuet's confidence seems more apparent than real. The *Discours sur l'histoire universelle* appears not as an expression of sublime self-confidence but as a piece of polemic on a cosmic scale, with Bossuet making as much use as possible of his rhetoric in order to silence the nagging doubts which Spinoza had created. He was indeed aware of the criticisms which were being made of the scriptural texts, and he added a special chapter in later editions in order to strengthen his case against them.

Bossuet's anxiety in the face of textual analysis may also be seen in his denunciation of Richard Simon, in 1678. Simon, son of a Dieppe blacksmith and a member of the French Oratory, published his *Histoire critique du Vieux Testament* in 1678, which he intended as an orthodox response to Spinoza's *Tractatus*. Simon accepted Spinoza's methods and some of his conclusions, even to the notion that the Scriptures were a late compilation, but he chose to rest his defence on the ground that the Scriptures were those writings which the Synagogue regarded as sacred. For Bossuet, this appeared to be throwing out the baby with the bathwater. It was to answer Simon as much as Spinoza that he published his *Histoire universelle*. Orthodoxy by the 1670s was facing an intellectual crisis, which in effect marks the beginning of the Enlightenment.

But Simon was a scholar writing for scholars, and if we seek a man who popularized Spinoza's ideas in the way Fontenelle did those of Descartes, we shall look in vain. Yet in Pierre Bayle Spinoza found a mouthpiece of his views. Bayle's *Dictionnaire critique et historique* was a massive work, too massive to be able to appeal to the same audience as Fontenelle's *Entretiens*. But it was influential, it was reprinted, and it was translated. And it was to Bayle among others that the *philosophes* turned as a model to follow.

Bayle was a former professor at the Protestant academy of Sedan, who went into exile in Holland when the academy was closed in 1681. He published his *Dictionnaire* in 1697 as an attack upon the intolerance of both Louis XIV and his own opponents within the Calvinist camp, notably Pierre Jurieu (1637–1713), a former colleague at Sedan.

Bayle recalls Spinoza and anticipates one aspect of Enlightenment thought in his advocacy of religious toleration, an attitude which shows him moving in the same direction as his fellow-exile John Locke (Locke, like Bayle, took refuge in Holland during the 1680s). Bayle was also clearly influenced by Spinoza's biblical scholarship. He may have criticized Spinoza when he wrote an article on him for the *Dictionnaire*, but the influence of Spinoza is manifest in many of the articles Bayle wrote on Biblical subjects. In his article on 'David', for example, Bayle made critical comments which were anathema to both the Catholic Bossuet and the Calvinist. Jurieu. He insinuated that the biblical text was so obviously corrupt that it would have been edited had it been a secular treatise. He criticized David's political outlook in an ironical vein, he attacked his barbarous treatment of captives, and he drew attention to his immorality. What made this all the more irritating for the orthodox was Bayle's show of scholarship. Bayle was scrupulous in embedding his most damaging remarks in learned footnotes.

In all this, Bayle sounds a note which we recognize as belonging to the Enlightenment. Where he differed from that movement was in the ambiguity of his general attitudes. It is not absolutely clear where Bayle stands on religion. Modern historians of ideas disagree fundamentally about the depth of his scepticism, a division which may perhaps be due to a lack of decision in Bayle's own mind—a lack of decision which is very marked in his attitude towards Spinoza. Perhaps we should conclude by saying that Bayle forged the weapons, but left it to the Enlightenment to use them.

With Fontenelle and Bayle, and behind them the massive figures of Descartes and Spinoza, the eighteenth century may be said to have begun. It is no illusion to see them as early *philosophes*. On the other hand, we must not see them as typical of French thought around 1700. Over the intellectual field as a whole, the forces of orthodoxy were still dominant. By looking ahead to the Enlightenment, we have in fact done less than justice to the contemporaries of Fontenelle and Bayle, to Malebranche, for example, the Oratorian theologian who reconciled Cartesian philosophy and Christian doctrine, or Mabillon, the Benedictine monk, who applied historical criticism as effectively as Spinoza, albeit in less sensitive areas. Religious issues were overwhelmingly important still—Jansenism was very much a living issue and was entering a second phase in which Crown and Papacy were to become embroiled deeply with the forces of Gallicanism. When all is said, Bossuet's thought was still typical.

It was not until the mid eighteenth century that Voltaire picked on him as a figure of fun. One of the articles in the *Dictionnaire philosophique* (entitled 'Gloire') described the reactions of a Chinese merchant to discovering Bossuet's *Histoire universelle* in a Dutch bookshop. The Chinaman expected much of the book to be taken up with Chinese history, stretching over several millennia, and he was surprised to learn that it dealt largely with the history of an obscure tribe—the Jewish people—with some mention of the Egyptians, the Greeks, and the Romans. The whole purpose of this article is to make fun of the provincialism of Bossuet's self-styled 'universal' approach, and it may stand as an example of the way in which 'the eighteenth century' made its judgement on 'the seventeenth century'. By the 1750s the grandeur of fifty years before had become dated. To Voltaire and the *philosophes*, the magnificent orthodoxy of Bossuet appeared merely narrow-minded prejudice. To enlightened ears, the Baroque organ now sounded like a tin whistle.

NOTE

DESCARTES, RENÉ, 1596–1650, was a philosopher and mathematician. As a young man (1617–28) he fought as a soldier. From 1629 he lived mostly in Holland. In 1649 at the invitation of Queen Christina he visited Sweden where he died of pneumonia in 1650. His *Discours de la méthode* (1637) served as a preface for three scientific works on optics, meteors, and geometry published at the same time. In 1641 he published *Méditations métaphysiques* and in 1644 *Principia Philosophiae* in which he outlined a scientific synthesis.

BARUCH DE SPINOZA, 1632–77, was the son of a Jewish merchant in Amsterdam. He received a rabbinical education but later became Cartesian in outlook. In 1670 he published the *Tractatus Theologico-Politicus* and in 1677 the *Ethics* (probably written earlier).

RICHARD SIMON, 1638–1712, entered the Oratorians in 1662 and was ordained as a priest in 1670. He was fascinated by biblical exegesis to which he devoted his life. In 1678 he published *Histoire critique du Vieux Testament* and in 1689 *Histoire critique du Nouveau Testament*. He was forced to retire into private life by Bossuet in 1678.

CHARLES LE BRUN, 1619–90, was born in Paris and studied in Rome. For nearly forty years (1647–83) he exercised a dominating influence over French painting. He was first director of the Gobelins Tapestry works (1662) and from 1668–83 Louis XIV employed him to supervise the decoration of Versailles.

PIERRE BAYLE, 1647–1706, was born at Foix in the Languedoc. After a Jesuit education which led him to turn Catholic for a time, he went to Geneva where he studied Cartesianism. In 1675 he was professor at Sedan, then from 1681 at Rotterdam. In 1684 he started a new literary periodical, *Nouvelles de la République des Lettres*. In 1693 he was dismissed from his post as a result of pressure from Jurieu, his fellow-exile, and from then on devoted his time to editing his *Dictionnaire historique et critique* (1696) which was attacked by Jurieu for the article on 'David'.

PIERRE JURIEU, 1637–1713, was born at Blois, the son of a minister. He taught theology at Sedan and later (1672) became professor of Hebrew there. In 1681, when the academy at Sedan was closed, he moved to Rotterdam. In 1686 he published *L'Accomplissement des prophètes* predicting the victory of Protestantism three years later.

BERNARD LE BOVIER DE FONTENELLE, 1657–1757, in the great debate of Ancients and Moderns, sided with the Moderns and came under attack from La Bruyère and other writers. In 1697 he was made secretary of the Académie des Sciences. He died in his hundredth year after having outlived Montesquieu (1689–1755).

Further Reading. Modern interpretative work for the later years of Louis XIV's reign begins with Paul Hazard, *La Crise de la conscience européenne 1680–1715* (1935), translated into English as *The European Mind 1680–1715* (1952).

The literature on Descartes is immense, but the best guide is Descartes himself in his *Discours de la méthode* (the standard scholarly edition is by E. Gilson (1947) but it is also available in many other editions). See also E. Gilson, *La Pensée médiévale dans la formation du système cartésien* (new edn. 1951). The standard edition of Descartes's *Œuvres* is edited by C. Adam, P. Tannery, *et al.* (12 vols., 1897–1913). More recent important work on Descartes includes P. Dibon, *et al.*, *Descartes et le cartésianisme hollandais* (1951), H. Gouhier, *La Pensée métaphysique de Descartes* (1962), and the chapter entitled 'The Fortunes of Descartes' in J. S. Spink, *French Free Thought from Gassendi to Voltaire* (1960). The standard edition of Fontenelle, *Entretiens sur la pluralité des mondes*, is by R. Shackleton (1955). Interest in Bayle has increased during the last decade, though there is no modern edition of Bayle's Dictionary. Convenient extracts in English, however, may be found in E. A. Beller and M. Lee, *Selections from Bayle's Dictionary* (1952). Elizabeth Labrousse's study of Bayle in two volumes (1963–6) is extremely important. An interesting selection of articles and documents has been edited by P. Dibon under the title *Pierre Bayle: le philosophe de Rotterdam* (1959).

For Spinoza, see R. B. Wernham's edition and translation of the *Tractatus* (1958). A convenient and brief modern study is Stuart Hampshire's *Spinoza* (1951). The standard work on Spinoza's influence in France is P. Vernière, *Spinoza et la pensée française avant la Révolution*, vol. *1* (*1663–1715*) (1954). Bossuet's *Discours sur l'histoire universelle* is reprinted in the Pléiade edition of the *Œuvres* (1961). Works on Bossuet include A. Rebelliau, *Bossuet* (1900) and A. G. Martinort, *Le Gallicanisme de Bossuet* (1953).

CHRONOLOGY

History	French literature	English literature
Treaty of Lyons between France and Savoie, 1601	Montchrestien, *La Reine d'Écosse* (1601)	
Henri IV recalls Jesuits to France, 1603		Shakespeare, *Hamlet* (1603)
		Jonson, *Sejanus* (1603)
Champlain's expedition to Canada, 1603–4		Shakespeare, *Othello* (1604)
French East India Company, 1604		
		Shakespeare, *King Lear* (*c.* 1605) Jonson, *Volpone* (1605)
Henri IV occupies Sedan, 1606		Shakespeare, *Macbeth* (*c.* 1606)
	D'Urfé, *L'Astrée* (1607–27)	Chapman, *Bussy d'Ambois* (1607)
		Shakespeare, *Antony and Cleopatra* (*c.* 1607)
Lippersheim invents telescope, 1608		
Champlain founds Quebec, 1608		
	Régnier, *Les Satyres* (1609)	Jonson, *Epicene, or The Silent Woman* (1609)
Assassination of Henri IV, 1610		Jonson, *The Alchemist* (1610)
Accession of Louis XIII (reigned 1610–43)		
		Authorized Version of the Bible (1611)
		Webster, *The White Devil* (*c.* 1611)
		Shakespeare, *The Tempest* (*c.* 1612)

Painting and music	Criticism and aesthetic theory	Theology, philosophy, and ideas
Peri, 1561–1633 (*Euridice*, 1601)		Charron, *De la sagesse* (1601)
Salomon de Brosse, *c.* 1562–1626		
John Bull, *c.* 1562–1628		
Pierre Guédron, *c.* 1565–*c.* 1620 (*Airs de cour*, 1602–20)		
Monteverdi, 1567–1643		
Caravaggio, 1569–1609	Vauquelin de la Fresnaye, *Art poétique français* (1605)	Bacon, *The Advancement of Learning* (1605)
Reni, 1575–1642	Malherbe, *Commentaire sur Desportes* (*c.* 1606)	Du Vair, *Traictez philosophiques* (1606)
Rubens, 1577–1640		
Hals, 1580–1666		
Orlando Gibbons, 1583–1625		
Frescobaldi, 1583–1643		
Antoine Boësset, *c.* 1585–1643		
Jacques Le Mercier, *c.* 1585–1654		François de Sales, *Introduction à la vie dévote* (1609)
	Deimer, *L'Académie de l'art poétique* (1610)	
Schütz, 1585–1672 (*Dafne*, 1627; *Symphoniae sacrae*, 1629)		
Antoine Le Nain, 1588–1648	Boccalini, *Ragguagli di Parnasso* (1612–13)	

History	French literature	English literature
Civil War in France begun by Condé, 1614		Webster, *The Duchess of Malfi* (*c.* 1614)
		Jonson, *Bartholomew Fair* (1614)
		Chapman, *The Revenge of Bussy d'Ambois* (1614)
Second Civil War and ending of Condé's rebellion, 1615–16		
Richelieu becomes Secrétaire d'État, 1616 (dismissed 1617)	D'Aubigné, *Les Tragiques* (1616)	Chapman, *The Whole Works of Homer Prince of Poets in his Iliads and Odysseys* (1616)
Outbreak of Thirty Years War, 1618		
Foundation of Congréga-tion de St-Maur, 1618		
Suppression of French Huguenot rising and union of Béarn and Navarre with France, 1620		
	Théophile de Viau, *Œuvres* (1621)	
	Théophile de Viau, *Pyrame et Thisbé* (1623)	
Richelieu becomes Premier Ministre, 1624–42	Sorel, *Histoire comique de Francion* (1623)	
Foundation of the Prêtres de la Mission (Lazarists), 1625		Bacon, *Essays* (final form, 1625) Massinger, *A New Way to Pay Old Debts* (*c.* 1625)
Defeat of Huguenots under Soubise, 1625		

Painting and music	Criticism and aesthetic theory	Theology, philosophy and ideas
Sarazin, 1588–1660		Ralegh, *History of the World* (1614)
Vouet, 1590–1652		
Georges de La Tour, *c*. 1590–1652		
		Montchrestien, *Traité de l'économie politique* (1615)
Callot, 1592–1635		
Louis Le Nain, 1593–1648		
Jordaens, 1593–1678		
Nicolas Poussin, 1594–1665		
		Bacon, *Novum Organum* (1620)
Henry Lawes, 1596–1662 (*Choice Psalmes put into Musick*, 1648)		Burton, *The Anatomy of Melancholy* (1621)
Luigi Rossi, *c*. 1598–1653 (*Orfeo*, 1647)	Chapelain's preface to Marino's *Adone* (1623)	Bacon, *De Augmentis* (1623)
François Mansart, 1598–1666	Opitz, *Das Buch von der deutschen Poeterey* (1624)	Lord Cherbury, *De Veritate* (1624)
Van Dyck, 1599–1641		
Velasquez, 1599–1660		Grotius, *De Jure Belli ac Pacis* (1625)
Bernini, 1599–1680		

History	French literature	English literature
Peace of La Rochelle and end of Huguenot rebellion, 1626	Sorel, *Le Berger extravagant* (1627)	
Capitulation of La Rochelle after second Huguenot rebellion, 1628		
Peace of Alais: Huguenots obtain religious freedom, 1629	Gomberville, *Polexandre* (1629–37)	Milton, *Ode on the Morning of Christ's Nativity* (written 1629)
	Mairet, *Sylvanire* (performed 1630)	
	Desmarets de Saint-Sorlin, *Ariane* (1632)	Milton, *L'Allegro* and *Il Penseroso* (1632)
	Tristan l'Hermite, *Le Page disgracié* (1632–3)	
	Corneille, *La Place Royale* (1634)	Milton, *Comus* (written 1634, publ. 1637)
	Rotrou, *Hercule mourant* (written 1634, publ. 1636)	
	Mairet, *Sophonisbe* (1634)	
Académie française founded by Richelieu, 1635	Corneille, *L'Illusion comique* (1636)	
	Corneille, *Le Cid* (1637)	Milton, *Lycidas* (1637)
	Rotrou, *Laure persécutée* (1639)	

Painting and music	Criticism and aesthetic theory	Theology, philosophy, and ideas
Claude Lorrain, 1600–82		
William Lawes, 1602–45	Ogier's preface to Schelandre's *Tyr et Sidon* (1628)	Harvey, *Exercitatis Anatomica de Motu Cordis et Sanguinis in Animalibus* (1628)
Philippe de Champaigne, 1602–74		
Cavalli, 1602–76 (*Giasone*, 1649; *Ciro*, 1654)		
François Anguier, 1604–69		
		Guez de Balzac, *Le Prince* (1631)
Brouwer, 1605–38		Galileo, *Dialogo sopra i due massimi sistemi del mondo* (1632)
Carissimi, 1605–74		
Rembrandt, 1606–69		
Mathieu Le Nain, 1607–77		
Teniers, 1610–90		Jansenius, *Mars gallicus* (1635)
Pierre Mignard, 1610–95		
Louis le Vau, *c.* 1612–70		
Hammerschmidt, 1612–75	G. de Scudéry, *Observations sur le Cid* (1637)	Descartes, *Discours de la méthode* (1637)
Gaspard Poussin, 1613–75		
Claude Perrault, 1613–88	Corneille's 'Épître dédicatoire' to *La Suivante* (1637)	
Le Nôtre, 1613–1700	Chapelain, *Sentiments de l'Académie française sur le Cid* (1637–8)	
Michel Anguier, 1614–86		

History	French literature	English literature
	Rotrou, *Les Captifs* (1640)	
	Corneille, *Horace* (1640)	
	Corneille, *Cinna* (1641)	
Mazarin becomes Premier Ministre on death of Richelieu, 1642	La Calprenède, *Cassandre* (10 vols., 1642–5)	Browne, *Religio Medici* (1642)
Battle of Rocroi, 1643	Corneille, *Polyeucte* (1643)	
Death of Louis XIII and accession of Louis XIV (1643–1715)		
	Corneille, *Le Menteur* (1644)	
	Corneille, *Rodogune* (1645)	
	Rotrou, *Saint Genest* (1646)	Vaughan, *Poems* (1646)
	La Calprenède, *Cléopâtre* (12 vols., 1646–57)	
		Cowley, *The Mistress* (1647)
Peace of Westphalia ends Thirty Years War, 1648		Herrick, *Hesperides* (1648)
Civil war of the Fronde ('Fronde parlementaire' followed by 'Fronde des princes'), 1648–53		
	Mlle de Scudéry, *Arthamène ou le Grand Cyrus* (1649–53)	
		Vaughan, *Silex Scintillians* (1650 and 1655)

Painting and music	Criticism and aesthetic theory	Theology, philosophy, and ideas
		Fuller, *History of the Holy Warre* (1640)
Salvator Rosa, 1615–73		
		Jansenius, *Augustinus* (1640)
		Descartes, *Meditationes de prima philosophia* (1641)
Le Sueur, 1616–55		
		Fuller, *The Holy State and the Profane State* (1642)
Froberger, 1616–67		
		Hobbes, *De Cive* (1642)
		Arnauld, *La Fréquente Communion* (1643)
Lely, 1618–80		
		Milton, *Areopagitica* (1644)
Murillo, 1618–82		Descartes, *Principia Philosophiae* (1644)
Charles Le Brun, 1619–90	Tassoni, *Pensieri diversi* (1646)	
Cuyp, 1620–91	Chapelain, *Dialogue de la lecture des vieux romans* (1646)	
	Vaugelas, *Remarques sur la langue française* (1647)	Pascal, *Expériences nouvelles touchant le vide* (1647)
Puget, 1620–94		Pascal, *Récit de la grande expérience de l'équilibre des liqueurs* (1648)
Antoine Lepautre, 1621–91		
		Descartes, *Traité des passions de l'âme* (1649)
	Ménage, *Les Origines de la langue française* (1650)	Jeremy Taylor, *Holy Living* (1650)
		Milton, *The Tenure of Kings and Magistrates* (1650)

History	French literature	English literature
	Corneille, *Nicomède* (1651)	
	Scarron, *Le Roman comique* (1651–63)	
Mazarin returns from exile, 1653		Walton, *The Compleat Angler* (1653 and revised 1655)
Fouquet becomes Intendant des Finances, 1653		
Coronation of Louis XIV at Reims, 1654	Cyrano de Bergerac, *Le Pédant joué* (1654)	
	Mlle de Scudéry, *Clélie, histoire romaine* (1654–61)	
	Quinault, *La Mort de Cyrus* (1656)	Cowley, *Davideis and Pindarique Odes* (1656)
Treaty of Paris between France and England against Spain, 1657		
Economic crisis in France, 1657–60		
English and French defeat Spaniards at Dunes and English take Dunkirk, 1658		Browne, *Urne Buriall* (1658)
	Molière, *Les Précieuses ridicules* (1659)	
Marriage of Louis XIV and Marie-Thérèse, 1660		Pepy's *Diary* begins (1660)
Death of Mazarin, 1661	La Calprenède, *Faramond* (12 vols., 1661–70)	

Painting and music	Criticism and aesthetic theory	Theology, philosophy, and ideas
J. R. Ahle, 1625–73		
		Hobbes, *Leviathan* (1651)
Steen, 1626–79		Jeremy Taylor, *Holy Dying* (1651)
		Guez de Balzac, *Socrate chrétien* (1652)
Legrenzi, 1626–90 (*I due Cesari*, 1683)		
		Pascal's 'Mémorial', 23 November 1654
Kerl, 1627–93		Pascal, *Lettres provinciales* (1656–7)
Cambert, *c.* 1628–*c.* 1677 (*Pomone*, 1671)		
Ruisdael, 1628–82	D'Aubignac, *La Pratique du théâtre* (1657)	
Girardon, 1628–1715		Guez de Balzac, *Aristippe* (posth. publ. 1658)
Pieter de Hooch, 1629– *c.* 1683		
	Corneille, *Examens et discours* (1660)	Pascal, *Trois discours sur la condition des grands* (1660)
Metsu, 1630–67		Milton, *The Ready and Easy Way to Establish a Free Commonwealth* (1660)
Matthew Lock(e), 1630–77		Nicole and Arnauld, *La Logique de Port-Royal* (1661)

History	French literature	English literature
Dunkirk sold to France by Charles II, 1662	Molière, *L'École des femmes* (1662)	
Condemnation of Fouquet, 1664	La Rochefoucauld, *Maximes* (1664)	
Colbert's tariff reform, 1664	Quinault, *Astrate, roi de Tyr* (1664)	
	Quinault, *La Mère coquette* (1665)	
	La Fontaine, *Contes et nouvelles* (1665–6)	
	Furetière, *Le Roman bourgeois* (1666)	
	Molière, *Le Misanthrope* (1666)	
French War of Devolution against Spain in the Netherlands, 1667–8	Racine, *Andromaque* (1667)	Milton, *Paradise Lost* (1667)
Louvois Secretary of War, 1668	La Fontaine, *Fables,* bks. i–vi (1668)	
Peace of Aix-la-Chapelle, 1668	Racine, *Les Plaideurs* (1668)	
	Molière, *George Dandin* (1668)	
	Molière, *L'Avare* (1668)	
	Molière, *Amphitryon* (1668)	
	Molière, *Tartuffe* (1669)	
	Racine, *Britannicus* (1669)	
	Molière, *Le Bourgeois gentilhomme* (1670)	
	Racine, *Bérénice* (1670)	

Painting and music	Criticism and aesthetic theory	Theology, philosophy, and ideas
Vermeer, 1632–75		Fuller, *The Worthies of England* (posth. publ. 1662)
Lully, 1632–87 (*Le Mariage forcé*, 1664; *La Princesse d'Élide*, 1664; *Monsieur de Pourceaugnac*, 1669; *Le Bourgeois gentil-homme*, 1670; *Les Fêtes de l'Amour et de Bacchus*, 1672; *Armide et Renaud*, 1686)	Ménage, *Observations sur les poésies de Malherbe* (1666) Prince de Conti, *Traité de la comédie et des spectacles selon la tradition de l'Église* (1667)	Bunyan, *Grace Abounding* (1666)
	Dryden, *Essay of Dramatic Poesy* (1668)	
Maes, 1632–93		Bossuet, *Oraison funèbre de Henriette-Marie de France, reine d'Angleterre* (1669)
Willem van de Velde, 1633–1707		Pascal, *Pensées* (posth. publ. 1670)
Charpentier, 1634–1704		Spinoza, *Tractatus Theologico-Politicus* (1670)

History	French literature	English literature
	Molière, *Les Fourberies de Scapin* (1671)	Milton, *Paradise Regained* and *Samson Agonistes* (1671)
Second war of Louis XIV against the Netherlands, 1672–8	Racine, *Bajazet* (1672)	Wycherley, *The Country Wife* (written *c.* 1672)
	Molière, *Les Femmes savantes* (1672)	
	Molière, *Le Malade imaginaire* (1673)	
	Racine, *Mithridate* (1673)	
	Racine, *Iphigénie* (1674)	Wycherley, *The Plain Dealer* (written *c.* 1674)
Death of Turenne at Sassbach, 1675		
	Racine, *Phèdre* (1677)	
Treaties of Nijmegen between France and the Netherlands and France and Spain, 1678	La Fontaine, *Fables*, bks. vii–xi (1678)	Dryden, *All for Love* (1678)
	Mme de La Fayette, *La Princesse de Clèves* (1678)	Bunyan, *The Pilgrim's Progress* (1678)
Peace of Nijmegen between France and Empire, 1679		
Beginning of 'Dragonnades' against French Protestants, 1680		
		Dryden, *Absalom and Achitophel* (1681)

Painting and music	Criticism and aesthetic theory	Theology, philosophy, and ideas
Adriaen van de Velde, 1635–72	Bouhours, *Entretiens d'Ariste et d'Eugène* (1671)	
	Sorel, *De la connaissance des bons livres* (1671)	Nicole, *Essais de morale* (1671–8)
J. H. d'Anglebert, 1635–91	Saint-Évremond, *De la tragédie ancienne et moderne* (1672)	
Colonna, 1637–95 (*Motetti sacri*, 1681)	Rapin, *Réflexions sur la poétique d'Aristote* (1674)	
Buxtehude, 1637–1707	Boileau, *L'Art poétique* (1674)	Malebranche, *La Recherche de la vérité* (1674–5)
Hobbema, 1638–1709		
	B. Lamy, *La Rhétorique ou l'art de parler* (1675)	
G. B. Vitali, *c.* 1644–92	Desmarets de Saint-Sorlin, *Défense de la poésie et de la langue française* (1675)	Spinoza, *Ethics* (1677)
	Boileau, *Épître VII* (1677)	Malebranche, *Conversations chrétiennes* (1677)
J. C. Bach, 1645–93		Cudworth, *The True Intellectual System of the Universe* (1678)
G. Muffat, *c.* 1645–1704 (*Florilegium I*, 1695; *Florilegium II*, 1698)		
		Malebranche, *Traité de la nature et de la grâce* (1680)
		Bossuet, *Discours sur l'histoire universelle* (1681)
Jules Hardouin-Mansart, 1646–1708		

History	French literature	English literature
Gallicanism causes conflict between France and Pope, 1682		Otway, *Venice Preserved* (1682)
Death of Colbert, 1683		
Louis XIV marries Mme de Maintenon, 1683		
Revocation of Edict of Nantes by Louis XIV, 1685		
	Dancourt, *Le Chevalier à la mode* (1687)	
Louis XIV attacks Holland. War of League of Augsburg, 1688–97	La Bruyère, *Les Caractères* (1688)	
	Racine, *Esther* (1689)	

Painting and music	Criticism and aesthetic theory	Theology, philosophy, and ideas
		Bayle, *Pensées sur la Comète* (1682)
Kneller, 1646–1723		Bossuet, *Oraison funèbre de Marie-Thérese d'Autriche, reine de France* (1683)
		Fontenelle, *Dialogues des morts* (1683)
Humfrey, 1647–74		Malebranche, *Méditations chrétiennes* (1683)
	Fénelon, *Dialogues sur l'éloquence* (1684)	Malebranche, *Traité de morale* (1684)
John Blow, 1649–1708	Saint-Évremond, *Sur les poèmes des Anciens* (1685)	Bossuet, *Oraison funèbre d'Anne de Gonzague de Clèves, princesse palatine* (1685)
		Fontenelle, *Entretiens sur la pluralité des mondes* (1686)
J. Pachelbel, 1653–1706 (*Musikalische Sterbensgedanken*, 1683)	Bouhours, *Manière de bien penser sur les ouvrages de l'esprit* (1687)	Bossuet, *Oraison funèbre du prince de Condé* (1687)
		Newton, *Philosophiae Naturalis Principia Mathematica* (1687)
Corelli, 1653–1713	Perrault, *Parallèles des Anciens et des Modernes* (1688)	
La Lande, 1657–1726 (*Le Palais de Flore*, 1689)	Fontenelle, *Digression sur les Anciens et les Modernes* (1688)	
Purcell, *c.* 1659–95 (*Dido and Aeneas*, 1689)		Locke, *Letters on Toleration* (1689–92)
		Locke, *Two Treatises of Government* (1690)
		Locke, *Essay concerning Human Understanding* (1690)

History	French literature	English literature
Death of Louvois, 1691	Racine, *Athalie* (1691)	
	Dancourt, *Les Bourgeoises à la mode* (1692)	
	La Fontaine, *Fables*, bk. xii (1693)	
Economic crisis in France, 1694		Congreve, *The Double Dealer* (1694)
		Congreve, *Love for Love* (1695)
	Regnard, *Le Joueur* (1696)	Vanburgh, *The Relapse* (1696)
Treaty of Ryswyck between France, England, Holland, and Spain, 1697	Regnard, *Le Distrait*, (1697) Perrault, *Contes de ma mère l'Oye* (1697)	Vanburgh, *The Provok'd Wife* (1697)
	Fénelon, *Télémaque* (1699)	
	Dancourt, *Les Bourgeoises de qualité* (1700)	Congreve, *The Way of the World* (1700)

Painting and music	Criticism and aesthetic theory	Theology, philosophy and ideas
Kuhnau, 1660–1722 (*Frische Klavier-Früchte*, 1696)		Furetière, *Dictionnaire universel* (1690)
A. Scarlatti, 1660–1725	Rymer, *A Short View of Tragedy* (1692)	
Desmarets, 1662–1741	Boileau, *Réflexions sur quelques passages du rhéteur Longin* (1694)	
	Bossuet, *Maximes et réflexions sur la comédie* (1694)	
Couperin, 1668–1733		
		Bayle, *Dictionnaire historique et critique* (1697)
Destouches, 1672–1749 (*Issé*, 1697)	Collier, *A Short View of the Immorality and Profaneness of the English Stage* (1698)	
	Boileau, *Lettres à Perrault* (1700)	

Index

PRINTED IN GREAT BRITAIN AT THE UNIVERSITY PRESS, OXFORD
BY VIVIAN RIDLER, PRINTER TO THE UNIVERSITY